Former athlete and churchman John Keddie brings both sporting expertise and spiritual insight to this lucid and meticulous biography of the great Eric Liddell.

Sally Magnusson
Broadcaster (Reporting Scotland, Songs of Praise)
Author of several books including *The Flying Scotsman: The Eric Liddell Story*

It is abundantly clear from these pages that the driving force in Liddell's life was love for his Lord and Saviour Jesus Christ and that he lived by the wisdom of Ecclesiastes 9:10: 'Whatever your hand finds to do, do it with all your might.' This is an inspiring and challenging account of the life of a truly inter-continental hero and will be enjoyed by the sporting enthusiast and Christian alike.

Euan Murray
Former Scottish Rugby Union Player

Running the Race is the definitive biography of Eric Liddell and one can say with confidence that Liddell himself would have approved. Not only is John Keddie the foremost authority on Scottish athletics, but he is also a Presbyterian Minister uniquely placed to set Liddell's sporting achievements in the context of the bigger priority of his Christian faith and witness. This superbly researched book inspires on many levels.

P▒▒▒ Lovesey
C▒▒▒ writer & ▒▒▒▒ ▒istorian
N▒▒▒ ▒ember

In a world increasingly fascin▒▒▒ ▒▒▒ ▒▒▒ d an athlete worthy of deep admirat▒▒▒ ▒▒ ▒▒▒ great Eric Liddell presents all of the ▒▒▒ ▒▒▒ ▒thletic accomplishment while also preserving the character and faith that fueled this remarkable life. More than the medals won, this book reveals the shining greatness of Liddell to be the humble, yet gutsy, spirit that drove him to 'press toward the goal for the prize' (Phil. 3:14) – whether in the classroom, on the track, or in the mission-field.

Joe Barnard
Executive Director, Cross Training Ministries
Author of *The Way Forward*

There are many reasons to read this gripping biography. Eric Liddell was a man of immense ability and profound conviction – an example in his own time and a hero for our age. Perhaps you have seen *Chariots of Fire*. If so, this book is for you. If you have an interest in Scottish athletics, this book will enrich your understanding. If you are curious about how someone so famous and so gifted could devote himself to service to others and to God, then you need to read this book. John W. Keddie is ideally positioned as a guide to this multi-faceted character whose life has been used to encourage so wide a range of people around the globe.

Jonathan L. Master
President, Greenville Presbyterian Theological Seminary, Greenville,
South Carolina

Like many, I shall never forget the impact of my first viewing of *Chariots of Fire*, where a portion of the life-story of the Scottish Christian sportsman Eric Liddell was told. It was deeply inspiring and proved to be the foundation of an ongoing interest in Liddell's life. So I am thrilled to recommend this fresh biographical study of Liddell by John Keddie: perfect to inspire a new generation, it is powerfully written and beautifully illustrated. A joy to read.

Michael A.G. Haykin
Chair and Professor of Church History,
The Southern Baptist Theological Seminary, Louisville, Kentucky

Being a Christian and former professional sportsmen, Liddell has always been a hero of the faith to me. So, I thoroughly enjoyed this book – a wonderful account which shows the reader that athletics was simply an extension of who Liddell was as a man running hard after Christ. That his life was a race within a race. Men like Eric Liddell are a rare commodity. They should be studied, imitated and never forgotten. So it is with great enthusiasm that I recommend this beautifully written and quite moving sports biography by John Keddie – a man well qualified to speak on Eric Liddell and athletics.

Gavin Peacock
Former professional footballer
Director of International Outreach, The Council on Biblical Manhood and
Womanhood

RUNNING THE RACE

BY JOHN W. KEDDIE

RUNNING THE RACE

ERIC LIDDELL
OLYMPIC CHAMPION & MISSIONARY

TRUTH FOR LIFE®

CHRISTIAN
FOCUS

Scripture quotations are taken from the *King James Version*.

Copyright © John W. Keddie 2020

paperback ISBN 978-1-5271-0531-7
epub ISBN 978-1-5271-0567-6
mobi ISBN 978-1-5271-0568-3

First published by Evangelical Press, 2007

Second edition published in 2012

This new edition published in 2020

by

Christian Focus Publications Ltd,
Geanies House, Fearn,
Ross-shire, IV20 1TW, Scotland.
www.christianfocus.com
with
Truth for Life
P.O. Box 398000
Cleveland, Ohio 44139
truthforlife.org

Cover design by MOOSE77

Printed in the USA

Eric Liddell in his Olympic vest before the 1924 Games in Paris.

TO MY WIFE JEAN,
to whose encouragements the writing of this book owes so much. 'A virtuous woman is a crown to her husband' (Prov. 12:4).

CONTENTS

ILLUSTRATIONS

PICTURE CREDITS

FOREWORD

Eric Liddell took 47.6 seconds to win the 400 metres race at the 1924 Paris Olympic Games, but his famous victory has now become a timeless moment in modern sporting history and achievement.

The portrayal in the *Chariots of Fire* movie of how Liddell turned what seemed to be a desperate situation into a triumph of the human spirit has inspired many people from many different backgrounds over the years, highlighting the equally timeless message of sport to never give up – on or off the sporting field.

The role of sport in Liddell's life as a child and in the years before and after the legendary Paris performance, however, is less well known – a situation which is addressed in an elegant and expert way by John Keddie in this new book on Liddell's life.

Instead of a full biography, the approach taken by Keddie, a leading authority on Scottish track and field history and a consultant on the *Chariots* movie, is to provide a detailed sporting biography of Liddell, charting his progress from gifted childhood athlete to rising track star at the University of Edinburgh, international rugby player for Scotland, and culminating in his dramatic Olympic challenges and achievements, on and off the track.

This is an impressive and informative account of the sporting side of Eric Liddell, which also blends his religious commitment, family and missionary work in China, the other great passions that shaped Liddell's life. Liddell's decision to sacrifice his strong chance of winning the Olympic Games blue ribbon 100 metres sprint event because the competition schedule clashed with his Christian beliefs continues to fascinate and capture the imagination, while the circumstances surrounding his amazing, against-the-odds gold-medal run seem even more remarkable when viewed through the tunnel of time: defeating the best athletes in the world at an unfamiliar distance and breaking the world record in the process – after winning a bronze medal a few days earlier in the 200 metres.

In an era where more heroes and role models are needed to inspire our young people, Keddie's new book on Liddell is well timed, taking us to the heart of life as well as the heart of sport.

Appropriately, given Liddell's life-long attachment to China, where he was born and died, this biography was first published in the lead-up to the Beijing Olympic Games, which brought the world's athletes to China for the first time.

It was republished in 2012 when it resonated with our vision to use the power of the Olympic and Paralympic Games in London in 2012 to inspire change; to regenerate some of the poorest parts of London; to inspire young people and change lives through sport – as Liddell did in his own way.

Now the Olympic world is again looking to the East as we approach the Tokyo Olympic Games, scheduled for 2021, and Liddell's story is as relevant as ever. To paraphrase that most renowned of eastern philosophers, Confucius, it is only by understanding our past that we can shape our future. In the sporting sphere, this book is an excellent place to start.

LORD SEBASTIAN COE
World Athletics President

PREFACE

The enduring fascination of the life of Eric Liddell is remarkable. It is remarkable because he was in many respects an ordinary soul and also no doubt because the lifestyle and faith that he espoused cannot be said to be popular, or even well understood, in our sceptical and secular age. However, part of the fascination attached to Eric Liddell must surely lie in the fact that he accomplished so much in sport and committed himself so wholeheartedly to the work of Christian mission. These two worlds are not often seen to touch so directly. There are many biographies of sportsmen today. There are also many Christian biographies. But there are very few which bring together the sporting and the Christian. That is the case, however, with Eric Liddell. And that, at least in part, must account for the fascination.

There is another factor, too. It is this: that he has achieved, posthumously, a celebrity status through being depicted in an award-winning movie. Most people know about *Chariots of Fire* (1981). Having had a little to do with some of the characterisation of Eric Liddell for that film, I was intrigued at the time to read this quite poetic description applied to it: 'Chariots of Fire is a fragment of history trapped in amber.'[1] It occurred to me that this might equally be applied to Eric Liddell's life. We are reminded when we consider such men and events of the past that every generation ought to have the humility to learn lessons on living from such exemplary figures. As someone has put it, a people who forget their history will tend to repeat its mistakes.

The book arises out of my own interests in sport and Christian faith. The two were intertwined in Eric Liddell's life. In some ways this is predominantly a 'sporting biography'. But it is not possible to write a sporting biography of Eric Liddell without reflection on his Christian faith. Here was a man who devoted his life to missionary service, apparently turning his back on fame and fortune. What we have in Eric Liddell is the life and character of a man directed by the teaching of the Bible, not least on the fact of a purpose and meaning that extend beyond this present scene of time and sense and transience. Certainly, his life testifies to the transforming power that such teaching has. He cannot be understood apart from his devotion to Christ and the beliefs of evangelical Christianity.

I am deeply thankful for having known D. P. Thomson, the first biographer of Liddell, and the one on whose shoulders all other biographers have stood. Much of the detail in this book has been drawn from D. P. Thomson's work, though the other biographies produced more recently have been very useful in places. The parts dealing with the sports records are, however, largely original, but there are lengthy quotations from Eric Liddell about his experiences in developing as an athlete which are culled from Thomson's biography of Liddell and in addition from a series of six articles Eric wrote for *All Sports Weekly* between May 29 and July 3, 1926. He described these as 'brief and imperfect memories of five happy years on the running track.'[2]

I am also thankful for the privilege of meeting Eric Liddell's widow, Florence, and his sister Jenny. Conversations with these delightful ladies and many others whose lives were touched by Eric Liddell in one way or another were enormously helpful in rounding out the character of the man. To all such I owe a deep debt of gratitude.

Thanks are due to Lord Coe, now President of World Athletics, for his Foreword to the new edition.[3]

In this third edition apart from corrections and updating here and there the text remains essentially the same as the previous editions (2007, 2012). Exceptions include the revision of the final chapter of the 2012 edition and of Appendices. Though the text remains more or less unchanged in the rest of the book there are fewer illustrations in this edition.

Eric Liddell was a notably modest and self-effacing man who would have been amazed and even embarrassed by the subsequent adulation and more recent interest in his life as a sportsman and missionary. 'Celebrity' status would not have sat comfortably with him! However, after *Chariots of Fire* (1981) and the Olympic Games of 2008 in the country of his birth an unlikely renewed interest was in many ways inevitable. His image in action even appeared on the front cover of a BT Telephone Directory in Scotland, 2011/12!

It seems to the author that striking the right balance in presenting Eric as an athlete and Christian missionary has not often been well drawn by biographers or journalists or film makers. Either they emphasise his sport and humanity with limited appreciation of his Christianity; or they emphasise his Christianity with limited reference in detail to his sporting experiences. It has been the concern of this biography, written by a Christian minister and former athlete, that such a fair balance be struck in these diverse aspects of Eric's life.

In the end of the day one suspects that Eric would have wondered what all the fuss was about. Yet there is a continuing admiration, not to say fascination, of his achievements on the sports field and in his work in China. In this respect his remembered life continues to be both inspirational and challenging.

JOHN W. KEDDIE
Kirkhill
Inverness-shire
October 2019

1.

ENCOUNTERING ERIC LIDDELL

I first encountered Eric Liddell in 1959, or thereabouts, at Craiglockhart, then the playing field for Edinburgh University Athletic Club. The facility was off Colinton Road on the south-west side of the city. Of course, I did not encounter him in person, as he had passed away in 1945, some eighteen months before I was born. But that May Saturday afternoon at Craiglockhart I accompanied my father to the Annual Sports of the Edinburgh University Athletic Club. My father was reporting the event for a local Edinburgh newspaper.

The situation at Craiglockhart had changed little since the 1920s, when Eric Liddell had competed at university events there. The field and pavilion had been opened and first used in 1897. It was all more or less the same sixty-two years on. The pavilion had a bank of seats and steps leading up to a clubhouse, above which was a large clock set into the front of the building. Underneath the clubhouse, and approached from the sides at ground level, were the changing rooms for the athletes. These, too, were much the same as what they had been in Eric Liddell's day: the same benches, the same hooks and the same baths. The track was all grass, with lanes marked out by white emulsion paint. It was a 440 yard, six-lane track. There were some differences from how things had been in the 1920s. In those days there were no lane markings except for a straight 100 yards and 220 yards. In the earlier days the 220 yards was not run around a bend, but was on a straight course from the far-distant south-west corner of the field coming right up in the direction of the clubhouse. Overlooking the playing field was the impressive building of Craig House, set on a wooded hillside. The house had been built as an 'asylum for the insane', and still served that purpose in the 1950s.

To return to my first encounter with Eric Liddell, it was in the clubhouse, up the stairs, where the tea and cakes were served. A picture of the great man was placed prominently on the wall just above the tea-table at one end of the room. It was like an icon. And what amazed me was that some of this man's records still stood nearly forty years on. He still held the 220 yards record outright and still shared the 100 yards record. I must have forgotten myself that afternoon as I exchanged a cake on a plate in full view of the then Principal of the university, Sir Edward Appleton. My father was distinctly displeased by my lapse in manners!

Eric Liddell's portrait that hung in the Craiglockhart Clubhouse.

Being interested in sport, my father had told me about Eric Liddell in my boyhood and he became something of a hero, even though I knew few of the details of his life. At that time there was not yet any biography written, at least none that my father knew of or possessed. Perhaps it might be said that I was 'inspired' by the Eric Liddell story, such as I then knew of it, and I took part in sports at school with some eagerness.

Though my own talent was limited in the extreme, in comparison to Eric Liddell's, there was one unusual coincidence in our respective track careers. Eric Liddell ran his very first senior quarter-mile at the Craiglockhart track in the Edinburgh University Sports on 27 May 1922. He won the race quite easily in what was for him a modest 52.6 seconds. Forty-four years later, on 24 May 1966, on the same grass track, in a contest between my club, Edinburgh Southern Harriers, and the Edinburgh University Athletic Club, I won the quarter-mile in exactly the same time. It happened to be one of my few senior successes.

By then I was a professing Christian and knew more about Eric Liddell. Whatever stimulus he may have been to my sporting interests, by then his Christian testimony was far more engaging and important to me. It was during 1966 that my older brother, who had not been much interested in sport at all, sent me a small biography of Liddell that he had picked up at a Students' Christian conference in Crieff,

The Cover of D. P. Thomson's first biography of Liddell (1945).

Perthshire. It was entitled *Eric Liddell: The Making of an Athlete and the Training of a Missionary*. Comprising forty pages, it had been printed for 'The Eric Liddell Memorial Committee (Publications)'. There was no date of publication on it, but it was the fourth edition, bringing the total circulation at that time to 55,000, and presumably it had been continuously in print ever since its first publication shortly after Eric's death in 1945.

The author was D. P. Thomson, who had been an evangelist in the Church of Scotland and was then living in retirement, though he was still very active as warden in what was called the 'Research Unit' attached to St Ninian's, Crieff. Under the banner of the Research Unit, Thomson produced many useful works on various aspects of Christian church history, biography and practice. He had been very closely involved with Eric Liddell in the 1920s, and had taken a crucial part in encouraging Eric's involvement in evangelism, especially among students and young people.

The booklet had a powerful effect on me. It was influential in encouraging me to think more deeply about athletics, but especially about Christian faith, of which Liddell was such a shining example. Certainly, from that time I never again took part in any sport on Sundays. Not that there was so much sport on Sundays in those days. Nevertheless, there was always pressure to train on that day and Sunday sports events were beginning to be held. However, I never did compete or train on the Lord's day after that summer of 1966 – not just because of the example of Eric Liddell, but out of persuasion that what he stood for was the correct biblical position and therefore God's will for man.

It is interesting to note the effect that Eric Liddell has had down the years, not least in connection with his Christian witness. In the biography of her late husband, Catherine Marshall speaks of the early influence of Eric Liddell on his life in the 1920s:

> Peter Marshall, along with thousands more young people in Scotland, followed every detail of all this [Eric Liddell's Olympic performances in 1924]. To them Eric was a hero, not just because of his great athletic ability, but also because of his modesty, his undeniable charm, and the great strength of his Christian witness. His influence on Peter's life can scarcely be measured.[1]

The BBC Scotland website commented that 'Without doubt one of Scotland's sporting heroes, Eric Liddell, owes much of his fame more to a race he didn't run, than any he did,'[2] with reference to his refusal to run in the 100 metres race in the Paris Olympic Games of 1924. Several years ago, in a letter to the author, the great Bible scholar F. F. Bruce said of Eric Liddell that 'His refusal to run on Sunday made a great impression on several of my schoolmates and myself in those far-distant days of 1924.'[3]

There have been others down the years, such as myself, who have been greatly influenced by his Christian witness, especially after the screening of the 1981 movie *Chariots of Fire*. The stand Eric Liddell took on the sanctity of the Lord's day was a powerful element in his Christian testimony.

In 1967 a coaching committee of the Scottish Amateur Athletic Association sent round a circular encouraging young schoolboys to attend coaching sessions at Redford Stadium in Edinburgh in preparation for the Commonwealth Games due to be held in Edinburgh in 1970. In the circular the Secretary of the Scottish Amateur Athletic Association (usually known as the 'SAAA', now *scottishathletics* – Scottish Athletics Ltd, in the post-amateur era) the famous former marathon champion,

Duncan McLeod Wright, encouraged the schoolboys by referring to the example of Eric Liddell. He said, 'I was one of Eric's colleagues at the Paris Games and enjoyed his friendship for many years, and without hesitation I declare that he was the greatest sportsman I have ever met.' Wright was referring to Liddell's great Olympic triumph, but writes that 'Eric Liddell is not remembered for this achievement but as the man who would not run on a Sunday.' This was a fine testimony. Though he was hoping that 'another "Eric Liddell"' would appear on the scene for 1970, I wondered how exactly that might be, given that the coaching course was to be held 'each Sunday 2.30 p.m. till 4.30 p.m.'!

Without doubt the Oscar-winning film, *Chariots of Fire*, released in 1981, gave stimulus to interest in the life and witness of Eric Liddell. A key part of that witness was his attitude to Sunday as the Lord's day, as Duncan Wright pointed out in his 1967 coaching circular. Sadly, the Lord's day issue has been played down in an increasingly unchurched and secular society in which there has been a growing disrespect for Sunday as the Christian Sabbath. Some prominent athletes, and no doubt many less prominent ones, have clearly been influenced by Eric Liddell's stand on that issue as depicted in the film. To mention just four that became known in the public arena, they were world triple-jump record holder Jonathan Edwards (before he did an 'about-turn'), champion long-jumper and Pentecostal pastor Barrington Williams, outstanding All-Black rugby star Michael Jones, and more recently the Scottish rugby international, Euan Murray. However, the issue of Sunday sports has been noticeably marginalised among professing Christians. In a recently produced daily devotional book produced in the United States by the Fellowship of Christian Athletes, there is included a devotional entitled 'The Flying Scotsman'. It is about Eric Liddell. His Christian witness is highlighted as something for sportsmen and women to emulate. However, in the piece there is no reference at all to his attitude to the Lord's day.[4] It is not that a careful observing of the Lord's day to exclude sports makes the Christian; nor was this the only aspect of Eric Liddell's Christian witness. At the same time, it is that issue which made Eric so notable and told the world in the clearest terms that he was a man of Christian convictions.

So, what is this book about? Are there not enough biographies available? Strange as it may seem, there are few people whose active interest in Eric Liddell goes back before the production of *Chariots of Fire*. All the biographies written since 1981 have stood on the shoulders of D. P. Thomson's biographies of Liddell produced in 1970 and 1971.[5] Thomson's knowledge of Liddell was personal and lifelong after they met in the 1920s. His knowledge of most of the events of Liddell's life, and of his Christian position, was exhaustive. He was not so knowledgeable about Liddell's sporting performances. It was in that area that I assisted 'D. P.' in the biographies of the early 1970s. Very kindly, in October 1971 he sent me a copy of the hardback edition with an inscription: 'To my friend John W. Keddie, to whose interest, knowledge and enthusiasm this book owes so much. In gratitude, D. P. Thomson.' In reality I had done little more than help him with details of Eric Liddell's track record and encourage him to put a biography into print. A gracious Christian gentleman, D. P. Thomson (1896–1974), did not live long after the publication of these biographies. My interest in Liddell was unabated after the first encounter in 1959, not least in eventually digging out all the details of Eric's track-running performances. I slavishly trawled libraries and newspaper archives in my late teens and early twenties for details and recorded the results carefully. I also acquired a considerable collection of programmes, now lodged in the Scottish Records Office in Edinburgh.[6]

I had also come to befriend the doyen of Scottish athletics historians of the day, David A. Jamieson (1879–1972), who was like me a native of Edinburgh. Jamieson had been involved with the sport from before the end of the nineteenth century and had a wealth of knowledge on all things to do with Scottish athletics, amateur and professional. He had known Eric Liddell in person and was a great admirer of his character and ability. I had endless hours of happy conversation with Mr Jamieson and became well acquainted with many of the characters and the events in track and field in Scotland in the first half of the twentieth century. Jamieson had been present in Paris at the Olympic Games of 1924 and was able to describe them with great feeling.

In due time I wrote a series of articles on Eric Liddell's life and track record for the premier magazine of the day, *Athletics Weekly*, then edited by Melvyn Watman, a top athletics historian.[7] These articles came to the attention of Colin Welland, an actor and scriptwriter who had been asked to do a 'Treatment' for a proposed film that was initially intended to involve as its main characters Harold Abrahams (winner of the 100 metres in Paris), Eric Liddell (winner of the 400 metres) and Douglas Lowe, an Englishman who won the 800 metres in Paris. Lowe was the only one of the three still alive at the time. As he was disinclined to co-operate with the venture, his character was dropped and a fictitious character by the name of Lord Andrew Lindsay was written in as a secondary figure (though this was a rather transparent reference to Lord Burghley, who did actually compete at the Paris Games – over 110 metres hurdles – but without success).[8]

The idea for a film had come from film producer David Puttnam, who had been inspired to produce a film on the theme after reading of the successes of the British athletes in Paris, being attracted by the disparate nature of the athletes in question and a certain heroism in their achievements. At any rate, Colin Welland was struggling to round out the character of Liddell. He had the information contained in the biography by D. P. Thomson, and my own articles on Liddell's track running, which were considered to be 'authoritative' by the athletics fraternity. But he needed more.

We met towards the end of 1978 and at the beginning of 1979. It seems he was helped by our meetings, given that I had such an interest in Liddell and stood for much the same things in terms of evangelical religion. I had also been an athlete in my earlier days.[9] Colin Welland could not at first really grasp what motivated Liddell in his sport and in his life. He had not previously met any 'muscular Christians'. Did Liddell not have 'feet of clay' somewhere? He had not come across a true evangelical driven by a desire to honour Christ and live by the Word of God. As an evangelical Christian, I knew what made Eric Liddell 'tick', so to speak. In this connection I believe Welland found our contact valuable. One thing that he was also concerned about was just what sort of things Liddell would have said in public addresses. I provided some outlines, some of which he used in modified form in the film. In the course of time the Treatment was accepted and Welland was asked to undertake the screenplay for the projected film, eventually entitled *Chariots of Fire*.[10] So thankful was Colin Welland for help given that he actually named a character in the film 'Colonel John Keddie, President of the SAAA,' in appreciation for my help.[11] Colonel Keddie appears – briefly – in the Scotland versus France contest in which Liddell is depicted as being knocked over in a race, but gets up to run out an exhausted winner. Although this was a fictitious meeting, the incident was based upon a real occurrence at the Triangular International held in Stoke on Trent in July 1923.[12] Something more will be said later of the representation of Eric Liddell in the film. Suffice it to say that Colin Welland (1934-2015) gained the Oscar in Hollywood for 'Best Screenplay' in 1982. It was a considerable achievement.

In connection with the use of my name in the film, he said on one occasion to my dear wife that he had modelled the character of Liddell on myself. My thinking was that I had rather been modelled on Liddell!

Still from Chariots of Fire *(1981), signed by Colin Welland.*

I have in my possession a still from the film signed by Welland with the inscription: 'To John – thanks for introducing me to Eric! Colin Welland.'

In an article on Eric Liddell posted on the web, David Virkler of Dedication Evangelism has outlined my involvement with the film:

> Scriptwriter Colin Welland learned about Liddell's character by interviewing John Keddie, a Scottish runner whose life had been dramatically changed when his minister brother had given him a booklet on Liddell. Keddie was so impressed by Liddell's life that he joined a Christian group and also refused to run on Sunday. Keddie told Welland how Liddell preached, how he expressed himself and what he would and wouldn't say. It is Keddie's image of the long-dead Liddell that people saw in Chariots of Fire.[13]

Many biographies of Eric Liddell have appeared since the distribution of the film *Chariots of Fire* in 1981. For a long time it had been my desire to do something on Eric Liddell's life, but I never seemed to have had sufficient time for the research or writing. Yet in most cases I have been consulted by the various biographers and programme makers and have duly provided information. It is not my intention simply to reproduce biographical material now so widely available.[14] However, it might be of some interest to 'fill a few gaps' and provide a fuller sporting biography, weaving into it the Christian position of Liddell, without which even his athletics career cannot be fully understood. Uniquely among all biographers of Eric Liddell, I believe, I approach this as an evangelical Christian who has participated in rugby and athletics at a high level, as well as being keenly involved in sporting history.[15]

This, then, is an account of Eric Liddell as a Christian sportsman. For the greater part I will dwell on his record on the sports field. However, some analysis will also be given of the impact of his Christian faith on his own life and sport, and on the lives of others. His is a life and a story that deserve to be remembered, not only because he was a man who achieved so much on the sports field, but also because of his devotion to the principles of Christian faith that he so wholeheartedly embraced.

2.

'IT IS SURRENDER'

The venue was an internment camp in China, in August 1944, towards the end of the Second World War. The cheering crowds of the 1924 Olympic Games were a distant memory. Yet it was evident to all his fellow prisoners that Eric Liddell had lost neither his passion for the glory of Christ nor his amazing ability to run. David Michell, only a young boy at the time, recalled this story:

> The sports day on the playing field was a speck of glitter in the dull monotony of camp life… Then, as the veterans' race prepared to start, a hush distilled over the crowd. Our eyes shifted to the chairman of the Camp Recreation Committee, who was starting well behind the others as a voluntary handicap. 'He can never make up that distance!' gasped a boy beside me.
>
> 'He can too! He will, just wait!' I hissed back.
>
> Down the track they came. Middle-aged runners, weakened by the rigours and poor food of camp life, puffed and panted their way onward in response to our cheers. Then, unbelievably, the runner in rear position surged powerfully forward, arms flailing wildly, head thrown back. Out ahead now, he pushed for the finish line. He did it! One great, wild chorus of cheers nearly drowned out the judge's voice, 'Eric Liddell wins the veterans' event!'
>
> 'I knew he could do it! He always wins!'…We basked in the aura of Olympic glory as – cheering, chanting, chattering – we surrounded our hero.[1]

Eric touched the lives of men and women in the camp, apparently leading not a few to faith in the Lord Jesus Christ. 'Two men have made

Shadyside Hospital and parts of the walls of the Weihsien Internment Camp.

a profound and lasting impression on my life,' wrote one who was in Weihsien (later known as Weifang) as a boy, 'my father, who died in China, aged 53, and Eric Liddell, who died at 43. Both were outstanding in the humility, utter selflessness, and supreme devotion to Christ, whom they served "faithful unto death". My constant prayer is that I may be worthy of them and have grace to follow their example.'[2] Such testimonials could be multiplied.[3] It seems that no one had any sort of bad word to say about Eric Liddell, young or old. He consistently showed a seriousness in Christian faith, a joy in life and a humility and pleasantness in manner which endeared him to all and commended his Lord. His care for others, physically and spiritually, shone in the internment camp. However, it took its toll. Annie Buchan, a Scots lass from Peterhead, had known the brothers Rob and Eric Liddell when they had worked at and around Siaochang between 1937 and 1941. Allowed to attend an elderly patient in Peking (Beijing), she did not arrive back at the Weihsien Camp until late 1944. Annie noticed a difference in Eric. He had slowed down and there was clearly something wrong. In the December he began to suffer headaches. This necessitated a month in hospital. Though there seemed to be a slight improvement in his condition, he still had little of the strength or energy he had known hitherto. He was evidently declining physically and there were quite simply not the medical facilities on hand to treat him properly. As Eric Liddell himself would have recognised fully, such things are in the Lord's hands and, to him, these were the best hands to be in. A brain tumour was suspected, especially after he experienced a slight stroke on Sunday, 11 February 1945. The symptoms perplexed Eric, especially as he believed himself to have broken down under the strain when he felt that he should have been able to cast all on the Lord. The fact was that by then he was not long for this world. The end came on 21 February. A lady missionary recalled that:

> On the morning of the day on which he died, Eric again climbed the stairs to return a plate on which I had sent him something the previous day. A cheery word, a smile, and the assurance that he was getting better, and by the close of the day 'he was not, for God took him'. The earth was white with snow next morning when we heard the news. I walked across the camp in its glittering whiteness, and eternal realities were more real that day because 'All the bells in the City rang again for joy'.[4]

'I was with him when he died,' wrote Annie Buchan afterwards. 'The last words he said to me were, "Annie, it is surrender." He then lapsed into a coma, and about half past nine that evening he went peacefully home.'[5]

Eric Liddell had run his course on this earth. At 9.20 p.m. in the evening of 21 February 1945, aged forty-three, he passed into the presence of his Lord, to enjoy 'a fellowship immeasurably richer, and a service more wonderful by far, than any which earth can know'.[6]

But where did the story start, and how did it unfold?

Cross marking Eric Liddell's grave in the Weihsien Internment Camp.

3.
THE SHAPING OF A CHRISTIAN SPORTSMAN

Eric Henry Liddell was born in the Madaifu Hospital, Tientsin (Tianjin), in China on 16 January 1902. He was the second son of missionary parents, James and Mary Liddell. James Dunlop Liddell, Eric's father, had been born in Greenock to Robert and Elizabeth Liddell on 6 September 1870.

Robert Liddell was a native of Killearn in Stirlingshire, where he had been born in 1833. His wife, Elizabeth Strachan, hailed from Kilmarnock. They married in Greenock on 20 April 1859 and in the course of time they were blessed with four daughters and the one son. James, the only boy, had three older sisters and one younger. Robert worked as a joiner in Greenock and the family was associated with the Evangelical Union Church in the town.[1] The Evangelical Union emphasised simple gospel preaching and was notably committed to the cause of temperance.

Sadly, Elizabeth Liddell died in 1874, aged thirty-six, not long after the birth of their fourth daughter. Shortly afterwards Robert moved to the village of Drymen in Stirlingshire near the 'Trossachs'. Drymen was not far from his birthplace, and he brought up his five children there on his own. Though a joiner by profession, he became a grocer in Drymen and the family associated with the United Presbyterian Church in the town, there being no Evangelical Union or Congregational Church congregation in the neighbourhood.[2] The influence of the Evangelical Union clearly, however, continued in the Liddell family. It was said that 'the Liddells, a highly respected family, were noted for piety at a time and in a place when evangelism was considered unorthodox'.[3] Grandfather

Liddell family group at Drymen in 1907.
Eric's grandfather is seated in the centre. His parents James and Mary are second and
third from the left in the back row. At the front are, left to right, Jenny, Robert and Eric.

Liddell passed away, aged eighty-six, in Drymen on 7 December 1919, full of faith and with a lively hope for the life everlasting.

In the late 1880s James became an apprentice in a draper's business in Stirling. He attended the ministry there of the Rev. William Blair (1856–1936) in the Stirling Congregational Church.[4] Under Blair's influence James was encouraged to think about missionary service. With that in view, in 1894 he began studies at the Evangelical Union Theological Hall in Glasgow. While in Glasgow he became a member of the Dundas Street Evangelical Union Church, but served as missionary in the Anderston Mission of the Elgin Place Congregational Church in the city between November 1895 and October 1897, as part of his training. With the merger of the Evangelical Union and the Congregational Union at the beginning of 1897, this hall became a college of the Congregational Union of Scotland, and James finished his course there in the following year, being ordained to the ministry of the Congregational Union in 1898. After completing his studies, James applied to the London Missionary Society as a prospective missionary in the foreign field.

The Rev. William Blair (Stirling) in his earlier days had been a member of the Elgin Place Church before pursuing studies for the ministry. In those early days he became friendly with a family by the name of Reddin who were involved in that congregation. The father, Henry Reddin (1833–1908), was a native of Bowden in Roxburghshire and had plied his trade there as a master blacksmith. Henry had a daughter, Mary Jane Smith (1870–1944), one of five children born to himself and his wife Janet (née Mabon) in Paxton, Berwickshire, before the family moved to Glasgow in the late 1880s, when he

James and Mary Liddell after their wedding in Shanghai, 1899.

became a worker with the Scottish Colportage Association, distributing Bibles, Bible portions and other Christian books and tracts. It was a visit by Mary to a Sunday School outing of Blair's congregation in Stirling in 1893 that brought her in touch with James Liddell. This was the start of a romance which culminated in their engagement and marriage in Shanghai Cathedral in 1899, after James had begun his work in North China under the auspices of the London Missionary Society. Before Mary went out to China for the wedding she took a nursing job in Stornoway on the Isle of Lewis, which lies off the north-west coast of Scotland. She was there for barely a year. However, she must have been powerfully conscious of the deep respect the islanders had at that time for a careful observance of Sunday as the Lord's day. It is not fanciful to believe that her experience there may even have influenced her own love for the Lord and His day, which was subsequently conveyed to her family.

Just why Eric Liddell was so conscientious about refusing to compete in sports on Sundays is, strangely, a question little touched on by biographers. None of them really explains the theology behind such a position. D. P. Thomson mentions that Eric was in effect working out what he had been taught from childhood.[5] Biographers, however, do not discuss this to any great extent. It is clear that Eric took his position from the Fourth Commandment (Exod. 20:8-11; Deut. 5:12-15), being convinced that it was of perpetual obligation and the basis for the observance by Christians of the Sabbath. The Christian Sabbath, or Lord's day, was the first day of the week, Sunday, by virtue of two great events of redemptive history: the resurrection of the Lord Jesus Christ from the dead and the coming of the Holy Spirit at Pentecost. The observance of the first day of the week is, however, also motivated by the Fourth Commandment. It seems clear that the Liddell children would have been instructed in such a view of Sunday by their parents. This was fairly widespread in Scottish church life at that point and was commonly maintained across the denominational divides.

Congregationalists could be as ardent for the Sunday Sabbath as any Presbyterians. It is of more than passing interest to note that James Gilmour (1843–1891), the pioneer missionary of the gospel work in Mongolia, was one of those. It is not at all unlikely that James Liddell was impressed by the position held by Gilmour, into whose work he was appointed in 1898. Gilmour had passed away seven years earlier, but James Liddell would certainly have been aware of the details of his predecessor's work and position. This was said of James Gilmour:

> …like Jesus, he preached and lived ideals which even his associates could not accept. His periods of fasting, his intense reverence for the Sabbath which, however, always included its right use, his strong position with reference to the use of tobacco and liquor, and his gradual rise from asceticism to a life singular in its imitation of Christ, constitute a legacy to every missionary and stimulus to higher living for all Christians.[6]

Of Gilmour it was noted that 'his strong Sabbatarian views never permitted him to travel by rail or omnibus on that day'.[7] It is quite possible that either James Liddell in his youth or his father had heard Gilmour speak at meetings held on his visits home on furlough. His last furlough had been in 1889–90. It is also more than likely that

James Liddell read Gilmour's popular books, such as his famous *Among the Mongols*, first published in 1883.

Another notable characteristic of Gilmour was to become a distinct feature of Eric Liddell's life, and very likely was exemplified in his father: 'His modesty in relation to episodes in which he was chief actor deprived the public of hearing many a thrilling tale. People often wanted to know what James Gilmour had done, but James Gilmour insisted on telling what God had done.'[8]

Though James Liddell would not have taken on all of James Gilmour's ways, there seems little doubt that Gilmour must have had some influence on his life and work, and through him on his sons. This may help to explain at least in part Eric's reverence for the Sabbath, his modesty in his work and his discipline and desire for Christlikeness in demeanour. The general tenor of Gilmour's position one way or another became true of Eric Liddell, no doubt encouraged by his father's teaching and example.

There is another area of possible influence through James Gilmour, as well as the earlier family connection with the Evangelical Union. Throughout his life Eric Liddell, like Gilmour before him, had an aversion to smoking and drinking. He would have been in what may be termed 'the total abstainers' camp'. Very often he appeared on platforms speaking out against the use of alcohol or tobacco. Sometimes he was sharply criticised for this. However, given what we now know about the effects of these substances, it may be suggested that this was beneficial to Eric Liddell in relation to his sporting interests. The fact that he had been brought up in a smoke-free, alcohol-free environment would have been no disadvantage to his lung and heart power, to say the least. It may even be argued that this gave him an 'edge' over less abstemious athletes!

The London Missionary Society was closely associated with the Congregational Union of Churches, though it was constitutionally independent. Perhaps the most renowned missionary of the LMS was David Livingstone (1813–1873), who had 'opened up' Africa under its auspices. The LMS mission field in Mongolia was pioneered by James Gilmour. Mongolia was a large, remote and sparsely populated country situated between Russia in the north and China in the south. It was a province of China up to 1911, when it became an autonomous state. The religion of the country then was largely Buddhist. Gilmour began his work there with the London Missionary Society in May 1870. It was said that 'He made lonely, heroic efforts to preach the gospel to a people steeped in Lamaist forms of Buddhism; spending summers with nomadic Mongols on the plains of Mongolia and winters with Mongols in Peking.'[9] It was his life's work, which ended only with his death from typhus at Tientsin on 21 May 1891. Gilmour's work was continued first, briefly, by a colleague, the Rev. John Parker, and then, in 1898, by James Liddell.

The work in Mongolia, however, came to a rather abrupt end with the Boxer Rebellion. That rebellion was initiated by a society known as the 'Righteous Harmonious Fists'. They were commonly known as 'Boxers' on account of their devotion to martial arts. The rebellion lasted from November 1899 to September 1901 and was motivated by objections to foreign influences in trade, politics, religion and technology. There was concern that Chinese culture was being submerged under Western values (or lack of values). Much of the aggression of the Boxers came to be directed against Christian churches and missions, somewhat 'soft' targets, but targets which they saw as a particular threat to their traditional values. The Boxers were intent on resisting with force any such thing that tended to undermine their own authority and power. The end of the rebellion came in September/October 1901 through the intervention of a coalition of Western armies. As a result of the rebellion 182 Protestant missionaries and 500 Chinese Protestants, as well as 18,000 or so Chinese Catholics, were murdered. It was said that the China Inland Mission lost more personnel than any other single society: fifty-eight adults and twenty-one children. However, when the allied nations were demanding compensation from the Chinese government, Hudson Taylor refused to accept any payment for loss of property and life 'in order to demonstrate the meekness of Christ to the Chinese'.[10]

At the time of the Boxer Rebellion, James and Mary Liddell were at Ch'ao Yang (Chaoyang) in Manchuria, North China. They were then staying with LMS doctor Tom Cochrane, a Scotsman from Greenock, and his wife Grace, with their three children. James took on the church-based side of the work there. When stories filtered through, early in 1900, of atrocities committed by the Boxers nearby, it was clear that they would have to flee for their lives.

Tom Cochrane saw it as his duty to remain behind with his Christian friends. It was arranged that his wife Grace and their children, together with Mary Liddell, would be taken by James Liddell to the railhead sixty miles away in an attempt to get them to safety. James would then return to the mission premises. Their journey was fraught with many dangers. However, in view of the very precarious situation in which he found himself, Tom later decided to make a dash for the railhead in the hope of catching up with his family. He dressed in Chinese clothes and went on horseback, once again facing terrible danger. Eventually he met up with his family and the Liddells at the railhead, where Grace Cochrane had refused to go on in the hope that her husband would join them. In the goodness of the Lord he did. They duly boarded the next train for Shanghai and relative safety.[11]

In their time at Shanghai Mary Liddell gave birth to their first child, a son whom they named Robert Victor. That was on 27 August 1900, at the London Missionary Society Compound in Shanghai, where the Liddells had taken refuge after their narrow escape from death in the flight from Ch'ao Yang. A few months later, however, the intrepid James and Mary returned to the north to be settled in Tientsin. Meanwhile James took a trip into Mongolia to see what had happened to

James and Mary Liddell with Eric, Rob and Jenny on a visit home in 1907.

the Chinese Christians there. He toured the Mongolian area for four months or so, accompanied, among others, by 200 soldiers!

It was in Tientsin that Eric Henry was born, sixteen months after Robert. When things returned to some semblance of normality in 1902, Mary Liddell and her boys moved to Siaochang [Zaoqiang], some 185 miles inland to the south-west, as James Liddell had been posted there in the interval. A daughter, Janet Lillian (Jenny), was born at Siaochang on 3 October 1903 and another son, Ernest Blair, was added to the family circle in Peking on 12 December 1912.

It is hard to grasp fully just how dangerous and volatile life was at that time in that area of the Far East. But this was the situation in which Eric Liddell and his older brother came into the world and spent the early years of their life, before they were brought by their parents, with their younger sister Jenny, to the United Kingdom for the first time in 1907.

Before James Liddell returned to China in the autumn of 1908 he arranged for the boys' education at the 'school for the sons of missionaries' then situated in Blackheath, London but which since 1912 has been located in Mottingham, Kent, where it came to be known as Eltham College.

The four Liddell children in 1914.
From left to right: Rob, Jenny, Ernest and Eric.

Start of a sprint race in front of the main Eltham College building (c1913).
Eric Liddell is on the left. This is the first known athletics photo of the future
Olympic champion.

Life at Eltham College was very congenial for the Liddell boys, hard as it must have been for them to be separated from their parents. The nearness in age of Eric and Robert must have been an important factor in the younger brother's development. In their early play Eric would inevitably have been 'running to keep up'. As far as Eltham College was concerned, as a boarding school, the education there was one that catered for academic, physical and also, to some degree, the spiritual interests of the boys. Whatever aptitude they may have had for playing games, the Liddell boys had every opportunity to take part in a wide range of sporting activities. They took full advantage of the opportunities offered. Again, it cannot be stressed too strongly just what an advantage such all-round sporting opportunities provided for those who had the basic ability and competitive drive, or at least for those who wished to develop them.

Both Rob and Eric performed outstandingly in the sports they took up. There were the athletic sports in the spring, cricket in the summer session and rugby in the winter months. The teaching and training received at such a school, moreover, encouraged a balanced view of life. It would have involved a restful Sunday, free from sport and study,

Eltham College cricket eleven in 1917. Eric and Rob are seated on the left.

Eltham College rugby first fifteen in 1918, Eric was captain (holding the ball).

and focusing on the spiritual needs of the boys. Besides church attendance at the Congregational Church next to the school at Blackheath, there would be prayers in the chapel, and it appears that the brothers were involved in forming a Crusader group in the college. The Crusaders' Union

56 George Square, Edinburgh, Eric's residence for much of his time at Edinburgh University.

was an evangelical non-denominational Bible class for boys.

All this ensured distinctly evangelical influences on the boys throughout their schooldays. It appears that they became members of the Congregational Church in 1917,[12] though what that involved in terms of profession of faith is not clear. In sports they excelled. Rob was captain of the college first fifteen between 1916 and 1918 and the cricket first eleven in 1916 and 1917. Eric followed Rob as captain of the rugby fifteen in 1918–1919, and cricket eleven in 1919. In successive years Rob and Eric received the Blackheath Cup as 'the best all-round sportsman of the year' – Rob in 1917 and Eric in 1918. Even as early as 1917 Eric was known as 'a fast right-wing three-quarter'. In 1918 Rob and Eric dominated the college games, Eric winning the 100 yards (setting a college record of 10.8 seconds), 440 yards and long jump, and Rob the cross-country race, the hurdles race and high jump. Rob won the senior championship that year, but Eric captured it in 1919, in the process setting a new 100 yards record of 10.2 seconds, a brilliant time for a seventeen-year-old.

Rob left Eltham in 1918 and the following spring went up to Edinburgh University to study medicine. The university was recognised to have one of the best medical faculties in the land. Life must have been hard for Eric after Rob left the college. It was the first time they had been separated, which meant a great deal to the younger brother. They were brought into each other's company again in 1920 when Eric went up to Edinburgh in the springtime to join his mother, sister and younger brother, who had returned a year in advance of the return of James Liddell on a regular furlough.

In the summer of 1920 Eric took a subject he needed for university entrance (French). He matriculated at Edinburgh University on 23 February 1921 for a BSc degree in pure science, after taking some courses at Heriot Watt College relevant for his degree.

Rob and Eric stayed with the family members in Edinburgh until mid-October 1922 when their father and mother, with Jenny and Ernest, returned to China. At that point Rob and Eric made their home in the congenial atmosphere of the hostel of the Edinburgh Medical Missionary Society at 56 George Square, in close proximity to all the various university buildings.

At certain points Rob's influence was crucial in Eric's life. There is no doubt that Eric had the greater athletic ability. Rob, however, did compete in athletics for a time in Edinburgh. Perhaps he was encouraged to do so by Eric's success, though Eric was at first a rather reluctant runner. It may be that Eric encouraged Rob to compete occasionally. Rob often ran as 'unattached', or in the colours of Edinburgh University Athletic Club. However, there is a record of his competing in some track meetings. At West Kilbride, for example, on Saturday, 16 July 1921, the Liddell boys competed in the 100 yards and 220 yards handicap races. In the 100 yards Eric won from scratch (i.e. the full distance) in a Scottish record-equalling 10.0 seconds, though the race was run downhill and no record was awarded. The 220 yards race was a close affair. C. Fraser (of Maryhill Harriers), who had a sixteen-yards start, won the race by inches from Rob Liddell, who had a twelve-yards start, in 24.2 seconds. Eric, who ran the full distance, was only inches behind Rob. The time seems slow, but the track would have been very rough and ready.

Rob regularly played rugby for the university in the 1921–22 and 1922–23 seasons. When he did play he played as a centre three-quarter, with Eric as his wing three-quarter. Eric also frequently played centre for the university team during his playing days, though in all the representative matches, including internationals, he was invariably on the wing. Rob was not as involved as Eric in the sports, and in any case was heavily committed to a hard course of medical studies. There is no reason to believe, however, that he did not give the strongest encouragement to his younger brother in all his sporting interests, recognising that he had a distinct talent for sports.

In spiritual matters, though, there is every reason to believe that Rob's encouragement of his younger brother was formative. There is no doubt that at university, while Eric became more involved with athletics and rugby after the spring of 1921, Rob was already more involved in student evangelism. He clearly had strong evangelical convictions. Eric would have been conscientious in the habits of daily Bible reading and prayer, inculcated from early years. He would also be diligent in the church services at Morningside Congregational Church, situated at 'Holy Corner', and would be involved fully in its life. However, there was a matter of commitment.

D. P. Thomson identified the spring of 1923 as a Rubicon for Eric, spiritually. 'Eric...passed through what was perhaps the first great spiritual crisis of his life,' wrote Thomson.[13] It had to do with a group of Scottish university students who were members of what was known as the 'Glasgow Students' Evangelistic Union'. They were bound for a mission in Armadale in West Lothian, an industrial town of some 5,000 souls. The mission was to be concluded with a meeting for men in the town hall on the Friday night. No doubt through Rob, who had already taken part in the GSEU campaigns, it was believed that his brother was a Christian. Given Eric's profile in the world of sport – by then he was representing Scotland at the international level in both rugby and athletics – it was suggested that he might speak at the closing meeting in Armadale. D. P. Thomson, who knew Rob already, made for 56 George Square and spoke to Rob first:

'Will Eric come and speak for us?'

'You'll have to ask him for yourself.'

A few minutes later Thomson was meeting Eric for the first time and asking him directly. There was a moment's silence.

'All right, I'll come.'

Thomson felt relieved. That was 6 April 1923, a crucial day in the spiritual life of the young Christian athlete. Thomson believed that at that time Eric did have real faith in the Lord Jesus Christ, but had been something of a secret disciple. 'Of his influence for good there could be no question – it was acknowledged on every hand – but he had never disclosed its secret, and he had never openly confessed his Lord.'[14]

Whatever understanding Eric had then of the nature of Christian experience, he certainly later expressed himself clearly on the necessity for the new birth, repentance and faith, and the importance of the work of the Holy Spirit and the Bible for Christian discipleship. In relation to the new birth he was later to write this:

> *True Christianity starts with the new birth.* 'Ye must be born again' (John 3:7). *The new birth is God coming into your life and giving you a new nature, a nature of love to God and man.* Nothing in life can make up for the lack of this; nothing can take its place...Christian living is made possible by the new birth. You never can understand the meaning of Christian living until God comes into your life.[15]

'When you are converted and give your life to God,' he says in another place, 'this is the work of the Holy Spirit.'[16] Eric must have known such a work in his own experience, as his life well demonstrated. He also maintained the imperatives of the moral law in the life of the Christian.[17]

At any rate, after Armadale there would be no turning back. Both Rob and Eric spoke at the Armadale meeting. 'Eric did remarkably well for a first appearance, and said some telling things,' recorded D. P. Thomson in his diary.[18] He recorded elsewhere that 'Both brothers spoke, and Eric made a deep impression more by his simplicity and sincerity, than by any words he actually uttered. Next day the news flashed around Scotland in the press – Edinburgh University's great runner had appeared on an evangelistic platform.'[19] No doubt Eric learned what is spoken of in the Bible:

> If thou shalt confess with thy mouth the Lord Jesus, and shalt believe in thine heart that God hath raised him from the dead, thou shalt be saved. For with the heart man believeth unto righteousness; and with the mouth confession is made unto salvation. For the scripture saith, Whosoever believeth on him shall not be ashamed (Rom. 10:9-11).

At a farewell meeting for him in June 1925, Eric related his feelings on that first occasion. This is how his words were reported:

> Years ago he had been faced with the greatest problem of his life. He had been asked to assist at a campaign in Armadale, and at that time he had not addressed a gathering and was very reluctant about accepting. On the following morning he received a message from his sister, which contained the text – 'Fear not, for I am with thee; be not [dismayed] for I will guide thee.' That text had helped him to make his decision, and since then he has endeavoured to do the work of his Master.

The text referred to could have been one of several verses found in Isaiah, Jeremiah and Ezekiel, but most likely it was Isaiah 41:10, which reads in full: 'Fear thou not; for I am with thee: be not dismayed; for I am thy God: I will strengthen thee; yea, I will help thee; yea, I will uphold thee with the right hand of my righteousness.' We can well appreciate how such a promise would have been a great encouragement to Eric, faced with D. P. Thomson's challenge.

Whether or not it was that particular verse, that was the start of Eric Liddell's involvement in evangelism, something he sustained in the years he remained in the United Kingdom. Indeed, it was the principal reason for his remaining in Scotland in the year after he graduated, though at that time he was also engaged in some theological studies at the Scottish Congregational College in Edinburgh. We shall return to this when we consider Eric's activities throughout the period he took part in track meetings before he left for the Far East in July 1925.

The involvement of D. P. Thomson was without doubt vital in Eric's change of direction at this point in his life. The example and encouragement of his older brother, Rob, as an evangelical Christian, were also crucial in Eric's spiritual experience and commitment, both in Scotland and later in China. With the use of Eric Liddell in such work, and of some other prominent sportsmen of the day as well, there was a strong reflection of the 'muscular Christianity' so common, for example, in evangelistic work in the colleges of the United States in the early years of the twentieth century.[20] There is no doubt of Eric's earnestness at that early stage, nor of his usefulness. There is no doubt, either, that it was a crucial factor in his following through his felt calling to the mission-field, in which he was to return to the land of his birth and devote his life to Christ and to China.

The question may be posed at this point: did this spiritual change, or open profession of Christ at least, make young Eric a better runner? Did his subsequent success derive from this 'Rubicon' of April 1923? The answer to these questions must be: 'Yes and no.' Being a Christian does not make a great athlete, nor does it necessarily make a more successful athlete. At the same time, peace with God and living to please Him will have a certain liberating effect on a person. It will not necessarily make him successful, but it will give him the means of dealing with adversities, coping with disappointments and not being over-expectant of rewards. Christian sportsmen and women, like anyone else, have a limited range of abilities. It may be that their Christian faith will encourage them to develop these abilities in a more diligent way as people who recognise that they are stewards of their bodies and answerable to God for the deeds done in the body. In addition, it may well be that their lifestyle, as those who live by the Word of God, will enable them to maintain a good state of health. At least they will have a perspective on things that is not dependent on worldly success. In this sense Eric Liddell's earnest Christian faith, and his evident reliance upon the Lord, would have brought out the best in him, something that might be expected of a Christian. He was motivated in his sport, just as in other aspects of his life, by a true desire to honour and glorify the Lord Jesus Christ. In a real sense this does explain his manner of competing in his sport and his success in it.

This much was suggested by his great track adversary, Harold M. Abrahams: 'Eric Liddell was a man whose intense spiritual convictions contributed largely to his athletic triumphs. While his ability must have been great, but for his profound intensity of spirit he surely could not have achieved so much.'[21] It is hard to take issue with that sentiment. D. P. Thomson had this to say about the matter:

> There were some who said, and very many more who feared, that Eric's participation in evangelistic work might have an adverse affect on his running. Apart from anything else, an additional interest and activity of such an absorbing kind might impede his progress as an athlete,

and as a coming British 'star', if not actually stultifying his efforts. It had exactly the opposite effect...In the three months immediately following his open confession of Christ, and his emergence as an evangelist, Eric ran more brilliantly and achieved greater distinction as a sprinter than in all the years that had gone before.[22]

Thomson goes on to suggest that this was to be expected: 'Spiritual liberation has as profound an effect on a man's mind and body as it has on his soul.' Ability, from the Christian perspective, is God-given. That is, of course, true for the non-Christian as well as the Christian, whether or not the individual acknowledges it to be so.

When Eric was asked by one journalist whether he ever preached from the text, 'So run, that ye may obtain' (1 Cor. 9:24), he answered adroitly: 'I'd sooner preach on "The race is not to the swift."'[23] Often, when he was asked about the secret of his success in track athletics, he would reply, 'Why, it's the three sevens.' To this enigmatic answer the obvious response was: 'What are the three sevens?' 'Why, the seventh book of the New Testament, seventh chapter and seventh verse: "But every man hath his proper gift of God, one after this manner, and another after that."'[24]

A missionary colleague in China once asked him whether he ever prayed that he would win a race. The ready answer was: 'No, I never prayed that I would win a race. I have, of course, prayed about the athletic meetings, asking that in this, too, God might be glorified.'[25] That typified Eric Liddell's attitude to the relationship of the Christian faith to his sport. It typifies a principle of Christian action in sport or any branch of culture, which is that all human cultural activities are to be brought into submission to the lordship of Christ to find their truest expression. Through sin everything may become perverted. The Christian, however, will seek to bring everything into the obedience of faith and will desire the glory of God in all things. In doing that the Christian will seek to use well the gifts which the Lord has given him or her. Eric Liddell certainly felt that the Lord had given him a gift for running. He obviously had the necessary inclination and drive as well.

All this, then, went into the making of the Christian sportsman whom Eric Liddell was to exemplify. Liddell's sportsmanship and

Christian integrity must stand as a constant stimulus to the youth of every age to live by Christian principles in every area of life. His story is always worth retelling. It all rested on his faith in Jesus Christ as his Saviour. In the words of a hymn he so obviously loved, this is how it was for him:

My faith looks up to thee,
Thou Lamb of Calvary,
Saviour divine!
Now hear me while I pray,
Take all my guilt away,
Oh, let me from this day
Be wholly thine!

May thy rich grace impart
Strength to my fainting heart,
My zeal inspire;
As thou hast died for me,
Oh, may my love to thee
Pure, warm, and changeless be,
A living fire!

While life's dark maze I tread
And griefs around me spread,
Be thou my guide;
Bid darkness turn to day,
Wipe sorrow's tears away,
Nor let me ever stray
From thee aside.

When ends life's transient dream,
When death's cold, sullen stream
Shall o'er me roll,
Blest Saviour, then, in love,
Fear and distrust remove;
Oh, bear me safe above,
A ransomed soul.[26]

4.

AN EXCITING PROSPECT

Eric Liddell clearly possessed great natural athletic ability. He had begun to show that on the sports field of Eltham College. He was slow, however, to take up sports after he went up to Edinburgh University in the autumn of 1920. He did not compete on the track at all in 1920. Nor did he play rugby that winter (1920–21). Truth to tell, he did not have a great build, standing just five feet nine inches (1 metre 75) and weighing at his peak around eleven stones (154 lbs).

It is not clear whether Eric intended to run competitively at university. In the event it came about almost accidentally. Eric left his own graphic account of how his track career began:

I had only been in the University a few months before the Athletic Sports came on. Six weeks before this event, a friend, hearing that I had done a little running at school, came round to try to persuade me to enter. I told him I was busy. I had a lot of work to get through and no time for that sort of thing. The very words I used seemed to startle me. Busy? Work? Yes, I had been working for about five months, and most of that time I had also been busy. These two words were new to me; they seemed to be strangers, trying to settle down in a home that wasn't their own. Needless to say, they were soon dislodged, and I was out in the open air practising once again what I had started at school. I was only a novice then, and a novice was my trainer. Both of us knowing very little or nothing about it, we got on extremely well together for the first week. Then came the holidays. I had made arrangements for a week's cycling tour. My novice friend said that that was the very worst thing for training. But all that he said slid off my back like water off a duck's, for, after all, at that stage we were both novices, and I was quite sure that I knew as much about it as he did. Leaving him with his thoughts, I went off with four other friends for a cycle run to Ben Nevis. It took us exactly six days, from a Monday morning to late on Saturday night. All of us agreed that it was a great success, despite the fact that when we reached the top of Ben Nevis at six o'clock one morning, and waited for the sun to rise, we found that that was one of the days on which the sun did not rise.

Arriving back, I went to see if I would be able to run, but, alas! what I had been told was only too true. I was stiff, there was no spring in my muscles. Only three or four more weeks before I was to make my first appearance in public as a runner. Gradually the springiness came back, and that May I entered for the 'Varsity Sports.[1]

Such were the beginnings of one of the most illustrious track careers of any Scottish athlete. It is thus that Eric Liddell made his way to the Edinburgh University Sports Ground at Craiglockhart on Saturday, 28 May 1921, to pit himself against the best sprinters at the university. One of the best that year was the 1920 champion G. Innes Stewart. The tussle between this raw novice, Liddell, and the more seasoned man, Stewart, has gone down in the folklore of Scottish athletics, though the event in itself was of only slight significance. But this was Eric Liddell's first track event in Scotland. It was his first sortie into competitive running since 1919. There was no weight of expectation on his shoulders. He might compete just the once and disappear into the obscurity from which he had come.

How Eric came to take part has already been noted in his own words. Innes Stewart also left an account of that particular track meeting. This is what he remembered:

I had been in strict training and had been running well, hoping again to be sprint champion. Shortly before the Sports, Dick Grace warned me that there was a young Arts student, Eric Liddell, whom I would require to watch. The last Saturday in May arrived, and we were soon trotting out for the 100 yards heats. Liddell was on my right, dressed in longish black pants and a white vest. Evan Hunter got us off to a good start and I could see that I was not going to have it all my own way, for

Liddell was running me very close indeed, and I reached the tape only a few inches in front of him. In the final the reverse occurred, Liddell reached the tape an inch or two in front of me. The time was 10.4 secs.

Stewart had won the heat by half a yard in 10.6 seconds. Liddell won the final by much the same distance.

Then there was the 220 yards. Again, let Stewart describe how he saw events unfold:

My self-esteem was to get another rude shock in the furlong, generally considered my best distance. Liddell got off to a slightly better start and soon gained two yards on me. When we came to the last 80 yards, I had narrowed the gap to about a yard, and finally got home by a matter of inches. The time, 23.4 secs., was not remarkable, but, on a slightly uphill grass track with little wind, it was probably better than it looks. After that I realized that a new power in Scottish athletics had arrived.[2]

Eric Liddell also left an account of these events:

There was there one who was greatly fancied as a coming champion of Scotland, and I was down to meet him in the first heat. The pistol went and within the first thirty yards he gained a short head; then for the rest of the journey we seemed to travel at the same rate; thus he won. But that was only a heat, and the first three were chosen to compete in the final, and when we met then the order was reversed.

In the next race that I took part in that afternoon I was second to G. I. Stewart, the above mentioned. This is the only time in the five years that, at the 'Varsity, Inter-'Varsity or Scottish Championship, I won a second prize.

Leaving aside the loss of the 100 yards heat, it is a remarkable fact that this defeat at the hands of Innes Stewart was one of only two that Liddell suffered in any scratch (i.e. non-handicap) sprint race at the hands of a Scot in distances of 100 yards to 440 yards between 1921 and 1925. But this was where it all began. It was the start of one of the most wonderful chapters in Scottish amateur athletics history.

In the remainder of that 1921 season Eric Liddell more or less swept all before him. The success at the Edinburgh University Sports meant that he would compete in the Scottish Intervarsity Sports to be held that year at University Park, St Andrews, on Saturday, 18 June. Liddell himself sets the scene:

> I was next chosen to run for the University in the Inter-'Varsity Sports against Glasgow, St Andrews and Aberdeen. That meant a little strenuous training. I was taken to a place called Powderhall. It was the first time in my life I had ever seen a cinder track. Many who trained there were professionals. Up to then I thought all professional runners would be first-class runners. They danced about on their toes as if they were stepping on hot bricks. Whenever they started to run, they dug big holes for their toes to go into, as if they were preparing for the time when their toes would dance no more. Surely they did not expect me to make such a fool of myself as all that? Yes, I found that they did.

It is of interest to note in passing that though sprinters then used 'crouch' starts, there were as yet no such things as starting blocks. What is more, it was only on the cinder tracks that holes would be made for sprinters at the start of the races. That did not happen on the grass tracks. There was no such thing then as an 'all-weather' surface! In truth there were precious few cinder tracks in those days. Invariably the cinder tracks were quicker than the grass – always provided the weather was fine and they had been well rolled. Naturally, both these surfaces were vulnerable to adverse weather conditions – the grass tracks often becoming soft and spongy and the cinder tracks liable to be flooded and be muddy. This has to be borne in mind in assessing the merit of performances in those days. Weather also had a greater impact at that time, for there were no fields or stadia which were entirely enclosed by stands. Most were perfectly open to all the elements.

Another point to be made has to do with time-keeping. In those days all performances were expressed in fifths of a second. That is to say, two-fifths of a second was 0.4 second. Stopwatches that recorded in tenths of a second would always be rounded up to the nearest fifth. Thus, in his competitive days in Scotland, Eric Liddell was frequently recorded at 10.0 seconds over 100 yards. It is very likely that a more accurate time, as measured by hand-held watches, would often have been 9.9 seconds. It was not until 1934 in Scotland that times were given in tenths of a second for races of up to 220 yards. The corresponding English Amateur Athletic Association, however, changed their rule in 1923 so that sprint races would be taken with 1/100th watches, with readings rounded up to the nearest tenth of a second.

At any rate, if Eric was going to be serious about his athletics, he would have to do what he saw among the professionals at Powderhall. It is important to recognise just how seriously, relatively speaking, Eric took this right from the start. Notwithstanding his renowned modesty, it is clear that he was conscious of having some native ability as a runner. He was therefore prepared for some hard work:

> At first I felt that every eye was turned on me, when, as a matter of fact, there was nobody watching me at all. Still, even when no one is watching at all, it is rather difficult to do things like working your shoulders, dancing about on your toes, doing short ten-yard dashes, and in general doing everything but run. The exercises seemed unimportant at first, but later one finds how useful they have been. It was at this time that I got to know the trainer who trained me during my five seasons on the running track. He took me in hand, pounded me about like a piece of putty, pushed this muscle this way and that muscle the other way, in order, as he said, to get me into shape.

The trainer in question was Thomas McKerchar.[3] Tom was employed in a printing establishment in the city, but he was passionately interested in track running. By the time he took on the young university sprinter he was forty-four and an astute and knowledgeable trainer who had worked among the professionals at Powderhall, not far from his home in Leith.

In *Chariots of Fire* the impression is given that Eric's approach to his training was somewhat rustic and carried out under the eye of a well-meaning, but amateurish mentor. In the film Eric's training is portrayed as relatively informal, by contrast to the 'professional' approach of Harold Abrahams. Eric is pictured running across

*Eric with his trainer,
Tom McKerchar.*

highland hills and sandy beaches under the eye of his 'novice' trainer, whereas Abrahams is depicted as going through 'scientific' training at the hands of the 'professional' trainer Sam Mussabini. That is not how it was. The truth is that Eric's training from the start was worked at very positively, to bring out the best in him.

Many years ago the author received a personal note from David Jamieson (1879–1972) that highlighted Eric Liddell's approach: 'My personal recollection of Eric was the tremendous verve he put into his training. Two sessions and occasionally three at Powderhall, and his mentor Tommy McKerchar usually laid down his routine of practice.'

The sport, for Eric Liddell, was not an all-consuming interest. He always held it in balance with his other interests, educational and Christian. But when he did train or run he certainly put everything into it – and it showed. Eric, again, gave insight into what Tom McKerchar did with him:

> He told me that my muscles were all far too hard and that they needed to be softened by massage. He added that if they were not softened soon, some day when I tried to start, one of the muscles would snap. He took me out and told me to do a short run. After finishing the run I stopped much quicker than any of the others. When I asked him what he thought of it, he answered that if I wanted a breakdown I was going about it in the best possible manner, for it appears that one must never stop abruptly on reaching the tape.
>
> Thus, being thoroughly humiliated, feeling that my reputation had been dragged through the mud, that my self-respect was still wallowing in the mire, and that if I didn't get into the clutches of a trainer soon, every muscle in my body would give way and I should remain a physical

wreck till the end of my days, I was then in a fit mental condition to start an athletic career.

Twice, and sometimes three times a week, I was down at Powderhall training for the Scottish Championships. The short-distance men trained on one side of the track, while the whippets were being trained on the other side. Thus, while we trained there was the continual barking of the whippets, which were straining their leashes in their eagerness to get on the track.

Training is not the easiest thing to do. It is liable to become monotonous, with the continual repetition of certain exercises. One of the hardest lessons to learn is how to start. Time after time you go to your holes, rise to the 'get set' position, and wait for the pistol to go. Someone tries to go off before the pistol, and so we all have to get up and start from the beginning again. Even after I had been at it for four years, the papers now and then reminded me that my weak point was the slowness with which I started.

The first 'open' meeting that Eric competed in during the 1921 season was the Queen's Park Football Club Annual Sports held on Saturday, 4 June at Hampden Park, the stadium of the national football team. Eric met with no success in this meeting, but his running was noticed by one astute observer, Duncan McLeod Wright, who was himself to become an outstanding marathon runner and administrator in Scottish athletics. He said this of his first sighting of Eric Liddell:

> In my half-century's connection with Scottish sport, I have met many famous athletes, but I state in all honesty that I don't remember my first view of anyone as vividly as my first sight of Eric Liddell.
>
> It was at Queen's Park Sports in 1921. I had heard that there was a real flyer in the Edinburgh University's colours called Eric Liddell. Through a small window from the competitors' room underneath the Stand, I saw Eric for the first run in the 100 yards and was completely thrilled. Off to a slow start, he ran with blazing speed, chin up, head back on the shoulders, and his arms thrashing the air.
>
> 'Dreadful style,' said the cynical critics. But his space-devouring legs raced on a straight path to the tape, and to me he typified the speed runner putting all his strength into his effort to gain victory.

Wright adds: 'His infectious enthusiasm endeared him to the sporting public, and for the next four years he packed the terraces at every sports meeting he attended.'[4]

The terraces were not packed, however, for his first Intervarsity Sports, held that year at St Andrews on Saturday, 18 June. There were only 600 spectators! What initial training Eric did after the Edinburgh University Sports certainly paid off as he proceeded to win the Scottish Universities 100 yards (with a time of 10.6 seconds) and 220 yards (in 22.4 seconds) at St Andrews on 18 June, the 220 yards on a straight course.

That was one week before the Scottish Championships. So, when Eric went to the Scottish Championships at Celtic Park, Glasgow, on Saturday, 25 June, he had behind him three senior scratch 100 yards races and two 220 yards races. His inexperience made no difference. He proceeded to sweep all before him at Hampden, winning all his races, heats and finals, and helping the Edinburgh University team to victory in the one-mile medley relay.

The next big challenge was the 'Triangular International' involving England (and Wales), Ireland and Scotland. This was an annual 'home countries' international which had been revived in 1920 following a lapse after 1914 due to the Great War. In 1921 the contest was due to be held at Windsor Park, Belfast, on Saturday, 9 July. This was the first experience the young rising Scottish star was to have of competing against some of the best athletes of the other home nations. In the 100 yards he was up against the crack English sprinter, W. A. Hill, who had been 1919 AAA 100 and 220 yards champion. He was an 'even-time' sprinter. ('Even time' is a speed of 100 yards in 10.0 seconds, or ten yards a second.) Eric, however, not apparently showing any nerves, won the 100 yards race in 10.4 seconds, outpacing Hill. In the 220 yards Eric won his heat in 23.0. The final involved only three athletes and it was not run in marked lanes. It turned out to be a 'tactical' race and the young Scot was beaten into third place by more experienced English sprinters. William Hill ran out winner by a yard and a half (so reported *The Scotsman*) from fellow-Englishman Fred Mawby in a slow 23.8 with Eric a yard or so further back in third place. He could only put it down to experience. Nevertheless, the victory in the 100 yards helped Scotland to a rare win in the contest, the scoring being simply on the basis of events won. Scotland that day won six events to England's three and Ireland's two. Despite his indifferent running in the furlong, his 100 yards win in this contest established Eric on a wider front than the domestic Scottish one. However, stiffer tests were to come that year.

In those days there were many athletics meetings in the domestic calendar. Many of these were held by football clubs. Their meetings combined track and field events – mostly track events – with out-of-season five-a-side football tournaments, designed to keep the professional footballers active in the summer months. Some of the football club events were the most prestigious events of the season. Especially was this true of the Rangers and Celtic Sports traditionally held right at the end of the track and field season. But even the lesser events were important in the development of the track athlete. The reason for this is not often recognised and has been scarcely mentioned in relation to Eric Liddell's progress as a sprinter.

In all the sports meetings outside the university sports and other championships, the 'local' events had some 'scratch' races, in which all the competitors ran the full distance, but many contained so-called 'handicap' events. In the handicap events starts were given, or not given, to individual runners, on the basis of how good the handicappers reckoned the various competitors to be. Thus the champion, or near-champion, athletes would be on the scratch mark – that is, they would have to run the full distance, or very near it. The lesser athletes would be given a start of some yards, the distances varying according to their ability. In a 100 yards handicap race, for example, the 'back-marker' – the runner on the scratch line running the full distance – would sometimes concede anything up to eighteen yards to other competitors. A person receiving a start of eighteen yards would only have to run eighty-two yards of a 100 yards race.

Invariably there would be heats and finals, and in the bigger meetings semi-finals as well. Bearing all this in mind, one can well understand that the top athletes like Eric Liddell would of necessity have to run flat out week after week in order to qualify in, or to win, any of these handicap events. This meant that to take part in such competitions a high quality of running was required. In some measure it helps to explain why Eric Liddell developed into such an outstanding sprinter, and how he was so strong in the closing stages of the races. There was rarely any scope for slowing down and cruising through the finish. The competition was very intense. Liddell's sprinting success may well in some measure be put down to this system. Indeed, a prominent English newspaper of the day commented that in athletics one thing in which Scotland did not lag behind was the 'liberal inducements in the shape of short-limit handicaps'.

Incredible as it may seem now, the major football club meetings of the day often attracted above 800 competitors. This stands to reason, when we consider, on the one hand, the attraction of prizes to be won and, on the other hand, the 'equalisation' brought about by the handicap system, by which the journeyman runner could have some chance of winning a race against some of the stars, given the start he had on them through the handicap. This is worth mentioning in connection with Eric Liddell's track career, in view of the fact that from the start, more or less, he was a back-marker, obliged to run the full distance. He inevitably, therefore, had to run flat out in such meetings, whereas he was rarely pushed in the non-handicap sports and championships.

In the summer of 1921 Eric took part in several such meetings in June and July. He won many of the events. Some of these were brilliant performances, given the rough state of many tracks that would have been used, at least by modern standards. A glance at the appendix will confirm that he was constantly running even-time sprints. The big events, however, were the final two of the year: the Rangers Football Club Sports at Ibrox, and the Celtic Football Club Sports at Parkhead. The five-a-side football involving teams from the Scottish Football Leagues ensured huge crowds. Though the track races were to some extent 'fillers' in the programme, in their own way they captivated the crowds, especially when they involved athletes of international renown, as they usually did at Ibrox and Parkhead. At the Rangers Sports on Saturday, 6 August, Eric, with a start of 1½ yards, won the 100 yards invitation handicap[5] in 10 seconds after a 'sensational finish' with West of Scotland Harrier H. J. Christie. The English AAA sprint champion, Harry Edward, starting from the scratch line, was surprisingly unplaced in the race. Eric came close in the 300 yards open handicap, clocking around 32.0 seconds, from a start of four yards from the scratch line.

The following week saw the closing event of the year at Celtic Park. There were 18,000 spectators that Saturday. Again, a great deal of interest was created by the appearance of the famous Harry Edward (1895–1973), a native of British Guiana who had been a double bronze medallist in the Olympic 100 metres and 200 metres for Great Britain at Antwerp in 1920, and was the reigning AAA 100 and 220 yards champion. In a 100 yards handicap special event, run on the cinder track, Edward was on the scratch mark, with the Scottish champion having a start of one yard. Edward (running for Polytechnic Harriers) was expected to come through strongly this time. As in the race at Ibrox the previous week, however, Eric again ran with great determination to hold him off by inches in a time of 10.4 seconds. This was an indicator that a star of the first magnitude had appeared on the scene. (Incidentally, Rangers beat Celtic in the five-a-side football that afternoon by five goals to one!)

That a new track 'star' had arisen in Scotland was fully recognised by the *Glasgow Herald* in a review of the track season in Scotland. In the review the reporter wrote of Eric Liddell with remarkable prescience:

> E. H. Liddell, Edinburgh University A. C., is going to be a British champion ere long, and he might even blossom into an Olympic hero. His success has been phenomenal; in fact it is one of the romances of the amateur path. Unknown four months ago, he today stands in the forecourt of British sprinters...Liddell, as much because of his supreme grit as because of his pace, is a great figure in modern athletics, and is destined to be still greater in the near future.[6]

The end of his wonderful first season on the track was not, however, the end of sport that year for Eric Liddell. What about rugby? Enquiries soon brought to light his record at Eltham and naturally he was persuaded to play for the university's rugby club in the ensuing 1921–22 season.

Lest anyone should suppose that Eric spent his time as an undergraduate simply in advancing a sporting career, it should be stressed that all the while he was an able and diligent student. He went up to the university in the autumn of 1920 with a view to a four-year course in pure science leading to a BSc degree. The fact is that he was an outstanding student. Obviously in his life at the university he balanced his academic work with his sporting and Christian interests. There is every reason to believe that he did this all very successfully. D. P. Thomson had possession of Eric's class records. He provides insight into Eric's academic achievements at university:

> In the 1920-21 session his marks were 94% in Inorganic Chemistry and 83% in Mathematics. The following year he was 1st equal in two of his classes, and in his 3rd year 1st equal again in one, with 90%. This is a record of which any man might be proud, and it disposes at once of the idea that Eric Liddell was guilty of neglecting his studies, or even of relegating them to a secondary place, in the interest of athletic distinction. In the Olympic year [1924] there was, it is true, a slight falling away, but his figures never fell below 68%.[7]

There is no doubt that Eric saw his degree work as a priority during his time at Edinburgh University. Consequently, he approached it with the same sense of Christian stewardship as he did his leisure and Christian pursuits. It could always be said of him that he was 'more than an athlete'.

5.
ANOTHER STRING TO HIS BOW

Eric Liddell loved rugby. Perhaps it was because it was a team game and on balance he preferred team games. Track and field athletics could often seem lonely and involve over-much single-mindedness. Admittedly, there was a measure of camaraderie about these events, especially in the relay races or in Intervarsity or international contests, but not to the same extent as in rugby.

After his great track season of 1921 some of the university rugby players researched Eric's school record to see if he had any aptitude for the game. Sure enough, he did. It is not surprising that he was approached to play for the university, and no surprise either that he excelled in it, so much so that he was soon to be a regular in the national team. The track season ended in August and the rugby season began the following month. By January 1922 Eric was playing in an international match. The meteoric rise he made in rugby is easily as startling as what had happened for him on the track in 1921. How did it come about?

Eric had everything going for him as a rugby player. He had speed, of course. Though not bulky, he was strong. Above all, he had determination. Within weeks of taking up the game again he was included in the Edinburgh University 1st XV as a wing three-quarter, often with brother Rob as his centre. It is clear that the Liddell brothers could be a lethal combination. In a match against Glasgow University in February 1922, it was reported of one of the Edinburgh University tries in a 16–3 win that 'The ball came out to R. V. Liddell, who broke through and passed to E. H. Liddell, who dodged through the opposition for a great try.'[1]

Eric Liddell was just nineteen years of age when he first played for the Edinburgh University XV. Not many weeks after his first game, he was in the Edinburgh District side in the annual 'intercity' match against Glasgow, and in December 1921 he played in both Scottish rugby union trials matches, one at Galashiels and the other at Inverleith in Edinburgh, the pitch used for international matches. In these trials Eric was on the left wing, with another former pupil of Eltham College, Archibald Leslie Gracie, as his centre. Though their times at Eltham overlapped, Gracie (1896–1982) was over five years older than Eric and they had never played together at the college.

As far as the trials were concerned, reports published in *The Scotsman* describe the impression that Eric Liddell made in the matches. The first game was between 'Scotland' and 'the North and South'. It was played at the Netherdale Ground in Galashiels on Saturday, 10 December. Liddell was left wing, with A. L. Gracie as his centre. *The Scotsman* reported that:

> ...the 8,000 spectators present saw one of the finest exhibitions of football played on the Borders in a representative game. From start to finish it was palpitating in its excitement and brimful of clever and, at times brilliant, play...This game will long be remembered by those present for the brilliant combination which A. L. Gracie and E. H. Liddell made...The Edinburgh University man scored five tries during the afternoon and but for the greatness of Gracie would have been the hero of the match...It was a happy inspiration, therefore, on the part of the selectors to place him on the wing...Liddell had more than speed to recommend him, for if Gracie was taking fast passes he was sending them along like a shot, but Liddell never failed to take them. The pair give promise of being the fastest wing Scotland ever had.[2]

The score was 30 points to 9 in favour of the Scotland team.

The second of the trial matches, between 'Scotland' and 'the Rest', was played at Inverleith, Edinburgh on 24 December. Again, Eric Liddell played in the Scotland side. In reporting on this match *The Scotsman's* correspondent was fulsome in his praise of Eric: 'A Great Wing,' said the sub-title of the report. The account went on:

The outstanding personality of the trial was certainly E. H. Liddell. His great speed is not his only asset, for not only did he 'round' one and sometimes two opponents when he scored – and he got five tries – but time and again he had to use both resource and initiative. Never once was he found wanting. He showed an almost uncanny intuition for being in the right place at the right time, and no matter how unconventional.[3]

Eric showed up well even in comparison to A. L. Gracie, his centre, who was acknowledged as one of the rugby stars of the age, for the report says that 'Next in order of merit must come A. L. Gracie.' Apparently both Liddell and Gracie were 'heartily cheered' after their individual efforts by the crowd of nearly 8,000. The final score was 32 points to 6 for the Scotland XV. Not only had a star of the first magnitude arisen on the track in 1921, but it is clear that a star of the first magnitude had also arisen on the rugby field in Scotland.

Eric Liddell, then, impressed the selectors to such an extent that they just could not leave him out of the team against France on 2 January 1922. Frankly, there was no one else with the sheer speed. His potential was great and he was obviously no shirker in the defence department. Therefore, the day after New Year 1922, at Stade Colombes in Paris, Eric, a fortnight short of his twentieth birthday, made his debut for Scotland. It must have been a somewhat intimidating atmosphere, as there was a record crowd of 37,000 at the stadium that day, most of them there to cheer on the French. Apparently, the game was even in the first half, but the Scottish forwards dominated the second half. However, with rain falling throughout the match, conditions were not conducive to a handling game, and the result was a draw, with one try apiece (3–3). The Scottish captain was Colonel Charles M. Usher of Edinburgh Wanderers (1891–1981), who had played for Scotland before the Great War and who at Colombes actually led his team on to the field to the sound of the bagpipes, with two of the players carrying a huge wreath in honour of the war dead of the 1914–18 war. It was all quite an experience for the new cap.

Twelve days after the French match, on Saturday, 14 January, there was a third Scottish rugby union trial, this time at New Anniesland in

Scotland team versus Wales in 1922. C. M. Usher was the captain (seated holding the ball). A. L. Gracie is on his left and Eric right in front of Gracie squatting cross-legged.[5]

Glasgow, the pitch of the Glasgow Academicals. 'Of the eight three-quarters engaged,' said the report in *The Scotsman*, 'only E. H. Liddell was really satisfactory. Great speed, sure hands, and the ability to turn his opponents' failings to account marked his work. The only thrills of the game came from him. He was the only player with the hallmark "international" stamped on him.'[4] This trial was in advance of the three 'home internationals' (against England, Wales and Ireland). The first was against Wales on 4 February at Inverleith. This was a dour affair, which ended in a 9–9 draw. It was said that 'Liddell never got a chance.' Scotland were leading up to the very last minute, when Welsh centre Islwyn Evans dropped a goal to square the match.

The Irish match three weeks later was also played at Inverleith. Again, as was often the case, handling was difficult in a strong wind, and the wingers received few opportunities to get into the match. However, Scotland won the match thanks to a first international try from left wing Eric Liddell, though it was felt in general that his pace was not as potent as it was expected to be. Unfortunately, a broken finger-bone prevented Eric from taking part in the match against England at Twickenham on 18 March. It was thought that his absence was a factor in the Scottish defeat, given that the lack of pace of the Scottish wingers contributed to the loss, C. N. Lowe, the fine English left-winger, scoring a brace of tries that afternoon in an 11–5 win for the 'old enemy'.

So ended a remarkable rugby season for the promising Edinburgh University sprinter, who became an international after less than three months playing in the senior game. It has become increasingly rare for men to represent their country in more than one sport. In those days there was not the specialisation that has become so common in more recent times. It may be said, however, that the rugby playing of Eric Liddell could only have enhanced his strength for his track running. He also brought to the game a level of athleticism not too common among rugby players. Not all track sprinters are suited to the rough and tumble of a sport that involves as much bodily contact as rugby.

There had, however, been dual internationals in Scotland before Liddell, some outstanding sprinters among them. Just after the turn of the century there was Glasgow Academical Robert Summers Stronach (1882–1966), three-times AAA 120 yards hurdles champion and wing forward for Scotland between 1901 and 1905. There was William Halliday Welsh (1879–1972), a Merchistonian from a famous Edinburgh family. He won the 100, 220 and 440 yards events at the Scottish championships of 1900 and played on the wing for Scotland from 1900 to 1902. Later he practised medicine at Bridge of Allan and continued an interest in sport into old age as 'Chieftain' of the Strathallan Meeting in its amateur days. Then there was the all-rounder par excellence Kenneth Grant Macleod (1888–1967), who adapted himself to track and field, rugby and cricket in an all-too-brief competitive career. He three times won the Oxford v. Cambridge 100 yards for the 'light blues' and was Scottish long jump champion in 1906. He might have competed in the Olympic 100 metres in 1908 had he not been committed to playing county cricket for Lancashire that summer. Macleod remains the youngest man – at seventeen years and nine months – to play rugby for Scotland in the post-1900 period. There was also the 'Tasmanian Scot' William Allan Stewart (1889–1958), whose roots had been in Inverness. He played for

Scotland on the wing with sensational effect in 1913–14. A Scottish sprint champion and international, he competed for Australasia at the Stockholm Olympics of 1912. Just before the First World War, Walter Riddell Sutherland (1890–1918) lit up games in the Scottish Borders and for the Scottish team. He competed on the track and scored a great win in the 220 yards against Ireland in 1913 in a time of 22.5 seconds, the year he won his Scottish furlong title. Sadly, he was killed in action in the last year of the Great War.

Since those days those who have represented their country in two different sports have become even rarer. In Scotland since the Second World War the only sportsmen who achieved real success in rugby and athletics have been wing three-quarters Arthur Smith and David Whyte. Smith was Scottish long-jump champion in 1953 and played for the Scottish XV between 1955 and 1962. Whyte was also a long jumper. He won back-to-back AAA junior and senior titles in 1958 and 1959, and the Scottish title in 1959, 1962 and 1965. Whyte played for the international rugby XV between 1965 and 1967. Though resourceful and speedy players, neither had the sheer pace of Eric Liddell.

These men showed the advantage of having track sprinting credentials and training. They were uniformly among the outstanding rugby players of their respective generations. Thus it was with Eric Liddell. It is clear that a want of real athleticism has often been a great disadvantage and has been noticeably lacking from time to time in Scottish international teams. Perhaps the lesson for rugby players is that they should take part in track and field events in the summer to sharpen their athleticism. It might well be that if this had been the case with more Scottish rugby players, the international team might have been more effective than it has often been. For Eric Liddell, certainly, his interest in rugby meant that he kept very active over the winter months. Injury was always a danger, though in his competitive days in both athletics and rugby he suffered from remarkably few injuries.

The journalist William Reid (writing under the pseudonym 'Diogenes') summed up well the relative merits of Eric Liddell's rugby and athletics performances:

Liddell...liked running but he loved football. In the winter of 1921–22 he played in three Rugby internationals and in the following winter in four. In the winter of 1923–24 he stopped playing football in pursuance of his plan of study, and it was said of him that he could not so much as see football played. For all that he was not a natural footballer as he was a natural runner, and although he was too plucky and too good a tackler to be stigmatized as a 'mere sprinter', he had not the attributes – the knack and craft – of the great football player.[6]

This is a perceptive comment by one who witnessed Liddell's performances in both arenas, though it is only fair to say that Eric himself was to write that 'much as I loved Rugger and Cricket, sprinting seemed to be the sport which made the strongest appeal to me as a schoolboy.'[7]

6.
MORE BRILLIANT RUNNING

After a successful winter season of rugby there was eager anticipation of the track season in 1922, just to see what advance Eric Liddell would make as a sprinter. The season effectively began with the Edinburgh University Annual Sports on the last Saturday in May. There was considerable excitement about this, within the university and beyond, and a large crowd turned out to Craiglockhart for the sports on 27 May. Besides the 100 and 220 yards, Eric was down to run in the quarter-mile, his first senior race over the distance. His form was outstanding for the first track meet of the year. The 100 yards race was easily won in a record time for the event of 10.2 seconds. In the 220 yards, on the straight but slightly uphill grass track, Eric ran imperiously to breast

The start of Eric's first senior 440 yards race at the Edinburgh University Sports of 1922. Eric is second from the left.

the tape twelve yards ahead of the next man in 21.8 seconds. This was the first time that 22 seconds had been broken by a Scot in Scotland, beating by 0.2 second the record of James S. G. Collie (of Aberdeen University Athletic Club) set on a straight track at Aberdeen in 1913. In the 440 yards Eric did not need to push himself too hard and ran out an easy winner by eight yards in a modest 52.6 seconds.

My memory is a bit hazy now on the details, but as I remember it, a remarkable discovery was made in my last year in school, 1964–65. My school was Boroughmuir in Edinburgh. By then I had acquired something of a reputation as a 'track nut' – i.e. somebody obsessively interested in statistical details of performances in track and field events, and the like. One of the cross-country runners, knowing my interest in historical things to do with sport, told me that he had discovered a small box of glass lantern-slides in an old hall used by his scout troop in the Newington region on the south side of Edinburgh. These were slides of some athletic event, or events. When I looked at them I soon found out that they were glass plates taken at Craiglockhart at Edinburgh University Sports events of the 1920s. To my excitement I realised that a few of them depicted Eric Liddell. I had them all copied and, sure enough, some at least were from the 1922 Edinburgh University Sports. One showed three record-breakers that afternoon: Eric Liddell (220 yards), J. Hill Motion (three miles) and Charles S. Brown (one mile). There was also a photo of the start of the quarter-mile, a historic picture, given that it was Eric Liddell's very first senior quarter mile.

In the Intervarsity Sports and SAAA Championships, Liddell repeated his successes of the previous year in winning both 100 and 220 yards events in respectable times, and over the furlong in the Scottish Championships he equalled his own best championship performance with 22.6 seconds.

The first big challenge of the year, however, was a real disappointment. It was in the triangular international held that year on 8 July before a home crowd at Hampden Park, Glasgow. In the 100 yards race he was beaten by a matter of inches by the fine English sprinter Lancelot Royle, whose winning time, on a grass track, was 10.4 seconds, a time that was surely well within Eric's capabilities. *The Scotsman* suggested that 'It was Liddell's wretched start which beat him.'[1] The two English runners

– Lancelot Royle and William Hill – certainly got off to a far better start and led the Scot clearly at the halfway stage. In the end Eric came through strongly and if the race had gone on for a few more yards would have passed Royle. However, instead he finished inches behind Royle over the 100 yards. It was certainly a shock defeat. But then, as Eric was all too aware, a man cannot run at his best every time he competes. And Royle was a good sprinter. He showed it that day at Hampden, when in the 220 yards he again defeated the Scot, in both a heat and the final. The Englishman won the final by half a yard in a time of 22.4 seconds, one of his fastest ever performances over the distance. It was said that in this race Eric was only seen at his best in the last twenty yards. It may be that he had some niggling injury. On the Saturday before the international contest he had been forced to withdraw from the Heart of Midlothian Football Club Sports on account of a muscle strain. This was one of the very few events that Eric Liddell missed in his track career. It is possible that on occasion he did run in spite of injuries, though he would have received a fair amount of treatment on the massage table from the professionals at Powderhall. His few dips in form in his career may well be accounted for by slight injuries.

However, the losses to Royle that day would have been a reminder to him that he did not just need to turn up in order to win races – if, indeed, he was ever inclined to think that way. Lancelot Royle (1898–1978), of Surrey Athletic Club, was a highly respected runner of the 1920s. He later competed in the 1924 Olympics, where he was a member of the silver-medal-winning 4 x 100 metres relay team.

On the Saturday following the international, Eric was back in action. If he had any slight injury problem there was not much sign of it at the Edinburgh and District Inter-Works Sports at Powderhall. In a 150 yards handicap he ran from scratch and, in winning the final with an even-time 15.0 seconds, he equalled Alfred R. Downer's Scottish native record set in 1895. The event was rarely run. Nevertheless, it did withstand what assaults there were upon it until 1964, when the excellent W. Menzies Campbell (Glasgow University Athletic Club) clocked 14.3 seconds. Campbell was later to become a Member of Parliament and the leader of the parliamentary Liberal-Democrat party at Westminster.

In his other races that summer Liddell showed wonderful even-time form, recording a series of outstanding wins in excellent times. At Greenock on 29 July, though defeated by inches in the 100 yards handicap, running from scratch he equalled the Scottish native record of 10.0, held jointly by James M. M. Cowie (1884) and Downer (1895). Other successes of importance followed. Especially significant were his performances at the late-season meetings held by the Rangers, Hibernian and Celtic Football Clubs.

The great English sprinter Harry F. V. Edward was again in Scotland for the various football club sports in early August. It may be assumed that, though he was an amateur, he would have been paid a fair sum in 'expenses' for coming north! Earlier that year, at Stamford Bridge as recently as 1 July, he had achieved a unique feat in winning the 100 yards (in 10.0 seconds), 220 yards (22.0 seconds) and 440 yards (50.4 seconds) at the English AAA Championships, all in the one afternoon. Because of the handicap system in the meetings north of the border – the Rangers, Hibernian and Celtic Football Club Sports – he was always going to be up against it. On 5 August at Ibrox, before 35,000 spectators, Eric Liddell won the 220 yards (invitation) handicap from a two-yard start in 22.0 seconds. Edward failed to qualify in a heat. Midweek, at the Hibernian Football Club meeting in Edinburgh, on 9 August, there were 11,000 spectators. The crowd were keen to see a direct confrontation between Edward and Liddell. It came in a 120 yards (invitation) handicap. Edward was on the scratch mark, with the Scot starting a mere one yard in front. After a closely fought race, Eric just got home by inches in 12.2 seconds.

The following Saturday, however, Harry Edward had an opportunity to turn the tables on the flying Scot. It was Celtic Football Club Sports, held on 12 August. This time there would be two races in which these great runners would face one another. First came the 120 yards (invitation) scratch race. This would undoubtedly show who was the fastest. It was almost like a British championship race. In sprints even a 120 yards race seems to pass in a flash. In this case it was Eric Liddell who got home first, by a yard, in a time of 12.2 seconds. There is a wonderful action shot of the finish of the race which shows all of Eric

Eric Liddell defeats Harry Edward over 120 yards at the Celtic F.C. Sports in 1922.

Liddell's best qualities of grit, determination and power. The race was run in a drizzle of rain on a heavy track, which made the performance all the more commendable. He received a great ovation.

More was to come. There was a 220 yards (invitation) handicap on the programme. In this Eric Liddell was given a start of two yards, as was the crack English sprinter, William P. Nichol (of Highgate Harriers). Harry Edward was back marker, on the scratch mark. *The Scotsman* was to describe this as 'a great race' and continued: 'Liddell won by inches after a desperate struggle.'[2] The desperate struggle was with both Edward (placed second) and Nichol (third). Eric only won by inches. There was therefore little to choose between England's best and the pride of Scotland. The crowd, though, was in raptures.

Liddell's performances against Edward at these meetings provide some measure of the new maturity he had gained as a sprinter. They marked a real advance, the full implications of which were to become evident the following season. So far he had not been tested on a bigger stage. That was something that would change in the course of the next season. In the meantime, he had a new academic year to think about and, of course, his beloved rugby. It was not long before he was back in harness for the university rugby club and embarking, as it turned out, upon another successful season with the oval ball.

7.

ANOTHER RUGBY SEASON

In his book, *The Story of Scottish Rugby*, R. J. Phillips made a strange comment about a Scotland versus Ireland match of 1913. 'A good game,' he wrote, 'was spoiled by the sprinting of the Tasmanian-London Hospitals Scot, A. W. Stewart.'[1] This refers to the fact that in that match Stewart ran in four tries, his sheer speed being too much for the Irish to cope with. Was Phillips complaining that Scotland had won by such a great margin, 29 points to 14, scoring no fewer than seven tries? At any rate, it was clear that defences had problems dealing with a real 'flyer'. In that sense Eric Liddell, like Stewart before him, was a handful for defences on account of his sheer speed. It is probably the case that Liddell's speed was not exploited as effectively as it might have been. Phillips, notwithstanding his strange reference to speed in the case of Allan Stewart, recognised that 'A. L. Gracie was self-condemned in his repeated failures to utilise the speed of E. H. Liddell, the fastest man that has yet played football.'[2]

The sprinter with an element of resourcefulness will invariably be a scoring machine on the rugby field. That was true of Stewart, and it was true of Eric Liddell. It was the same in the 1922–23 season. It was a rare thing for him not to be on the score sheet, and he must have instilled a sense of fear into all the defences against which he played. There is a wonderful example of this in a report of a match between Edinburgh University and the Royal High School Former Pupils on Saturday, 7 October 1922. As *The Scotsman* reported under the headline, 'Great Try by E. H. Liddell':

In the last minute…E. H. Liddell got possession inside his own 25, and after cleverly eluding two or three challengers, set off for the home line. His speed was such that he was never seriously challenged, and he touched down at the posts.[3]

Naturally, he could only play as well as he was allowed to play, or at least, according to the help he received from his team-mates and the defences he was up against. But the Gracie/Liddell left-wing partnership was the strongest of all the Five Nations teams. Gracie was unorthodox in his methods. The famous English international player Adrian Stoop said humorously of his unorthodox methods 'that he did everything wrong, but did it so quickly that nobody could catch up with him'.[4] Some commentators thought Gracie not quick enough for Liddell, but Eric himself never said so. They were a lethal partnership, as they showed frequently in the 1922–23 season.

Early in December 1922 Eric was in the Edinburgh team for the inter-city match against Glasgow at New Anniesland, Glasgow. It was held on Saturday, 2 December, and attracted 10,000 spectators. It appears to have been an uninspiring match. Eric, however, did bag a brace of tries. Again, his searing pace was a telling factor as Edinburgh won the match 17 points to 8.

This was a week before the first of the Scottish rugby trial matches, held at Hawick on 9 December. Like most of these trials, the latter was a disappointing game. Perhaps this is not surprising, given that both teams were virtually scratch teams that would have just turned up on the day without any prior preparation or coaching. At any rate, it appears that Eric Liddell did not have the ball passed to him as often as he would have hoped. The best of wing three-quarters can do nothing without the ball! He did, however, have one try, laid on by Gracie. The result: Scotland, 4 goals, 2 tries (26 points); the 'Rest', 2 tries (6 points).

The second trial was played at Inverleith on 23 December. The 8,000 or so spectators saw Eric Liddell at his very best in this match. Apparently, his handling was sure and his pace too much for the opposition. He scored three tries, two for Scotland and one for the 'Rest'. The reason for that was because the Scotland and the Rest backs switched places *en bloc* at half time! The third and last trial was played at New Anniesland on 6 January. The Scotland team won easily enough, 18 points to 3, and again Eric scored a try. However, the comment was made by one reporter that the players selected for the winning team 'owed their victory, in large measure, to their greater pace behind the scrum, and it was quite apparent that had the Liddell-Gracie wing been transferred to the Rest team, "Scotland" would have been several points in arrears at the close'.[5]

All this was preparatory to the international season, which again began with a match against the French. This was played at Inverleith on 20 January and resulted in a very convincing victory for the Scots. Eric scored the last try in a 16–3 triumph.

Next up were the Welsh. The match that year was played on 3 February at Cardiff, where Scotland had not won for twenty-three years. The 1923 match, however, resulted in a famous victory for the Scots. On the Friday the pitch had been waterlogged on account of incessant rain. It dried out a bit the following day, with the help of fire engines and an army of volunteers! Wales took an early lead with a penalty (3–0), a lead they held up to the break. After the break, Eric Liddell scored a great try for Scotland to level the scores. Allan Massie well describes what happened: 'Gracie had found J. C. R. Buchanan at his shoulder when challenged by the full-back, and passed to him. Buchanan was tackled at once and could only throw out what was described as a ground pass to Liddell, who, in Gracie's words, "zooming along the horizon, picked up the ball at full speed without the slightest check, and ran over in the left corner".'[6] Perhaps this would have attracted more attention had it not been outshone by A. L. Gracie's winning try for Scotland towards the end of the match, to make the final score, Scotland 11 (1 goal, 2 tries), Wales 8 (1 goal, 1 penalty goal). Eric was to say of this game that 'It was a jolly good game, and one of the finest international matches I ever played in.'[7]

Three weeks later, it was the turn of Ireland at Lansdowne Road. This game was played before 20,000 spectators in a drizzle of rain, which made open rugby more difficult. Also, the Irish resorted to spoiling tactics and effectively 'bottled up' the Scottish centre three-quarters.

Scotland team for the rugby international against England in 1923. The captain was A. L. Gracie (holding the ball). Eric is second from the right at the back.

Though this meant that Eric Liddell had limited opportunities, he appears to have had one of his very best games playing in the Scotland team. Ireland took the lead with a try, but soon afterwards Scotland replied with a try by Liddell. Eric had missed the England international the previous season and this was his fourth try in successive matches for Scotland. Scotland's third and final try that day was also down to Eric's work, after he made an outside break and gave an inside pass to the Scottish outside half, Samuel McQueen, to score. That try was converted and Scotland ran out winners with a total of 13 points to 3. One comment made by a reporter on Eric Liddell's performance that day was that he was one of the outstanding successes of the Scottish three-quarters. 'Never again,' said the report in *The Scotsman*, 'should it be urged against the former that he is only a runner.'[8]

Victory against Ireland meant that Scotland went into their match with England at Inverleith on 17 March, knowing that a win would clinch the 'grand slam' for them that season. England had won their previous matches against Wales and Ireland, though they still had to face France after playing the Scots. This was a game Scotland had good prospects of winning. Though it was not known at the time, it would be Eric Liddell's last international match. A record 30,000 packed the limited Inverleith ground for the game. The match was played in brilliant weather and among the crowd were the Duke of York and his fiancée, Elizabeth Bowes-Lyon, the future King George VI and Queen Elizabeth (the Queen Mother).

England certainly had some great players – C. N. Lowe and W. J. A. Davies among the backs, and W. W. Wakefield and A. T. Voyce among the forwards. The game was a close one. The teams were evenly balanced and few opportunities arose. As for Eric Liddell's part in the game, little is said in the reports, though *The Scotsman* did say that 'Nothing can be urged against E. H. Liddell. He got few chances, and, although hardly so prominent as against Ireland, he ran with fine resolution, and in estimating his worth it should not be forgotten that he had against him the redoubtable Lowe.'[9] In the end England defeated the Scots by 8 points to 6 (1 goal and 1 try to 2 tries). It was a great disappointment to the Scots that the 'grand slam' was so near and yet so far. England subsequently went on to beat France and secure the 'grand slam' for themselves.

That, however, was to be the end of Eric Liddell's international career on the rugby field. The following winter he preferred to apply himself to studies and use such time as he had for special training for the forthcoming Olympics of 1924. In point of fact he did take part in one more match. When the Edinburgh University XV had difficulty raising a team for their fixture against Glasgow University at Craiglockhart on Saturday, 26 January 1924, Eric was prevailed upon to turn out. It was to be his last official rugby match, though it was reported that 'he had no opportunity to shine, and the ball rarely went his way.'[10] Nevertheless, the Edinburgh team won by 8 points to nil.

But what shall we make of Eric Liddell as a rugby player? It goes without saying that he was a very potent force on account of his great pace. In that sense he was very difficult to counter. No one could afford to give him any opportunity to exploit his great pace. He appears also to have had good ball sense and with A. L. Gracie comprised possibly one of the finest wing partnerships in the history of Scottish rugby. While resourceful in attack, given the opportunities, there is no doubt that he also showed a fearlessness in defence. He was no shadow-tackler, as some sheer sprinters playing in rugby union have been suspected of being. A. A. Thomson wrote of Eric Liddell's defensive qualities, 'It is usually said of flying wingers that they are not good in defence, but nobody can truthfully have said this about Liddell. He was a tireless and dogged defender, and when he smother-tackled you, you stayed smothered.'[11]

As always, those who seek to assess Liddell's sporting achievements also give fulsome tribute to his character. This is what Thomson says of him:

Liddell was a doubly splendid athlete, for he was in the highest flight both as a rugger player and a runner. The fact that his ideals were eventually to lead him into the missionary field did not detract from his human pleasure in his athletic prowess. Not many rugger players are noted as serious characters; indeed, the contrary is much more likely. But Liddell's quiet integrity of character was recognized by everyone whose circle touched his. He would not, for instance, run or play football on Sunday; but there was not the least priggishness in his attitude; he respected the opinions of those who disagreed with him as much as they respected his. There was never any argument about it.[12]

Thomson – no relation to Eric Liddell's biographer D. P. Thomson – made a valid point about Liddell's attitude to sports. He wrote of his 'human pleasure in his athletic prowess'. Eric Liddell did not see this as being in any way contradictory to a Christian profession. It was the simple and lawful pleasure of play, which God built into man's nature. Such things can be corrupted and abused in a sinful, fallen world. As for Liddell, seeing himself as a man seeking to live for the glory of God, all his sporting activities would be performed with serious pleasure.

Ted McLaren (London Scottish) played in the centre for Scotland in all the 1923 Internationals. He left on record this fine tribute to Eric Liddell as a rugby player and role model:

Never once did Eric [Liddell] show the slightest sign of bad temper or bad sportsmanship on the field; both, it seemed to me, were utterly foreign to him. Many a time he was lain for by his opponents, whose tactics were at least doubtful, but never would he repay them in their own coin – his method was invariable – he merely played better rugby and made them look like second-raters.[13]

It was not long after the end of the 1922–23 season that Eric began to take a more direct interest in, and involvement with, student evangelism, as described elsewhere. That, if anything, gave him a perspective that would sharpen his performance on the sports field. Certainly 1923 was a crucial year for Eric in more ways than one. His track appearances were awaited with great anticipation that summer.

8.
BEGINNING TO FULFIL THE POTENTIAL

The 1923 season opened for Liddell with a repeat of his 1922 'sprint treble' at the Edinburgh University Sports in May. After the initial Edinburgh University Sports of 1921 there was no one within Scottish university athletics circles to challenge his domination of the sprints. The same could be said at the wider national level. In all the years he competed in the Scottish Championships he remained undefeated.

Early in the season Eric gave an indication of the speed he was to show later in the year. At the Queen's Park Football Club Sports at Hampden Park, Glasgow, on 2 June, he ran a close second in the 100 yards handicap, running the full distance and clocking 10 seconds flat.

A fortnight later he showed similar pace at the Intervarsity Sports on his home track at Craiglockhart, Edinburgh. It was a beautiful day, favourable to good running and fast times. This year he took on the treble for the first time at this event. His form was sensational as he won the 100 yards with a time of 10.1 seconds, the 220 yards in 21.6 seconds and the 440 yards with a superb time of 50.2 seconds. It must be remembered that although the 220 yards race was on a straight track, all these events were run on grass. The time for the 220 yards was a Scottish native record, and it withstood all assaults until 1960, when Michael G. Hildrey (Victoria Park Amateur Athletic Club), nicknamed the 'Balfron Bullet', improved it by 0.1 second on the cinders of New Meadowbank, Edinburgh. It is worth noting that in the 440 yards Liddell defeated the reigning Scottish champion, J. Gordon McColl (Glasgow University Athletic Club), by no less than eighteen yards!

The following Saturday, 23 June, Liddell successfully defended his 100 yards and 220 yards titles at the Scottish Championships held at Celtic Park. In the process he improved his own best championship performance in the 220 yards with a time of 22.4 seconds.

On the Wednesday evening after the championships, Liddell ran a yard inside even time (11.9 seconds) in winning the 120 yards open handicap from scratch at the Edinburgh Pharmacy Sports, Powderhall. He was in excellent form, consistently achieving speeds faster than even time, and things were shaping up well for his first appearance at the English Championships just over a week later.

The English Amateur Athletic Association meeting was a prestigious event. It attracted athletes of international reputation. In the British context it was fully recognised that these were in effect the British championships. In 1923 the championships were held at Stamford Bridge, London, on 6 and 7 July. On the Friday evening Liddell impressed the crowds by winning both his first and second round 220 yards heats with ease in the fast times of 22.4 and 21.6 seconds respectively. His second-round time, which he was to equal in the final, was the fastest he was ever to achieve round a turn. In this heat he defeated the great Cambridge sprinter Harold Abrahams into second place by about five yards. The winners of the other two second-round heats were C. L. Steyn (South London Harriers), with a time of 22.1 seconds, and T. Matthewman (Huddersfield Athletic Club) in 22.0 seconds, with W. P. Nichol (Highgate Harriers) qualifying for the final as the fastest loser. There was an interval of just one hour and thirty-five minutes between the first and second-round heats of the 220 yards that Friday evening.

The heats of the 100 yards were the first events of the afternoon on the Saturday. These started at 2.30 p.m. There were eight heats, with Eric Liddell winning the second in even time (10.0). The times were impressive in the fine weather. Close rival W. P. Nichol actually won his heat (the fifth) in 9.9 seconds. Harold Abrahams won the eighth in 10.2 seconds. He was not a happy man, though, as he was apparently suffering from a septic throat.

In the second round Liddell created a sensation in defeating Tom Matthewman in 9.8 seconds, equalling the British record. Nichol won the other heat in 9.9 seconds from South African C. L. Steyn, with Harold Abrahams failing to qualify in third place. This meant that both sprint finals would be contested by the same four athletes: Liddell, Matthewman, Nichol and Steyn, though unfortunately Steyn had strained a muscle in his 100 yards semi-final and pulled out of both finals. Harold Abrahams was eliminated in the second of the semi-finals. Though he complained of a septic throat, it did not prevent him from winning the long jump that afternoon in an English record (23 foot, 8¾ inches/7.22 metres). Incidentally, in the first semi-final Lancelot Royle had been well beaten into third place behind Eric Liddell and had been eliminated.

The first of the sprint finals to be contested was the 100 yards. This was run only one hour and ten minutes after the first round! It is interesting to note the sequence of events that afternoon:

100 yards First-round heats 2.30 p.m.
100 yards Second-round heats 3.10 p.m.
100 yards Final 3.40 p.m.
220 yards Final 4.05 p.m.

This constituted a pretty exacting schedule. Eric, however, took it in his stride. With Matthewman and Nichol, Eric went to his mark in the 100 yards final. It was run in lanes infield of the 440 yards track. The race was close all the way but the young Scot came through with an electrifying finish to win by half a yard in a new record time of 9.7 seconds. As has been stated in an earlier chapter, that year watches timing in 100ths of a second were used for the first time in the championships. It is interesting to note the exact times recorded by each of the three official time-keepers: 9.67, 9.65 and 9.65 seconds respectively. This was rounded up to 9.7, a British record. Nichol was second, about half a yard behind, with Matthewman a foot behind his fellow countryman.

Just twenty-five minutes later the same three sprinters lined up for the 220 yards. The start of the 220 yards track was very near the

Finish of the AAA 100 yards at Stamford Bridge, London, July 1923. Eric Liddell wins in record time from William Nichol and Tom Matthewman.

run-up for the long jump. The long jump was scheduled for 4 p.m. that afternoon, five minutes before the final of the furlong. One of the long-jump competitors has left a charming picture of what happened before the start of the race:

> I remember with delight an incident which occurred that afternoon. Eric was preparing for the 220 yards race. I was not jumping for some minutes, so was able to see what happened.
>
> Eric had brought a small trowel with him to dig his holes for starting (they go for wooden blocks now, I believe), and he carefully went from one to another of his opponents in the race, and offered each the use of his trowel. Most of them (four, I seem to remember) accepted. All the nearby spectators appreciated the action (and a large number of athletes who recognized the Scottish champion had gathered to get as close a view as possible). All having prepared, he walked to each opponent again, and shook hands with him, smiling his very sunny smile. He then got 'on his marks' with them, was off at the gun, and won a very fine race from the outside berth.
>
> I had heard a lot about him, and now I had seen him. I came away feeling that I had witnessed a gentleman doing all a gentleman should do. Afterwards, when I heard he had gone to China, I realized that I had been watching a Christian in action.[1]

The 220 yards race was run round a bend and was won by Eric Liddell by one and a half yards from Matthewman, with Nichol a further yard behind. The time was 21.6 seconds.

Eric Liddell, therefore, emerged unbeaten in all his races at Stamford Bridge. For these outstanding performances he was later to receive the Harvey Memorial Cup, presented to the athlete adjudged to be the best champion of the year.

Harold Abrahams and Eric Liddell, who met for the first time at the 1923 AAA meeting, were to become the most famous of the British sprinters of the era. Abrahams (Cambridge University Athletic Club) was dominant in the Oxbridge university circles in his day, as Eric Liddell was in the Scottish university scene. Between them they won remarkably few English AAA championships. Abrahams won the 100 yards in 1924 and the long jump in 1923 and 1924. Eric Liddell won the 100 and 220 yards in 1923 and the 440 yards in 1924. Their fame rested more upon their victories at the Paris Olympics, belatedly popularised in *Chariots of Fire* (1981).

One of the problems the makers of the film had was putting the two athletes together in races. In the film they are depicted as running against each other in the 100 yards at the 1923 AAA Championships, with Liddell winning. However, they never did meet over the short sprint distance. They met one another in competition only twice. Both times Eric Liddell came out on top – in the AAA 220 yards heat in 1923, and the Olympic 200 metres final of 1924, described in chapter 10. For one reason or another, in 1923 Harold Abrahams avoided direct confrontation with Eric Liddell in the shorter sprints. He was beaten in the second semi-final of the 100 yards at the AAA event and so did not contest the final. However, the following week he declined to compete in the Triangular International 'in view of the coming British-American inter-universities' contest' and so again missed a direct match over 100 yards. Incidentally, in *Chariots of Fire* Eric Liddell is depicted as travelling down to London on his own on the overnight train. In point of fact in 1923 he was accompanied by his trainer, Tom McKerchar.

How did they compare, Abrahams and Liddell? One can only surmise. Eric Liddell was clearly the faster over the furlong. It is a different matter weighing up their respective merits in the short sprint. In my personal estimation, Eric was the faster in the shorter sprints in 1923. It does appear, however, that in the following year he lacked the pace that he had shown at points in the 1923 season, and Harold Abrahams had certainly made some progress in 1924. Eric Liddell would have been hard pushed to make the 100 metres final in Paris, given his performances over 100 yards during that year. That, however, may be explainable by two considerations. On the one hand, it is incontrovertible that after his 440 yards performance at the triangular international in Stoke the week after the AAA Championships in 1923, he never ran as fast again. He never seemed to 'lie down' under injuries, but it does appear that the 440 yards at Stoke took its toll and caused an injury which diminished his speed just a little. The race at Stoke, however, seemed to persuade him in any case that, given the fact that he would not be competing in events scheduled for Sundays in Paris, it made sense to train more seriously for the 440 yards/400 metres. It is likely, then, that his training for that event after 1923 in any case told against the sheer speed that he would have required for the 100 metres in Paris.

A recent biographer of Harold Abrahams has argued that the Englishman was happy to avoid direct competitions against the 'Flying Scotsman'. Apart from seeming to 'choke' in the sprints at the 1923 AAA Championships, Abrahams notably avoided the Triangular Internationals between 1921 and 1923, and made no visits to Scotland for any of the prestigious late season football club meetings. Abrahams' claims that he was better than Eric over the shorter sprint were, in the event, never tested.[2]

The week following his great victories at the AAA Championships, Liddell confirmed his outstanding form, and his superiority over the other established British sprinters of the day, with a sprint treble in the Triangular International held at the Stoke Football Club track. The times were not brilliant. It is rather puzzling that the reason given for this was that the cinder track was especially hard. It was reported that the slowish times were 'accounted for by the state of the track. It was board-hard, and the Edinburgh man found in the 100 that his spikes were too long, and did not give him enough grip.'[3] He had just enough grip, however, to defeat old rivals William Nichol and William Hill (representing England and Wales) in 10.4 seconds, with no more than eighteen inches between the three of them. Nichol, not feeling fit enough, did not turn out for the furlong and Scots finished first and second in the race, with Liddell winning by five yards from Robert McLean in 22.6 seconds.

'Veterans whose memories take them back 35 years, and in some cases even longer, in the history of athletics, were unanimous in the opinion that Liddell's win in the quarter-mile was the greatest track performance they had ever seen.' This is what one national newspaper stated about the 440 yards at Stoke. It was Eric Liddell's first really important race over the distance. In those days the quarter-mile was rarely run in lanes. As a consequence, there was often a considerable amount of jostling for position at the start. The race at Stoke was not run in lanes, and the early jostling for position created a problem at the beginning but inadvertently led to one of the most remarkable races spectators had ever witnessed. It became the stuff of sporting folklore, as a contemporary report stated that 'The circumstances in which he won the 440 event made it a performance bordering on the miraculous.' We let *The Scotsman* describe the unfolding drama of the race:

> It was a remarkable race, and only a runner possessed of indomitable courage and determination and extraordinary ability could have accomplished what the Scotsman did.
>
> The runners were started on the bend, Liddell having the inside berth, but the Scot had only taken three strides when J. J. Gillis, England, crashed into him and knocked him off the track. He stumbled on to the grass, and for a moment seemed half inclined to give up. Then, suddenly, he sprang forward, and was after his opponents like a flash. By this time the leaders were about twenty yards ahead, but Liddell gradually drew up on them, and by the time the home straight was reached he was running fourth [of six runners, two from each nation]. He would be about ten yards behind Gillis then. It seemed out of the question that he could win, but he achieved the apparently impossible. Forty yards from home he was third, and seemed on the

point of collapsing, but, pulling himself together, he put in a desperate finish, to win by two yards from Gillis. The latter was afterwards disqualified for 'boring',[4] and the second place was awarded to Sean Lavan, Ireland. The time, $51^{1/5}$ secs., indicates the merit of Liddell's running, and considering everything, it is virtually equal to 49 secs.

The effect on Liddell was dramatic: 'Liddell was greatly distressed at the end, but he was given a tremendous ovation, and the spectators, officials and competitors, including those who had run in the event, joined in the cheers.'[5]

One or two comments may be made here. Although the Englishman, John James Gillis, was ultimately disqualified for 'boring', there is no reason to believe that he knocked Eric over deliberately. It was inevitable, however, that he would be ruled out. It was such instances that hastened the introduction of individual lanes for 440 yards/400 metres races. To put the performance in perspective, it may be noted that on 29 July in Paris Gillis won a 400 metres race for England against France in 49.8 seconds. In other words, Gillis was a 50-seconds quarter-miler. This indicates that the estimate of what Eric Liddell's running represented that day – 49 seconds – would be a conservative one. To an astute observer it would be worth nearer 48 seconds in better conditions. Another interesting factor brought out in the contemporary press report is that because he felt his spikes had been too uncomfortable in the 100 yards race, Eric Liddell had run the 220 and 440 yards wearing borrowed shoes! Jack Gillis, incidentally, was later to be a starter at the 1948 Olympics in London.

In his authoritative book *A World History of Track and Field Athletics, 1864–1964* (published in 1964) Roberto Quercetani misinterprets this incident when he says, 'Liddell normally lacked the type of condition which now allows a runner of his calibre to run a fast "quarter" at practically any time of the season. It is said that he once fainted after winning an early season race in 51 seconds.'[6] Quercetani is correct, however, in saying that Eric Liddell did essentially lack conditioning for a quarter-mile race by contrast with more modern athletes. This makes all the more remarkable what he achieved at Stoke, given that he had no 'special conditioning' for the quarter-mile. It was simply raw power. But it makes one think just what he might have achieved with better conditioning. In some measure he was to show something of what could be achieved a year later. His time of 51.2 seconds for the race at Stoke tended to conceal the fact that – as would have been evident to a keen observer – he was even then a world-class performer over the longer distance.

It may be added that the incident in Stoke is near-perfectly represented in the film *Chariots of Fire*, although in the film the event is a competition between Scotland and France, and not a Triangular International involving Scotland, Ireland and England (and Wales). The film catches the drama and grit of the performance very well.

As a postscript to the international, Liddell's performance contributed to a Scottish success that day. It was the only occasion in the whole series of Triangular Internationals – held between 1914 and 1930 – in which such a treble was gained.

It seems, however, that Liddell paid the penalty for his great effort at Stoke. In the remainder of the season he was not quite the same power he had been earlier. He ran indifferently at the Greenock Glenpark Harriers meeting two weeks after Stoke, and the headline in the papers reporting the Rangers Sports of 4 August read, 'E. H. Liddell Off-Form'. 40,000 spectators turned up at Ibrox that first Saturday in August. Many would have been excited about the prospect of seeing Eric Liddell in action. In fact, a special 300 yards race had been arranged as a 'Scottish record attempt'. The record was held by one of the great figures of Scottish athletics, Wyndham Halswelle, who set the record in 1908 with a time of 31.2 seconds. Giving away considerable starts on the handicap, and obviously still suffering the effects of his 440 yards race at Stoke, Eric failed to make up the deficits and, uncharacteristically, faded at the finish to cross the line in 31.8 seconds. The race was won by Robert McLean, a former pupil of Glasgow High School (with a thirteen-yard start) in 30.6 seconds. The news report suggested that '[Liddell] has had a very hard season and appears to have gone stale.' There doesn't seem much doubt, however, that he was suffering from some injury after his heroics in Stoke.

Nevertheless, Eric was at Stamford Bridge on the following Monday (6 August) for the British Games Meeting. He had been invited to run in the 100 and 220 yards races. In the 100 yards he won his first-round heat from J. Titcombe (Surrey Athletic Club) in 10.2 seconds. In the second-round heat he was beaten into third place by his old rivals, Nichol (10.0 seconds) and Matthewman and only qualified as the fastest loser with a time of 10.1 seconds. In the final of the event later in the afternoon Eric had a great start and was leading with twenty yards or so to go. Normally he would have been expected to finish strongly. At that point, however, uncharacteristically he faltered and the other three finalists went past him in a blanket finish. This time Matthewman turned the tables on Nichol, winning in 10.1. G. Varney (Polytechnic Harriers) was third, with Eric a disappointing fourth. A matter of inches covered all four athletes. It was clear, however, that Eric was troubled with an injury, which prevented him from taking part in the furlong that afternoon.

This injury also affected him at the Hibernian Football Club Sports the following Wednesday, 8 August, at Easter Road, Edinburgh. Though he won his heat of the 100 yards in 10.8 seconds, he was still clearly not at his best and was unplaced in the final, as he was also in the 100 yards invitation handicap. At the final meeting of the season, the Celtic Football Club Sports on 11 August, Eric was again below his best, though he came quite close in both the 100 yards open handicap and 220 yards open handicap. He was placed third in both, starting from the scratch mark in closely contested races.

The latter part of the season was a difficult one for him after he picked up a muscle strain at Stoke. There were always high expectations of him whenever he turned out. It seems that he did tend to run even when he was not fully fit. The 1923 season, however, was a magnificent season for him. It established him as a world-class sprinter and a real prospect for the 1924 Olympics. Perhaps the most significant breakthrough, though, was the quarter-mile at Stoke. The race revealed all his great qualities of drive and determination. But to gain twenty yards or more on a runner of the quality of J. J. Gillis was remarkable, especially considering that Eric Liddell would never have trained for the quarter-mile. No doubt Eric himself saw it as providential in redirecting his efforts as he was invited to prepare for the Olympic Games at Paris the following year. It took the edge off his sheer speed, but his training during the winter and spring would need to concentrate on preparing him to run 400-metre races with only brief intervals between them, no mean task.

There is no doubt that Eric Liddell was pencilled in as a prospect for at least the 100 and 200 metres, and probably also for both the relay races in Paris. However, the programme of the Games was publicized towards the end of 1923 (in point of fact it would have been available from 1921). The following was the scheduling of the various events in which Eric might have been expected to take part:

Event 1
100 m. 1st/2nd rounds, Sunday 6 July
100 m. Semi-finals/final, Monday 7 July

Event 2
200 m. 1st/2nd rounds, Tuesday 8 July
200 m. Semi-finals/final, Wednesday 9 July

Event 3
400 m. 1st/2nd rounds, Thursday 10 July
400 m. Semi-finals/final, Friday 11 July

Event 24
4 x 100 m. 1st round, Saturday 12 July
4 x 100 m. Semi-finals/final, Sunday 13 July

Event 25
4 x 400 m. 1st round, Saturday 12 July
4 x 400 m. Final, Sunday 13 July

When Eric became aware of this he made it perfectly clear that he would take no part in any events scheduled for the Lord's day, the Christian Sabbath. As far as he was concerned, that was a day of rest and worship in terms of the Fourth Commandment. It was, for him, not a day for recreation or work, apart from such works as were of necessity or mercy. The theology of the Lord's day as Christian Sabbath, to which Eric Liddell subscribed, held that the Sabbath principle was preserved though the day was changed from the seventh day of the week to the first day of the week. Most evangelical Christians held that the change of day was necessitated by three things: first, commemoration of the resurrection of Christ on the first day of the week; second, the coming of the Spirit at Pentecost on the first day of the week, seven weeks after the resurrection; and, third, New Testament precedents. The term 'Lord's day' to describe the Christian Sabbath derives from Revelation 1:10. Naturally, the argument that the Sabbath principle continued rested on the principle that the Ten Commandments contained permanent spiritual and moral precepts which in their very nature could not be abrogated.

At any rate, Eric made his position clear – he would not run in any events scheduled for a Sunday. As his friend D. P. Thomson put it later, 'That decision there was no hope of changing. It was based on principles from which he never deviated a hair's breadth. Even in the Weihsien Internment Camp, where he was in charge of all sports and athletics, he refused to be responsible for planning Sunday sports.'[7]

There has been a debate about whether or not the British Olympic authorities appealed to the International Olympic Committee to reschedule some events. It was clear that Eric, for one, would also not be available for either the 4 x 100 metres or 4 x 400 metres relay races, heats or finals of which were also scheduled for Sundays. This would seriously affect Great Britain's prospects, and might make the difference in the colours of medals won.

A personal note which I received from David A. Jamieson contained the following statements: 'It was suggested to Liddell that the Continental Sunday finished at midday; he replied that "His Sunday lasted all day"! Efforts were made by the British Olympic Council to persuade the Olympic Committee in Paris but they were of no avail.' It seems that the British Olympic Council towards the end of 1923 did appeal to the International Olympic Committee that 'Athletes who object to running or taking part in any Game on Sunday, be given a chance to have their race or event arranged on another day.' In a reply dated 22 January 1924, the IOC indicated that they were not prepared to ask any other committee, or the host country, to make such changes at that point.[8] This may not have been attempted only on behalf of Eric Liddell, but the strong likelihood is that it was the case of Eric Liddell that was the motivation for the approach.

There is an irony in this matter of Eric Liddell's refusal to run in the events scheduled for Sundays. His widow Florence later recalled that 'Eric always said that the great thing for him was that when he stood by his principles and refused to run in the 100 metres, he found that the 400 metres was really his race. He said he would never have known that otherwise. He would never have dreamed of trying the 400 at the Olympics.'[9] In order to make preparation to 'run the distance' over 400 metres, Eric forsook rugby in the winter of 1923–24. He also had his university work to do as he entered into his finals year. At the very least, avoiding rugby meant that he would not run the threat of injury, always present in that game. No, he would quietly prepare for the Olympic 400 metres, under the watchful eye of Tom McKerchar.

9.

REACHING FOR THE PINNACLE

How it came about is not clear, but in the spring of 1924 Eric Liddell was invited to join the Oxford and Cambridge athletes in a trip to the United States for the University of Pennsylvania Relay Festival. This was due to be held at their Franklin Field in Philadelphia on Friday and Saturday, 25–26 April 1924. The trip took several days by the *Berengaria*, a Cunard liner of some 50,000 tonnes, 919 feet in length, and ninety-eight feet in width. The sailing was from Southampton to New York. This meant two things: first of all, little or no athletic exercise; and, secondly, the possibility of seasickness. In point of fact one at least of the athletes, Eric Liddell, was badly seasick – not a great preparation for the track meeting!

The trip was a great experience, despite the effects of the crossing. Eric was down to compete in two individual invitation events, over 100 yards and 220 yards. The furlong had been added to the programme specifically for Eric's benefit.[1] Several top-class American sprinters were present for these sprints. The 100 yards race was extremely close, with about thirty inches separating the first four at the finish, but Eric only managed fourth place behind Chester Bowman (from Syracuse) who clocked 10.0 seconds. There was also a 220 yards race. The Scot ran brilliantly well, but was just headed home by a yard or so by Louis Clarke of Johns Hopkins College, who clocked 21.6 seconds. In point of fact this was great running by Liddell, given the ravages of the crossing and the fact that it was so early in the season. It augured good things to come. The return trip from the United States was made on the *S.S. Republic*. Unfortunately, in transit two suitcases containing his mementoes and souvenirs of the trip unaccountably disappeared!

Eric was to write later:

> I was at the time concentrating on the Games, and [Tom] McKerchar was careful to insist that I should not overdo things in America, in order that I should be perfectly fit three months later in Paris. And so, although I ran well enough, I did not touch top form at any stage of the trip, merely regarding it as an incident in my preparation for Paris.[2]

Eric Liddell finishes second in the 220 yards race at Franklin Field, April 1924.

There was one thing that impressed him very much at the University of Pennsylvania. As he passed through the gate, he noticed the motto of the university inscribed: 'In the dust of defeat, as well as in the laurels of victory, there is a glory to be found if one has done his best.' He recalled this later when he was called on to give a speech at St Giles' Cathedral after his graduation.

There was another aspect, too, of his experience in the United States on which he later commented. The following year he spoke at a Young Abstainers' Union meeting at Dalkeith near Edinburgh on 'Alcohol and health'. Among other things he said that, on the question of prohibition in America, he could only speak from ten days' experience there. 'They could have had liquor if they had wanted it,' he said. His opinion of prohibition? 'Even those who did not profess total abstinence were agreed that the measure had done good.' As we have already noted, Eric Liddell was an old-school evangelical who favoured total abstinence and practised it throughout his life.

After the American trip Eric went into steady training three times a week, and took part in various sports meetings on Saturdays. 'My trainer was handling me beautifully,' he was to write later, 'and I was coming on steadily all the time, so that when I ran in the Scottish Championships I swept the board, winning three titles.'³ His trainer Tom McKerchar was astute enough to know, not only that he had great potential for the 440 yards/400 metres, but also that if he was to mount a serious challenge in that event he would need to be better conditioned than he had been before. The programme for the Olympic Games, of which they would be aware, showed back-to-back 400-metres races on successive days, and that after back-to-back 200-metres races on the previous two days, all run at high intensity.

The fact is that Eric Liddell had not yet been seriously tested in the 440 yards. It was true that he had run a great race to win the Triangular International at Stoke. But he would have to run two such races within three hours of each other on two successive days, and at this point his best time for the 440 yards was a mere 50.2 seconds. The Olympic record, set in 1912, was 48.2! It is clear from his performances over the longer distance in the 1924 season that he must have done some serious conditioning training that winter. Writing of his track experiences after he had moved to China, Eric was to comment on his approach to 'running the quarter':

> All through my career as a runner in later years [Tom] McKerchar has blazed the trail.
>
> I shall not forget his advice when without training for it, I had to run a quarter-mile. He took me to the track and plotted out the vital stages of the race to be run over it, telling me exactly how to run each part; and, doing so, I was able to win.

The upshot was that he adopted a very distinct approach to running the distance:

Always when running a quarter I have used the same method, save only on exceptional occasions when more was expected, as in the greatest race of my life, in the 400 metres at Paris…

It is the method in which every 'sprint' quarter-miler usually runs it – the first hundred yards almost, if not quite, 'all out,' the back stretch at well over three-quarter pace, the next bend which one takes as the slowest part of the journey, and the last hundred as a sprint.[4]

The idea conveyed in *Chariots of Fire* that he changed events at the Games was dramatic but entirely the stuff of fiction. Stoke proved that he had serious work to do. His performance in the 440 yards at Stoke in 1923 was the catalyst in Eric's switch to the longer sprint – the 'killer sprint' as some commentators have described it – and application to the necessary training to cope with more than one high-quality race within a very short period of time. There is no doubt that he would have done a considerable quantity of high-quality training runs at various distances from 100 yards to a quarter of a mile, the longer distances very likely being time trials. Be that as it may, the first real test would come at the AAA Championships at Stamford Bridge, London, on 20 and 21 June. This would involve, on the Friday night, two 220 yards races and two 440s, all within the space of three and a half hours!

His domestic season began on 19 May with unspectacular performances at the Maryhill Harriers Sports. Between 28 and 31 May he swept the board at both the Edinburgh University and Intervarsity Sports. Though admittedly unchallenged, the 440 yards wins in these events were nothing to write home about – 51.5 seconds at the Edinburgh University Sports and 51.2 at the Intervarsity. By all accounts, however, the former was a remarkable performance as the grass track was heavy after pouring rain all day.

Dr Neil Campbell, in his contribution to *The story of Edinburgh University Athletic Club*, provides a touching personal reminiscence of those Edinburgh University Sports: 'On the track and off, Liddell was the complete sportsman, in the best sense of that much-misused word. The writer remembers before the 440 yards race at the Sports in 1924 drawing the outside position and Liddell, who had drawn the inside berth, quietly offering to change places.'[5]

There is also a lovely incident typical of Eric Liddell described by a fellow-competitor in the Intervarsity Sports of that year:

> Eric Liddell, whom I had met and competed against the year before at St Andrews, was an Edinburgh competitor, and I was representing Aberdeen. Towards the end of the Sports I was, rather thoughtlessly, sitting on the cold turf wearing nothing but a light singlet, shorts and spiked shoes, and waiting for the last event of the afternoon to start, the Relay Races for teams of four runners from each of the Scottish 'Varsities. Liddell, strolling in my direction, saw me sitting and, to my surprise, took off his Edinburgh blue blazer and placed it over my shoulders to keep me warm. He did this with a smile and a word of advice about avoiding the cold. A small enough gesture, it might be said, but a spontaneous Christ-like one towards one who was virtually a stranger from another 'Varsity. I have never forgotten this kindly act, and not by any means only because Eric Liddell afterwards became so famous.[6]

This, incidentally, betrays the fact that in those days there were no such things as tracksuits. Athletes would change into their running gear and simply put on their university blazers or jumpers and perhaps a scarf. They would stretch and jog a little in preparation, but really not much attention was given to warming up. Dr Neil Campbell, who ran with and against Eric Liddell at Edinburgh University in the 1920s, recounted the sort of thing that prevailed in those far-off days:

> Tracksuits were unknown and on a cold day athletes would remain in the pavilion until the last possible moment and then emerge hoping that their overcoats would keep some of the cold wind from their bare legs. The modern athlete's habit is a great improvement which enables him to keep warm and 'limber up' round the track to his heart's content – a practice unknown thirty years ago. It is to be noted also that the athletes of that time did not devote the time, thought and energy which is now essential to the athlete with high aspirations. Liddell, for instance, trained regularly but not excessively.[7]

An easy win for Eric in the Scottish 220 yards of 1924 at Hampden Park, Glasgow.

The Scottish Championships were earlier than normal that year, to accommodate the Olympics, which were due to start at the beginning of July. Though the races in championship events appeared to be relatively easy for an athlete as dominant as Eric Liddell, what a sprinter faced in a one-day event of this kind is well illustrated by the schedule for the man attempting a treble (this year he opted out of the medley relay):

Event 1: 100 yards heat 1 (3.00 p.m.)
Event 3: 100 yards final (3.15 p.m.)
Event 7: 220 yards heat 2 (3.40 p.m.)
Event 10: 220 yards final (4.10 p.m.)
Event 14: 440 yards heat 2 (4.30 p.m.)
Event 18: 440 yards final (5.00 p.m.)

In the event there was no heat for the 440 yards. Nevertheless, it was a taxing schedule by any standards. In the 100 yards Eric equalled the best championship performance of 10.0 seconds both in his heat and in the final. He was stretched by the Glasgow High School former pupil Robert McLean, who by all accounts got off to a flying start in the final and led Eric for much of the way until the latter came with a late burst to pass him just before the tape. The official time was 10.0 seconds, though one stopwatch clocked Liddell at 9.9 seconds. The 220 and 440 yards were won easily in modest times of 22.6 and 51.2 seconds respectively.

The Friday and Saturday following the Scottish Championships saw Eric in London for the AAA Championships. He was down to defend his furlong title and to attempt the quarter-mile.[7] By success in these events he would stake his claim for inclusion in the British Olympic team over 200 metres and 400 metres. His showing in the 440 yards was awaited with keen interest. This was his first real test. Up till then he had not even recorded a time of less than 50 seconds for the distance. Furthermore, a real test of his being able to cope with the Olympic 400 metres event lay in the fact that at Stamford Bridge on the Friday evening, 20 June, he had two back-to-back furlong races followed by two back-to-back quarter-miles. The Friday evening therefore constituted a busy evening's running for Eric Liddell. This is how his races turned out:

5 p.m.:	220 yards, 1st round, heat 1 – 1st, 22.3
6.25 p.m.:	220 yards, 2nd round, heat 2 – 1st, 21.8
7 p.m.:	440 yards, 1st round, heat 3 – 1st, 51.0
8.25 p.m.:	440 yards, 2nd round, heat 1 – 1st, 49.6

In other words, he coped well with all these high-quality races in the space of just three and a half hours!

The following day he had only the two finals. The first was the 220 yards. The finalists were Eric Liddell, Arthur E. Porritt (New Zealand), Walter Rangeley (Salford Athletic Club) and Howard P. Kinsman (South Africa). They lined up at 4.15 p.m. In a closely fought race Kinsman, the South African champion, showed the greatest pace on the day by coming through to win by two and a half yards from Liddell, with Porritt another half-yard behind in third place. The winner's time was 21.7 seconds.

About twenty minutes later Liddell was on call again, this time for the final of the 440 yards. He lined up with the defending champion

An easy victory for Eric Liddell in the AAA 440 yards against highly rated athletes.

William E. Stevenson, who had won the 1921 American Amateur Athletic Union (AAU) title with a time of 48.6 seconds, David M. Johnson, a Canadian who, like Stevenson, was a Rhodes scholar at Oxford, and the Irishman Sean Lavan. In this race Liddell had a fairly comfortable win from Johnson by four yards in 49.6 seconds, with Stevenson in third place, a further five yards behind. The winning time, though respectable enough, was hardly anything special. This was no clear indication that Eric Liddell might challenge for the Olympic crown, the final of which, was, after all, only three weeks away. His performance was far enough short of fellow-countryman Wyndham Halswelle's long-standing British record of 48.4 seconds set in 1908. At the same time, in the quarter-mile he was not pressed very hard and, for the astute observer, had plenty more to show. Given that Eric had to negotiate two 220 yards rounds and two 440 yards rounds the previous evening, it is not to be wondered that he was a bit jaded for the final of the 220 yards. Harold Abrahams commented on the race that:

> In all fairness to Liddell it must be said that he had run two 220s and two 440s on Friday evening, and was obviously suffering from the effect on Saturday. He managed to win the 440 in 49.6 secs, and in this race he ran with great determination from start to finish. This

time speaks volumes for his greatness as an athlete. People may shout their heads off about his appalling style. Well, let them. He gets there.[9]

After the AAA Championships Eric did not run in any events of real consequence. He competed without success at the Edinburgh Pharmacy Sports on the following Wednesday, and the Heart of Midlothian Sports the next Saturday. So far, though, nothing indicated that he would pose a major threat in the 200 metres or 400 metres at Paris.

10.

THE MAN WHO WAS FRIDAY

In 1968 the British athletics historian Melvyn Watman was to write, 'More than forty years after the event Liddell's success still reads like a fairy story. If ever a man was inspired by the supreme test of Olympic competition, that man was Eric Liddell.'[1] That he was successful at all was a great surprise. Perhaps the most surprising thing about Eric Liddell's performance in the 400 metres at the Paris Olympics of 1924 was the fact that he dominated the event. It was a case of a man's potential being realised at the most opportune time. It was no fairy tale, as the events proved.

Initially scheduled for Amsterdam, the VIIIth Olympiad was transferred to Paris at the request of Baron Pierre de Coubertin. He entertained the hope that the French authorities would do a better job in 1924 than they had done in 1900. Over 3,000 competitors from forty-four countries converged on Paris in early July 1924 for the Games. For the track and field events the Colombes Stadium, built in 1907, was modified to accommodate around 45,000 spectators. The *attendances* for the track and field events at Colombes were, however, frankly disappointing. The highest total daily attendance was on the day of the opening ceremony (5th July) when 16,677 *paying* customers turned up. On the days Eric competed on the track the highest number was on the Thursday (10th) when there were 13,190 in all in the stadium. On the day of the 400m semi-finals and final (11th) there was, sadly, only a total of 6,403 there to cheer on the athletes.[2]

The Colombes track bore little resemblance to the modern 400 metres oval athletics track. One circuit was 500 metres, so that the

1500 metres race was run over three laps. Consequently, the 400 metres started at the beginning of the back straight and was run around only one bend.

For the first time there was an Olympic Village. This was a rather unsophisticated assembly of wooden huts put up nearby the Olympic Stadium for athletes, trainers, coaches and physios to allow easy access to the Stadium. Eric and other of the British athletes would have used these huts preparatory to their various events or to rest between events. The British Headquarters, where the various athletes were accommodated, was the Hôtel Moderne on the Rue de la République.

When it came to the events themselves, the athletes would gather in the appropriate changing room beneath the Stadium, awaiting a call for their event. There was a long concrete corridor connecting some 30 or so changing rooms with showers and bathrooms. For the greater part nations would have a changing room for themselves. In these rooms officials and physiotherapists would mingle with the athletes, attending to their preparations before the events. As far as the calling of the events themselves was concerned, a French official would run down the corridor barking out orders for the event in question. One British athlete at the 1924 Games provided a picturesque account of what was involved for Eric Liddell and all the other athletes:

> [Competitors were]…painfully disturbed by a maniac dashing down the corridor and bawling [the event details]. How one loathed that man!…Feverishly you collect your gear, and inserting your upper incisors into your lower lip, you advance to the fray. From the corridor a subterranean tunnel labelled *Entrée de la Piste* leads into the centre of the arena. The journey affords one a strange mingling of weird sensations. The earthy smell of this haunt is so comforting as one ponders on what is to be seen on ascending that last flight of stone steps leading up to the arena. Suddenly you emerge into a blaze of sunlight and, if you are a favourite, a roar of applause goes up, making you feel more unsteady than before.[3]

The opening ceremony of the Games was held in the stadium on Saturday, 5 July. The first track event was the 100 metres, the first and second rounds of which were held on the next day, a Sunday. Representing Britain were Harold Abrahams, William Nichol, Walter Rangeley and Lancelot Royle. Abrahams and Nichol safely negotiated these preliminary rounds to qualify for the semi-finals on Monday. Rangeley and Royle, however, did not qualify through their second-round heats and were eliminated. In his second-round heat Harold Abrahams showed what great form he was in by equalling the Olympic record with a time of 10.6 seconds.

That opening Sunday Eric Liddell was ordering his priorities in a very different way. He was not at the stadium but rather in attendance at the Scots Presbyterian Church in Paris. He was in the stadium, however, on the Monday to see Harold Abrahams gain his great victory in the 100 metres final. Abrahams thus became the first European to win that coveted title.

In the film *Chariots of Fire*, there is a very effective scene depicting Eric Liddell 'reading a lesson' at a service on a Sunday during the Olympic Games. The writer of the screenplay very effectively blends the biblical text – the reading is selected from Isaiah chapter 40 – with flashes to the events in the stadium. This is particularly poignant when he comes to the last three verses of the chapter: 'He giveth power to the faint; and to them that have no might he increaseth strength. Even the youths shall faint and be weary, and the young men shall utterly fall: but they that wait upon the LORD shall renew their strength; they shall mount up with wings as eagles; they shall run, and not be weary; and they shall walk, and not faint' (vv. 29-31).

It was an inspirational choice of text, though a fictionalised incident loosely based on the fact that on the second Sunday of the Games (13 July) Eric did preach in the Scots Kirk in Paris. However, in that scene we are given a contrast between merely earthly pursuits and much higher ones. The depiction of athletes falling about half exhausted is ironically an illustration of a certain futility. The reading from the Bible, however, shows a more serious and lasting purpose or meaning found among these who 'wait upon the LORD'. This is, therefore, in fact a central and powerful part of the film in indicating just how Eric Liddell ordered his priorities, without any hint of an overbearing legalism.

Incidentally, there is a mistake in the film when Abrahams is depicted as telling Aubrey Montague before the 100 metres final that he had been 'tricked' by Charley Paddock in the semi-final and lost out to him. No such thing occurred. In fact Abrahams won all his 100 metre races in Paris. In that same scene in the film, in the only reference to the 200 metres, Abrahams speaks of being 'beaten out of sight' in the race. However, in fact the 200 metres event did not start till after the 100 metres was concluded, though it was true that he was 'beaten out of sight' in the final, as it happened.

THE 200 METRES

The 200 metres course at Colombes was an unusual one. Because the track had such a long bend and straight, the 200 metres started on the bend with the runners positioned at the start in a way in which they ran straight to the crown of the bend and then followed the track round to the left into the home straight down to the finishing line, which was the same for all the track races. The first and second rounds of the 200 metres were scheduled for Tuesday, 8 July. This was Eric Liddell's first competitive experience in the Games. Besides the Scot, Abrahams, Nichol and Tom Matthewman were Britain's representatives in the event.

In heat 3 of the first-round ties Liddell won comfortably in 22.2 seconds. Two and a half hours later he won through to the semi-finals by coming second, in heat 2 of the second round, to the fine Australian sprinter E. W. 'Slip' Carr, whose time was a fast 21.8 seconds. Meanwhile Nichol (with a time of 22.6) and Abrahams (22.2) had won their first-round heats, while Matthewman had qualified behind the American George L. Hill in heat 13. Nichol and Abrahams also joined Liddell in the semi-finals, Nichol by coming second to Charley Paddock (USA) in the first heat of the second round, and Abrahams by winning heat 4 in 22.0 seconds. This was a fine performance from the British team.

The following day Liddell lined up for the second semi-final of the 200 metres. He had just seen Abrahams qualify for the final by running third in the first semi behind the Americans Scholz (the latter in a time of 21.8) and Hill (who was seventy-five centimetres behind Scholz). In

Charley Paddock (USA) wins the second semi-final of the 200 metres in Paris. Eric Liddell (2nd) is on the left of the picture.

that race Nichol came sixth and was therefore eliminated. Now Liddell faced a top-class field in what was his most important race to date. There was the great American Charles W. Paddock, who held the world record of 20.8 seconds (set in 1922), another crack American, Bayes M. Norton, the Frenchman André Mourlon, Liddell's conqueror at the AAA championships, Howard P. Kinsman (South Africa) and the Canadian co-holder of the world record at 100 yards, Cyril H. Coaffee. In a close race Paddock just edged in front of the Scot by a metre, with Norton qualifying in third place a metre and a half behind.

The finish of the 200 metres at the Olympics in Paris. From left to right: Charles Paddock (2nd), Jackson Scholz (1st), Eric Liddell (3rd). George Hill (4th), Harold Abrahams (6th) and Bayes Norton (5th).

113

For the eagerly awaited final an hour and a half or so later it was USA versus UK, as all four Americans entered for the event qualified for the final, as did two of the British athletes. Norton was on the inside, Harold Abrahams in lane 2, Hill in lane 3, Jackson V. Scholz in lane 4 and Liddell in lane 5, with Paddock on the outside. After a good start Paddock, trying to make up for his lowly fifth place in the 100 metres, quickly spurted ahead and led for most of the way until in the last few strides he was caught and overtaken by Scholz, who won by thirty centimetres in an Olympic record-equalling 21.6 seconds. In a keen race for the third spot Liddell just edged out Hill and Norton, having moved from fifth with a late burst. The bronze medal was his! He had finished just one and a half metres down on Scholz. A rather jaded Abrahams finished last (with a time of 22.3). In commenting on this race afterwards Eric was to say: 'I was able to keep in third place, but although I was at the top of my form, I could not increase my speed by a fraction of an inch. It is a race that I shall always remember.'[4]

Because of the acclaim given to his later successes at these Games, Eric Liddell's performance in the 200 metres has tended to be overlooked. The 200 metres is only mentioned in passing in *Chariots of Fire* (as noted earlier), and no reference is made to Eric Liddell's having taken part in the event. On a track affected by heavy rain in the morning the times were better than they might at first sight appear to be. If this had been all that Eric had achieved in Paris, it would have entitled him to generous praise for a truly great run. After all, only two British athletes had previously gained an Olympic medal in the event: Willie Applegarth (third in 1912) and Harry Edward (third in 1920). This, then, was a magnificent performance by Liddell, whose running against the Americans suggested that if he had been able to benefit from their superior facilities and weather conditions, he might have accomplished very much faster times than he ever did in the UK.

THE 400 METRES

There was no rest between the 200 and 400 metre races at Paris as the heats for the 400 metres (i.e. the first two rounds) were held on the day after the 200 metres final. As Eric was the only fancied competitor who was entered for both the 200 and 400 metres events, it is an interesting question to ask whether this helped him with the longer race, or possibly put him at a disadvantage. I think it could be said that the timing of the events worked in his favour. Needless to say, taking part in both races would prove whether or not his stamina was adequate. That would certainly be well tested. But it is very likely that the way that he ran the 400 metres fast from the start was facilitated by the pace that he had been required to sustain in the various 200 metres races. Naturally the competitors from the other nations would have had no idea how Eric would run the 400 metres, given that they would have had only the sketchiest knowledge of his running over that distance. In any case, there were very few opportunities to compete against other athletes at an international level so that they could become familiar with their opponents' styles or strengths.

In those days the 400 metres or 440 yards was not really counted as an out-and-out sprint and few international athletes competed in both 200 and 400 metre events at major Games. It was not unknown, however. In 1912 at Stockholm the American Charles D. Reidpath finished fifth in the 200 metres (with a time of 22.3 seconds) and won the 400 metres (in 48.2 seconds). In fact it was Reidpath's Olympic 400 metres record that the men at Paris had in their sights. But few 400 metres runners would have had the flat speed of Eric Liddell.

Perhaps Eric had two advantages as he went to Paris for the 400 metres. One was that the track was 500 metres in length. As there was only one bend to negotiate, it would not have looked very different from an extended 200 metres race to him. The other possible advantage, ironically, was his lack of experience. He was an intelligent runner with an astute trainer, but really he was largely untested. It is possible that he had very little in the way of strategy or a race plan, apart from what formed in his mind as the event unfolded. His main weapon was sheer speed, and he could either use that at the beginning to establish a clear lead and hope that he was in good enough condition to hold on to it, or he could hold back and come through at the end with a fast finish. He was known as a good finisher.

At any rate, his preparations were going to be seriously tested. By his own testimony his trust was in the Lord – not that he would necessarily win, but that he might acquit himself well. At that time it was against the prevailing orthodoxy for the first 200 metres to be run fast. As it turned out, the athletics-loving public would see Eric Liddell adopt a different approach to 400 metres running at the Paris Games from the one they might have expected.

The day following his bronze medal in the 200 metres, Liddell was back on the track for the opening heats of the 400 metres. According to Webster, 'Because Liddell won the final on the next day in world's and Olympic record time of 47.6 sec., the Americans, who evidently knew their G. K. Chesterton, nicknamed him "The Man who was Thursday."'[5] Webster must surely be mistaken in applying this phrase to Eric Liddell, as it was clearly applied to Paavo Nurmi, who on that Thursday won the 1,500 metres and 5,000 metres within a couple of hours of one another.[6] We might therefore call Eric Liddell 'the man who was Friday'!

On the Thursday Eric Liddell faced the preliminaries for the 400 metres, the heats of the first round being scheduled for 3 p.m. He was in the fourteenth of seventeen heats and won comfortably enough in 50.2 seconds. The second-round heats were to be run starting at 5 p.m. Eric was to be lined up in the fourth heat with four other athletes: Raymond Robertson (USA), Adriaan Paulen (Netherlands), Raymond Fritz (France) and Luigi Facelli (Italy). Fritz, however, did not start the race. There were, therefore, just four runners. Robertson was a distinct threat. He had come third in a very close US trial held on 14 June, clocking an estimated 48.4 seconds just behind J. Coard Taylor (48.1) and Horatio Fitch (with an estimated time of 48.4), after winning his heat the previous day in 48.1 seconds. It may be said that, apart from Fitch, the Americans running in the 400 metres in Paris did not perform up to expectations. However, the truth is that Eric Liddell very nearly did not get through to the semi-finals. In this second-round heat (in which two athletes would qualify) it was Dutchman Paulen (later to be a President of the International Amateur Athletic Federation) who showed the best pace, coming through to win in 49.0 seconds. In the tussle for second place, Eric narrowly defeated Robertson with a time of 49.3 seconds to the latter's 49.5. So, the Briton got through by a mere fifth of a second. Observers might have thought that Eric was running at his limit. After all, his time in that second-round heat was equivalent to his best performance in the 440 yards up to that point. In the last heat of the day (the sixth) the Swiss runner Joseph Imbach actually broke the Olympic record (and the accepted world record at the time) by a fifth of a second with a time of 48.0, ahead of two other athletes who came in at just under 49 seconds. How could the Scot match that pace? There was no indication that he could. Nevertheless, he was through to the semi-final on the next day, and might acquit himself well enough. But he would have to face two races on the Friday as well – if, that is, he progressed to the final. Meanwhile another Briton, Guy Butler, runner-up in the Olympic 400 metres four years earlier, had also qualified for the semi-finals with victories in the first and second-round heats (with times of 50.2 and 49.8 respectively).

A rather grainy picture of the finish of the second semi-final of the 400 metres at Paris. It can readily be seen how easily Eric (451) won this race, no head thrown back nor flailing arms!

The first semi-final the next day started at 3.45. This saw a magnificent run by the second-ranked American, Horatio Fitch, who, in defeating Britain's Guy Butler after an exciting and close duel, created a new Olympic record of 47.8 seconds. In coming second Butler set a British best of 48.2, improving the previous record of 48.4 set by Wyndham Halswelle back in 1908. Third in that semi-final was the Canadian David M. Johnson with a time of 48.6. A few minutes later the runners lined up for the second semi-final. In this race the 'dark horse' Liddell created a great surprise when he crossed the line first, easing up in a personal best time of 48.2. Running in the second lane, he won with relative ease, something which must have caused his opponents some anxiety. In truth it was a huge leap forward for him. It was patently obvious that he was drawing on a potential that few thought he possessed. He was at the very peak of his form. Second in the race was Imbach (with a time of 48.7) and third was J. Coard Taylor (49.0), who the previous month had won the US Olympic trial from Fitch in 48.1 seconds. Eric's own recollection was that 'despite the times the others had put up, I felt fairly confident, because I had been running well within myself, and felt absolutely keyed up to run the race of my life in the final three hours later.'[7] As it turned out his semi-final performance was scarcely indicative of the drama that was to unfold in the final just two and three-quarter hours later.

As we have already noted, the 400 metres at Paris was run round a single bend. This meant a saving of perhaps 0.2 or 0.3 of a second over the same distance run round two bends. The first 200 metres were run more or less entirely on the straight. It is clear that the track, newly laid for the Olympic Games, was not a particularly fast one. The race was run in lanes partially demarcated by strings. This practice had generally prevailed in Olympic competitions since the notorious 400 metres race at the 1908 Games in which Wyndham Halswelle had allegedly been fouled by an American finalist. That had almost produced a diplomatic incident, not least because, besides Halswelle, the other three finalists were all Americans! Ultimately – and unsatisfactorily – Halswelle had a walkover when he reran the final in blissful isolation. His time of 50.0 was respectable in the circumstances, but it was a melancholic sight for the crowds, and for Halswelle himself, as they cheered on the Scot while he strode over the course in one lane stringed off by itself. This was the only case of a gold medal being won by such means in the history of track and field events at the Olympics. It was a shame, because Halswelle was in superb form, having clocked 48.4 for an Olympic record in the semi-final. The idea of stringed lanes had its downside, however, as the Olympic final of 1924 was sadly to demonstrate. That was the last occasion of the use of strings to demarcate lanes in such events.

It was about 6.30 p.m. when the 400 metres finalists lined up. The pipe band of the Second Queen's Own Cameron Highlanders was on the field at the time and struck up with 'Scotland the Brave'. There is no reason to suppose that this produced any inspiration in the Scottish runner! What it did for the others, however, is harder to say! At any rate, as to the race, the strategic inside lane was drawn by Johnson; next came Guy Butler; Imbach was in lane 3, Taylor in lane 4, Fitch on the outside of Taylor, and on the very outside Eric Liddell, perhaps the least experienced runner in the field, though certainly the fastest in terms of sprint speed. Of these athletes Imbach was the oldest at twenty-nine. The youngest was Johnson, who was just three months younger than Eric Liddell. Eric was therefore one of the two youngest athletes in the field. The outside lane was reckoned to be no advantage, especially to an inexperienced runner. The runner on the outside would have to set his own pace. He would not have the advantage of having runners outside him to help him judge the correct pace. However, such things did not faze Liddell. He would run the race in his own way.

Lieutenant-Colonel F. A. M. Webster drew attention to one incident before this final, which indicates something of Eric Liddell's attitude to the competitions – and his respect for the other runners:

> Just before the starter sent his field to their marks Liddell walked back to shake hands with each of his opponents. That evoked a wisecrack from the irrepressible Frank Dartnell of the *Daily News*. 'Here,' he asked, 'do you know what he is saying to these other fellows? No! Well I'll tell you! He's saying "Goodbye you so-and-sos, because I don't reckon you're going to see my so-and-so heels for so-and-so dust!"' And so it turned out to be, although I am quite sure that Liddell said nothing of the sort when he made his charming gesture.[8]

A charming gesture it was, and a very refreshing one in contrast to the intense over-seriousness which usually marks such occasions. After all, these competitors are human beings, and it is good to wish your opponents well for the race. It must be counted a great sadness that this spirit has been all but lost in top international sport today. It is thought a sign of weakness, at least in the psychology department, though in Eric Liddell's case it certainly did not indicate any softness in his competitive spirit, which was one of his strongest features. As to Eric, he was later to write of his own feelings before the final: 'Curiously enough I was quite cool, and I remember saying to myself, "I must go all out, so as not to be behind at the last straight."'[9]

It is appropriate at this point to mention the note that was handed to Eric Liddell before the race. On the morning of the 400 metres final back at the British team headquarters, he received a note from one of the team masseurs. D. P. Thomson tells the story of what happened:

> 'Today,' wrote my correspondent, on 8th October, 1945, 'I saw and purchased a book entitled Eric Liddell. I was deeply interested as being one of the runners' masseurs who attended to Eric Liddell and others at Colombes, Paris, in 1924 (July). I liked Eric so much, and on the morning of his final 400 metres I handed him the note mentioned on page 24 of that book. I'm afraid I did not quote the text as written; this is what I put – "In the old book it says, 'He that honours me I will honour.' Wishing you the best of success always," and I signed it.
>
> 'I gave it to him at the Hotel Moderne, Rue de la République, Paris, and he said, "I'll read it when I get to the Stadium." I saw him start his race, and shake hands with all his opponents. We said, "He said goodbye to them," for he certainly ran away from them easily. In the dressing room he thanked me for the note, as I and his own trainer, McKerchar, massaged him. I did the left side and remember what a great heart he had.'[10]

This is the sort of effect Eric Liddell had on those who came into contact with him. The quotation was from the Old Testament book of 1 Samuel and said, 'Them that honour me, I will honour' (1 Sam. 2:30). That had reference to his decision not to run on the Sundays.

It seems to me that this account of the note is far more moving than the way it is recreated in *Chariots of Fire*, which depicts Jackson Scholz as giving Eric the note. Scholz himself would have had only the scantiest interaction with Liddell during the Games. Besides this, the idea of Eric holding the note as he ran is inaccurate. In one of the lapses in continuity in the film there are some filmed sequences of the final in which Eric Liddell is shown clutching the note and others in which he is not! It is almost as if Eric Liddell had to carry some little 'charm' corresponding to the charm that Sam Mussabini is depicted as giving to Abrahams – another case of dramatic licence in the screenplay.

It appears that the note made a deep impression on the young athlete and proved a great encouragement to him. A week later, at a complimentary dinner given for him in Edinburgh's Mackie's Restaurant, in replying to various speeches, Eric Liddell referred to the note. He said that perhaps one of the finest things he had enjoyed at the Olympic Games was receiving that note. It surprised him and 'he was glad to find there were many there who voiced the same sentiments as himself'.[11]

To return to the 400 metres final, the starter's pistol cracked and they were off! From the start Liddell set a furious pace and was soon well out in front. All his considerable sprinter's speed went into the first 200 metres, which he covered in an unprecedented (unofficial) 22.2

Finish of the 400 metres at Paris, as depicted on a contemporary postcard. Eric Liddell (left) is well ahead and is finishing in excellent style.

seconds – the same time as he took to win his first-round heat in the shorter sprint, though in this case the first 200 metres were over a course that was more or less straight. He seemed to be running at optimum sprinting speed and many knowledgeable onlookers thought his tactics – if such they were – the height of folly. As the race unfolded, however, it appeared that Liddell might just keep the pace up, or, rather, keep it from declining too much. Sadly, on entering the straight, Joseph Imbach became entangled in the strings which had been placed along the back and home straights and he tumbled to the ground. He did not finish the race. Though Fitch, just inside the Scot, closed the gap a little going around the bend, Eric Liddell was still a good way ahead. In the last fifty metres he even managed to increase that lead a little and, to the amazement of the cheering crowd, broke the tape some four metres clear of the American champion. It was a run of exceptional courage in which he ran in an inspired manner. 'I watched the final from the stand,' recalled Harold Abrahams some ten years later. 'Liddell had the outside lane. From the start he ran like a man inspired. He set off at a pace which looked so ludicrously fast that we expected him to crack when the home straight was reached. But he seemed to maintain it right to the finish and he won by yards and yards in the new Olympic record time of 47.6. Every muscle of his body seemed to be working overtime in his wild rush to supreme victory.'[12]

Eric was to leave on record his own recollection of the course of the race that day: 'We went off to a perfect start, but it was not until I got to the top of the straight that it suddenly dawned on me that I was several yards in front of the field. Evidently the pace I had set had been too much for the others up to this stage. The question was, could I last home? About seventy yards from the tape, I felt that the second man was at his nearest to me. I attempted to lengthen my stride and could do no more; but the comforting thought flashed into my mind that I could no longer hear the second man behind me. I was amazed to find that I had won by six yards.'[13]

With just a touch of exaggeration one contemporary correspondent reported that 'E. H. Liddell today won the Quarter-mile [400 metres] for Great Britain in what was probably the most dramatic race ever seen on a running track.' The same reporter went on to say that 'There was never more than one man in the race and it was the pace he set which fairly ran them off their legs.' So impressed was he by Liddell's performance that he felt that 'After Liddell's race everything else is trivial'![14]

The time was as sensational as the manner of Liddell's victory – a world and Olympic record of 47.6 seconds.[15] The extent of his victory over Fitch was one of the widest ever in the history of the event. After the first semi-final Fitch had been the favourite to win the gold medal. Also highly favoured were Imbach and Butler, who had both clocked 48.0 seconds.[16] Then there was Fitch's compatriot Coard Taylor, who had won the 400 metres at the U.S. Olympic trials, beating Fitch in a time of 48.1 on 14 June. Perhaps he might have been expected to emerge as the winner. In this final Eric Liddell was the 'dark horse'. He was a dark horse, however, who devastated the field! The sight of Liddell 'taking off' the way he did must have shaken all the other athletes. And the way he did not 'come back' to them in the second part of the race must have shaken them even more. Horatio Fitch (1900–1985) left a recollection of his experiences at Paris:

Liddell shot out of the block first, and because of his outside position, he gained an early lead. He set a terrific pace down the first stretch, but I matched his speed. He was only two yards ahead. I heard the other runners behind us. I knew the duel would be between the two of us.

Around the turn he held the same pace. I couldn't believe a man could set such a pace and finish. The reporters expected the race to be between the Swiss [Imbach] and me because we had both broken the world's record. But Liddell pushed himself like a man possessed, head tilted back with determination.

He was still two yards ahead when we entered the final turn. I knew I could close the gap. I had always had a good kick.

The tape loomed 100 yards ahead. I pushed with everything I had, but Liddell fought to hold the advantage. Suddenly, behind us, Joseph Imbach snagged the string with his spikes and skidded to the track. I remembered that my coach had told me. 'When you are getting tiredest, keep your arms driving high.' I wasn't tired, but I couldn't go any faster. Every second I expected the Scot to slow down, to 'tie up'. He had sprinted the entire race, an unusual feat because most coaches believed then that a runner could not sprint 400 yards.

Liddell didn't weaken. And we were closing on the tape much too quickly. I pulled closer, but he strained until we were again the same distance apart. With the tape only 20 yards away, I again spurted closer, but Liddell threw his head further back, gathered himself together, and shot forward.

Just as he broke the tape, I jumped for it in desperation. The gap was just too great. My reign as world's champion [world record holder] had lasted a little more than two hours.[17]

There are some flaws in Horatio Fitch's recollection. His remarks about matching Eric's speed and 'spurting closer' are stretching the facts just a little! Also his reference to jumping for the tape in desperation is hardly accurate. The truth is that he was a good four metres (and four-fifths of a second) behind as Eric Liddell crossed the line. Guy Butler finished a gallant third (in 48.6), but poor Coard Taylor, who seemed to be carrying a slight injury, stumbled and fell to the track some fifteen metres before the finish. He limped across the line to finish in fifth place, with Canadian David Johnson finishing fourth (in 48.8). In modern parlance, Liddell dominated the field.

It is, of course, an exaggeration to say that 'Liddell did not weaken' and that he 'seemed to gain in speed and power'. It may have seemed like that, but in reality Eric Liddell slowed significantly, covering the second 200 metres in 25.4. As Roberto Quercetani puts it in his authoritative volume on the history of the 'One-Lap Race':

A single breath is enough for a well-trained sprinter to travel at his maximum speed for about 100 metres. With more breaths, the oxygen intake allows a good runner to maintain his top speed for about 250 metres. Beyond such a limit the maximum of oxygen debt is inevitably reached, at which point more oxygen is required than is in fact obtainable through respiration. Consequently, the runner who has been going all out until then will have to slow down considerably.

The point is made that the strongest man at the end of a 400 metres race is the runner who decelerates the least. Quercetani remarks that 'As early as in the nineteenth century the quarter mile was defined as "the severest course that can be run". It has remained just that even in our time and age. That's why it is sometimes referred to as "the killer event".'[18]

In relation to Eric Liddell's performance in Paris, the point is that he never did 'tie up' or decelerate more than the other finalists! Eric Liddell's performance over 400 metres in Paris was exceptional. Being on the outside lane was a distinct disadvantage for an inexperienced runner. That is how it seems, at any rate. However, there are a couple of surprising things about the 400 metres race that to date have passed unnoticed by track and field commentators. One is the strange fact that two of the finalists had trouble with the strings, Imbach and Taylor. It has been suggested that either or both of these athletes may have fallen prey to injury. However, the strings were not rigid and would have been blown by the wind. They were placed on the straights and not round the long bend. If an athlete strayed to the inside of the lane, as he would be inclined to do, he could very easily be snagged on the string. It is noticeable from film of the race, including stills, that Eric Liddell ran the race perfectly in his lane, keeping away from the inside. This meant that he may have run marginally more than 400 metres, making his performance even more creditable. The point is that his was a disciplined race, notwithstanding the tendency he had to throw his head back in the closing stages.

The other notable feature in the final was the unusual phenomenon of men in the two outside lanes coming through to outstrip the rest of the field. It is perhaps significant that on the Thursday before the final of the 400 metres there were finals of 1,500 metres and 5,000 metres. It is easy to see how the inside lanes, perhaps as far out as the fourth lane, would be rather more cut up than the outside ones. If this is so, as seems likely, it may be that the two outside lanes in the 400 metres event were not necessarily so disadvantageous for Fitch and Liddell! However, they still had to do all the running, and one would have thought that those on the inside would have been able to pace themselves well. In any case, Eric Liddell's sheer pace from the outset seemed to devastate the field. On the day he was quite simply in a class of his own. Eric Liddell's was a performance of world-class grit and superb execution. He ran it like an extended 200 metre race – something that was more or less unprecedented. He almost single-handedly, if unintentionally, introduced a new concept into one-lap racing. Prior to this, convention had dictated a 'paced' race. Liddell changed that concept at Paris. The *Edinburgh Evening Dispatch* takes up the story:

> Liddell...had his plans arranged, and he had not gone far before they were made perfectly clear. He was going to do what had been considered the impossible – go all out for a quarter of a mile. As the half-dozen men came into the straight Liddell was just in front by a yard, going like a perfect piece of machinery. Fitch was next, then Butler and Johnson level.
>
> With thirty yards to go Liddell was 3 yards in front and going away from the others as if they were novices. Liddell never faltered. He went along in the perfect style of his own, a smile on his face, his head thrown slightly back, his arms working in unison with his legs, and he broke the worsted with almost 6 yards separating him from Fitch. Guy Butler was, perhaps, half a yard behind Fitch. Imbach was limping and broken down. Johnson was fourth, and Taylor, in his eagerness to reach the tape, was sprawling on the ground.

The same writer goes on:

> I have seen some remarkable races and world beaters in them, but never have I seen a race where the winner showed such power and supreme confidence as Liddell. From perfect silence on the part of the spectators a roar went up, and whilst it was quietening down the microphone announced that Liddell had not only won but had beaten the world's record by doing 47.6 secs.[19]

It is noticeable, incidentally, that there is no reference to Liddell's being exhausted or distressed after this race, indeed, after running two high-quality races. It just shows how splendid his fitness and his spirit were on the day. 'The strange thing was,' he was to recollect afterwards, 'that despite the race I had run, and the time I had run it in, I was quite cool and collected, and not in the least distressed. I felt perfectly strong, and there was really no need to lie down and rest.'[20]

With reference to Liddell's Olympic triumph, the famous American coaches Payton Jordan and Bud Spencer, writing forty-five years after the 1924 Games, stated categorically that he had achieved 'a breakthrough of established 440 technique'.[21] They then go on to bewail the fact that this had not been immediately taken up by American coaches at the time and, as a consequence, the event continued to lag behind. This observation is worth making as it sets Liddell's great run within the context of the development of the history of the event. Incidentally, his performance ranked as a European best until as late as 1936, when Godfrey Brown clocked 47.3 in a semi-final of the 400 metres at the Berlin Olympics. The film of the race shows that there was no collapsing into the arms of his coach utterly exhausted after the race. Eric was remarkably fresh afterwards, standing with his hands on his hips, smiling for the photographers. There was no lap of honour, nor any medal presentation. In fact the medals were sent on by the organisers through the post several months later! On the contrary, after a few photographs, with characteristic modesty Eric 'with every haste took his leave of the cheering multitude'. Inevitably there was great excitement among the British Team. Eric afterwards wrote of the 'wild reception' he had received from them after the race as he reached the top of the exit of the competitors' tunnel leading to the dressing rooms:

> The first to congratulate me was a Surrey man, who was entered for the cross-country event. Before I knew where I was he had grabbed me, and got me upon his shoulders, and I was carried into the dressing-room by a big, excited crowd of my fellow-countrymen. It was an experience I shall always remember, and the other pleasant recollection will be the congratulations I got from the Americans, who were more than generous in their references to the race.[22]

As it turned out, this was the last cheer for Scottish sporting followers of Olympic track and field events before the unlikely appearance of Alastair McCorquodale in the 100 metres final at Wembley in 1948 and, of course, of Allan Wells in Moscow in 1980, but as his great rival, Harold Abrahams put it at the time: 'Eric's brilliant victory at the Paris Olympiad will always remain an epic.'

As for the rest of the Olympics, the two relays – 4 x 100 metres and 4 x 400 metres – were run between the last Saturday and Sunday of the Games, 12 and 13 July, both finals taking place on the Sunday. Once again on that Sunday Eric Liddell was not present. Instead he was preaching for the Rev. T. H. Wright in the Scots' Kirk at 17 rue Bayard, near the Champs-Elysées. It could be said that he was sorely missed. In the sprint relay the Great Britain squad won the silver medal behind the Americans. In the 1,600 metres relay the British team won the bronze. Would they have done any better if Eric had taken part? Possibly. The following Saturday, 19 July, there was a relay contest arranged between a USA Olympic team and a team representing the British Empire. Included was a 4 x 440 yards relay event in which perhaps an answer might be given to that question. The 'Empire' team would comprise three members of the Great Britain bronze-medal winning team, along with Eric Liddell. The match was awaited with especially heightened anticipation.

11.

COMING DOWN FROM THE MOUNTAINTOP

Eric Liddell's life immediately after the conclusion of the Games in Paris was frantic. Obviously, he must have faced all sorts of adulation, but it was never allowed to turn his head. Eric seems always to have been able to keep mere sporting success in perspective. He had already decided to follow brother Rob to the mission-field in China. But that week after the Games was to see several memorable events in his life.

First, there was his graduation at Edinburgh University. The ceremony took place on Thursday, 17 July, at the McEwan Hall, where he was awarded his BSc degree. This was no ordinary graduate, however, and he wasn't going to get away with just a run-of-the mill graduation ceremony. In conferring his degree, the Principal of the University, Sir Alfred Ewing, said that it was clear that no one could pass Liddell but his examiners! He also presented the young graduate with a wreath made of the wild olive Oleaster, specially commissioned from the Royal Botanic Gardens. In addition to this a scroll was put in his hand. It was in Greek, but read in translation:

> The University of Edinburgh congratulates
> Eric Henry Liddell, Olympic victor in the 400 metres.
> Happy the man who, the wreathed games essaying,
> Returns with laurelled brow.
> Thrice happy victor thou, such speed displaying
> As none hath showed till now;
> We joy, and Alma Mater, for thy merit,
> Proffers to thee this crown;

> Take it, Olympic victor. While you wear it,
> May Heaven never frown.

These were unprecedented scenes, as was the cheering that accompanied it all. After the conclusion of the ceremony Eric was chaired by fellow-students to St Giles Cathedral in the High Street where there was to be a worship service. Needless to say, this attracted the attention of passers-by.

When the company arrived at St Giles, Eric was prevailed on to make a speech. What he said was typical of his self-effacing modesty. He said that he had noticed over the entrance of the University of Pennsylvania the inscription: 'In the dust of defeat as well as in the laurels of victory there is a glory to be found if one has done his best.' To this he added: 'There are many present here who have done their best, though they have not succeeded in gaining the laurels of victory, and to them there is as much honour due as to those who have received the laurels of victory.'[1]

Eric's Graduation photo, July 1924.

The following day he was the honoured guest at a complimentary dinner arranged at short notice by a number of prominent churchmen and others. It was in Mackie's Restaurant and Tea House on Princes Street, Edinburgh. Over one hundred guests were present and the dinner was presided over by Lord Sands. What a gathering it was of prominent citizens! The Lord Provost, Sir William L. Sleigh, was there, as was the Principal of Edinburgh University, Sir Alfred Ewing. In addition, there was a fair collection of titled dignitaries and clerics. Even in those days an Olympic victor was seen to be an A-list celebrity! But it must have been all very intimidating for a young man only in his twenty-third year. Various speeches were given.

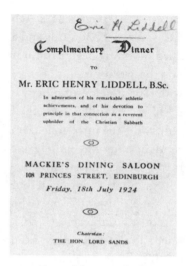

Complimentary Dinner

TO

Mr. ERIC HENRY LIDDELL, B.Sc.

In admiration of his remarkable athletic
achievements, and of his devotion to
principle in that connection as a reverent
upholder of the Christian Sabbath

MACKIE'S DINING SALOON
108 PRINCES STREET, EDINBURGH

Friday, 18th July 1924

Chairman:
THE HON. LORD SANDS

*Front of the menu for the
complimentary dinner held for Eric
Liddell after the Games.*

It is interesting that the menu card for the event stated that the dinner was given 'in admiration of his remarkable athletic achievements, and of his devotion to principle as a reverent upholder of the Christian Sabbath'. In the course of his introductory remarks, Lord Sands said that 'they all honoured him for the public stand he had made in the face of the world for what he believed to be right. In these days of moral flabbiness, it was something to find a man who was not content to shield himself behind such easy phrases as "It is only once in the way" or "When you go to Rome you must do as they do in Rome."'[2]

The Rev. Norman Maclean said that Eric had shown that Christians were not milksops and that Christianity had to do with all departments of life. That afternoon a cable was sent from the meeting to Eric's parents in China. It said, 'Large gathering, Edinburgh, Chairman Lord Sands, cordially congratulates father and mother on Eric's wonderful feat, and still more on his noble witness for Christian principles.'

That complimentary dinner took place on the Friday afternoon. The report of the event ended thus: 'After the dinner, Mr Liddell left for London to take part in the international athletic contest at Stamford Bridge.' That event was the relay contest between a United States team and one representing the British Empire. It was held on Saturday, 19 July, just eight days after his Olympic triumph. With so many Olympic athletes competing, a large crowd of 38,000 spectators pressed into the Stamford Bridge sports ground that afternoon to witness the proceedings. Those who came specially to see the Olympic 400 metres champion in action were not to be disappointed by the events of that day.

The programme contained eight events: 4 x 100 yards; 4 x 440 yards, a one-mile medley (consisting of 440 yards, 2 x 220 yards and a final stint of 880 yards), high jump (decided on the aggregate of three competitors), putting the weight (judged on the average results of three competitors), an eight-lap steeplechase (with four athletes running two laps each) a three-mile team race and 4 x 120 yards hurdles. Out of all the events the British Empire team won only two – the three-mile team race and the 4 x 440 relay race. The success in the latter was entirely due to the superb running of Eric Liddell. It was the second event of the afternoon. The Empire team for the 4 x 440 yards relay comprised four British athletes. In order of running, they were: Edward Toms (who had set a personal best of 49.9 in the second-round heats in Paris), Richard Ripley, Guy Butler and Eric Liddell. The first three had been in the bronze-medal-winning team in Paris. Pitted against them was an American team comprising Eric C. Wilson, Raymond A. Robertson, William Stevenson and Horatio Fitch. Of this team only Stevenson had been in the gold-medal-winning 4 x 400 metres team in Paris. Wilson and Robertson, however, had each run in the individual 400 metres at Paris and were both performers who had clocked times of less than 49 seconds. If anything, this team would be considered an even stronger one than the American team at the Olympics.

Off to a good start, Toms ran well to hand over to Ripley a lead of about five yards or so over the first leg. On the second stage, however, Robertson overhauled the Englishman in the home straight to hand over to Stevenson a lead of three yards, which he increased to six in outpacing Guy Butler, who was struggling with a leg strain. The Americans also had the best of the final changeover, with the result that Liddell found himself seven yards down on the Olympic silver-medallist, Horatio Fitch. It was just this sort of situation that the partisan crowd savoured. Here was a test for the new Olympic champion. Could he achieve the apparently impossible?

In this case there were two bends to negotiate, unlike the single-bend race at Paris. Undaunted by the magnitude of the task, Liddell set off after Fitch. Round the first bend he made little impression, though with a terrific burst of speed down the back straight he actually pulled

Eric brings the British Empire 4 x 440 yards relay team home to defeat a crack USA team.

up to the American's shoulder. Fitch responded by holding off the Scot round the final bend, but could not match the latter's finishing power and had to yield in the home straight, where, to the great delight of the roaring crowd, Liddell pulled away in front to win by four yards, 'amidst tumultuous cheering'. The time recorded by the Empire team was 3 minutes, 18.2 seconds, just 0.2 second outside the listed world record set in 1915 by the University of Pennsylvania. It was reckoned that Eric Liddell ran 447 yards in 48.4 seconds. There seems little doubt that this was his fastest-ever 440 yards. It was another gutsy, determined performance. But it did take a lot out of him. This is clear from his performance later in the programme, in the one-mile medley. In that race, the last of the day, he ran the opening quarter of a mile. Tired no doubt from his earlier effort, he made the mistake of setting off too fast and this time he slowed down enough to be overtaken by a fresh Charles Brookins (USA) and to finish two yards behind him.

The British Empire team might still have won that race, as Arthur Porritt and Guy Butler did not lose any ground to George Hill and Jackson Scholz. However, the anchor-man for the Empire team, Douglas Lowe, made a mistake in trying too early to overtake the American

Alan Helffrich. He sprinted past Helffrich with 220 yards to go, but the American, twice before the United States 880 yards champion (1921 and 1922), still had something in reserve and retook the lead 100 yards from home to give the Americans another victory that day by a couple of yards. It was an exciting race, though the crowds would have liked to see Liddell and Lowe bring off something special. It was not to be.

Eric Liddell's hectic schedule continued after the Stamford Bridge meeting. Unfortunately, as a result of that meeting Eric was kept from attending a valedictory service for his brother, Rob, in which he was dedicated to missionary service in China. This service took place on Sunday, 20 July, at the Morningside Congregational Church. By this time Rob was married. Eric had been best man at Rob's marriage to Ria Aitken in Fountainhall Road Church, Edinburgh, on 17 May. Rob and Ria subsequently left for China that December.

The Saturday following his great run at Stamford Bridge, Eric Liddell made his first appearance on a Scottish track since his Olympic success when he competed for Scotland in a match against a Canadian team at the Greenock Glenpark Harriers meeting. He ran in the 100 yards, 440 yards and mile medley relay. All events were run on a grass track. In the 100 yards he finished third to the outstanding Canadian Cyril Coaffee, who had been a semi-finalist in both 100 metres and 200 metres at Paris. Coaffee won the race by a yard from James Crawford, who, in defeating Liddell by inches, inflicted upon him the second of only two defeats that Eric Liddell ever suffered at the hands of a fellow-Scot in a scratch race. The winning time was 10.0 seconds. In the 440 yards, however, Liddell had everything very much his own way, winning by a full ten yards in 51.2 seconds on a rough sodden track. He also helped secure victory for Scotland in the relay, overtaking Allan Christie (Canada) on the last leg to do so. His time for his stint was recorded at 50.2 for 445 yards. This was another epic performance, given that he took over about eight yards down on the Canadian, who was no mean performer over 440 yards.

That evening Eric Liddell remained in the west of Scotland and the following day addressed a meeting at Inverkip Road, Greenock. Despite heavy rain throughout, several thousand people turned up.

The crowd was so big that an adjournment was made to an adjacent park. John Kerr, a Scotland cricket international, acted as chairman of the meeting. Eric spoke on the text: 'Remember now thy Creator in the days of thy youth' (Eccles. 12:1). This is the sort of thing that Eric was to do habitually in the following year – take part in Christian outreach meetings on the Saturday evenings, or the day following track meetings. It showed his popularity when such huge crowds braved the elements to attend such gatherings.

During my time as a divinity student the author spent a few weeks one summer in the mid-1980s as a supply minister to Free Church congregations on the Island of Arran off the west coast of Ayrshire. On visiting the home of an older married couple in Lamlash, at one point the couple were asked about their experience of becoming Christians. The wife recounted how sixty years earlier she had been converted to Christ at a meeting in Greenock addressed by Eric Liddell! As far as could be ascertained, it was precisely that meeting on Sunday, 27 July 1924! She still remembered it. To me it brought alive the story of Eric Liddell in a new way, indicating how he had been used in the work of bringing the gospel to the young men and women of his own day.

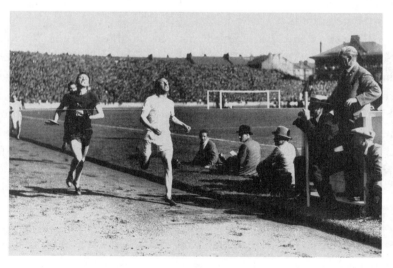

Eric often competed in the Rangers Football Club sports. Here he wins the 440 yards handicap from South African Clarence Oldfield in the 1924 meeting.

In the remaining track meets in Scotland that year Liddell drew large crowds. They were rarely disappointed. At the Rangers Football Club Sports on 2 August there were no fewer than 50,000 spectators. While it may be true that by and large the crowds for these prestigious meetings were mainly there to see their soccer heroes in action in popular five-a-side tournaments, it is likely that in 1924 Eric Liddell figured as an equally significant attraction. At any rate, he narrowly won an exciting 440 yards handicap, running the full 440 yards course in the excellent time of 49.6 seconds, up till then the fastest he had recorded for the distance in Scotland. Apparently, it was hoped that he might attack Wyndham Halswelle's long-standing British and Scottish record of 48.4. However, a troublesome wind put paid to any such notion.

There was a genuine surprise in this race that Eric was pushed so hard by the South African Clarence W. Oldfield, who, given a start of five yards, finished a mere foot behind Liddell. That should not really have been a surprise, however, as Oldfield had finished fifth in the Olympic semi-final at Paris won by Eric Liddell, with a time of 49.4 to Eric's 48.2. He was a world-class performer. It was a fine victory by the Scot and in good weather he might well have achieved a time under forty-nine seconds.

Three days later Eric Liddell was back at Ibrox for the West of Scotland Harriers meeting in which he won a scratch 300 yards race in 32.0 seconds, beating his old rival William Nichol, with Oldfield in third place. He competed in just one more meeting that year, in the Gala Harriers Sports at Netherdale Park, Galashiels, on 16 August. 2,000 people gathered on a rainy afternoon to see the sports. In a downpour of rain Eric delighted the crowd by winning a special handicap 440 yards race from scratch in 54.0 seconds.

So ended one of the most glorious chapters in the history of Scottish amateur athletics. By his magnificent running that season Liddell established himself as one of the great 400 metre runners. It will surely always be the case that wherever athletics stories are told an honoured place will be given to this track hero of 1924. But his life was to be shaped by altogether different and higher ends. He was now a candidate for the mission-field under the auspices of the London Missionary Society, with whom his father, and more recently his brother Rob, had gone out to China. In order to prepare for this work he undertook a year's theological study at the Scottish Congregational College at 29 Hope Terrace, Edinburgh, where he had a room that year.[3] He was to have one more season, or part-season, on Scottish tracks. Besides that, however, he would also be involved with fairly extensive campaign work, frequently speaking at evangelistic meetings, mostly with his friend D. P. Thomson.

12.

THE FINAL SEASON

By 1925 it had become clear that Eric Liddell's life's work would take him to the mission-field in China, where both his father and older brother were serving. That year saw his last season in competitive athletics in Britain before his departure for China. He ran with scarcely less verve than he had shown the previous momentous year. Wherever he appeared large crowds gathered to see him in action, doubtless expecting a record every time he ran! His popularity at this time was high and it is certainly not an overstatement to say that he was without a doubt Scotland's best-loved sportsman at the time.

The 1925 season opened for Liddell with his regulation sprint treble in the Edinburgh University Sports on 20 May and also in the Scottish Intervarsity meeting at St Andrews on 30 May. In the Edinburgh University Sports he improved on his own record for the 440 yards with a time of 51.4 seconds on the slow grass track at Craiglockhart. On 6 June, at the Queen's Park Football Club Sports at Hampden Park, Glasgow, he approached something like his best form with a time of 50.2 for the 440 yards on a slow track, in a handicap race in which he finished a close third. The following week, on a rough grass track at Corstorphine, he won the East of Scotland 440 yards championship in a modest time of 53.5 seconds. He also ran seventh in a field of thirty-four in a 600 yards handicap race, starting from scratch and finishing eight yards behind the winner, J. N. K. Clarkson (of Edinburgh University Athletic Club), who had a start of forty-five yards and won in 1 minute, 16.8 seconds.

The next Saturday, Liddell won the East of Scotland 220 yards title in the Edinburgh Southern Harriers Sports at Powderhall. His winning time was 23.4 seconds. That this was well within his capabilities on the day was shown in his later winning the 220 yards handicap from scratch in 22.25, after winning a heat in 22.8. For that win he was presented with a nine-carat gold gentleman's wristwatch, which cost £4 – a handsome prize and the last he was to win in Edinburgh. This is thought to be the watch that Eric gifted to Tom McKerchar before he left Scotland for China, and which has subsequently been in the possession of Eric Liddell McKerchar, a son named after Tom's 'charge'. Incidentally, his performance that day illustrates the value of handicap races for Liddell's athletic conditioning. In scratch races a time of 23 seconds would have been sufficient for a comfortable victory, but in handicap races the quality and intensity of his running would have to be of a higher order.

At that same Edinburgh Southern Harriers meeting he also ran a fine 300 yards race in a time of 31.5, just 0.3 second outside the long-standing Scottish record of Wyndham Halswelle, set in 1908. Although Liddell had several good times of under 32 seconds for that event over the years, that record of Halswelle's always eluded him.

Liddell's final appearance on an Edinburgh track took place on 24 June at the Edinburgh Pharmacy Athletic Club Annual Sports, again at Powderhall. He competed in the 120 yards handicap. Running from scratch, he was narrowly defeated in a heat by A. Kennedy, of the King's Own Scottish Borderers Regiment, to whom he conceded eight yards on the handicap. He just failed to catch Kennedy, who won by inches in 12.0 seconds. Liddell did, however, end on a winning note by helping his university to win the mile medley relay, to the delight of the large Edinburgh crowd.

Three days after his final track appearance in Edinburgh, Eric Liddell bade farewell to the Scottish track scene at the SAAA Championships at Hampden Park, Glasgow. For him, this was a day of 'uninterrupted triumph', as one reporter put it. A crowd of 12,000 turned out on a fine day, the gate receipts amounting to £490, a huge amount for those days. The attraction was Eric Liddell, and the crowd was not to be disappointed, for he won all three sprints with championship-best performances and contributed an important leg in the mile medley relay, helping Edinburgh University to a fine win. In the 100 yards he won the final in 10.0 seconds by one and a half yards from the Glasgow runner, Robert McLean, who pressed him all the way, as he had done the previous year. In comfortably winning the 220 and 440 yards he clocked the useful times of 22.2 and 49.2 seconds respectively. His time for the quarter-mile was in fact the fastest he ever recorded for the distance, though it was inferior when compared to his best time over 400 metres of 47.6. For these performances Liddell was awarded the Crabbie Cup as the most meritorious competitor at the championships, an award that had also been conferred on him in 1922 (jointly with miler Duncan McPhee), 1923 and 1924. Eric received a tumultuous reception from the crowd on this his final appearance on a Scottish track.

Eric Liddell's career in the one-lap race was near-perfect. His only loss in a scratch race was in the second round of the Olympic Games at Paris, in which he eased through just behind Adriaan Paulen of the Netherlands and was not going flat out by any means. The race in which he finished third was a handicap event in which he started from scratch. He finished in a time of 50.2, just 0.4 second behind the winner, to whom he was conceding eighteen yards.

One thing that ought to be mentioned at this point is the matter of Eric Liddell's running style. Duncan Wright's recollections of seeing Eric run for the first time in 1921 have already been quoted. Most commentators have considered that he had an unorthodox style, flailing his arms and throwing his head back in an ungainly manner. Clearly, however, Tom McKerchar saw no reason to persuade him to change the way he ran. There seems to be no contradicting the fact that he wasn't the most graceful of movers on the running track. Harold Abrahams had this to say: 'It has often been suggested that if some trainer could have taken Liddell in hand and given him a decent style he would have been capable of even greater achievements.' He does concede, however, that:

Personally I doubt very much if at his age it would have been possible to mould so unorthodox a performer into anything approaching a recognized form. Any attempt might well have resulted in ruining his running, for individuality is often such an elusive factor that once it is submerged or even modified so far the innate greatness of the athlete is completely obscured. I do not mean to suggest that good style is not a tremendous asset and if one had started when Liddell was very young something advantageous might have resulted.[1]

There is no doubt that Liddell's style was characterised by certain exaggerated features: an overly high arm action and a tendency to throw his head back being the most obvious. These aspects have been given particular prominence in recent years with the representation of his style in *Chariots of Fire*, with Ian Charleson's whirling arms and skyward

gaze. But was his style really so bad? After his great victories in the sprints at the 1923 AAA Championships, one English reporter commented that 'His style is splendid, for he is quick into his running, has a rare stride, and puts all his strength into the race. In the 220 yards he threw his head back in the last 60 yards, seemed to close his eyes, and yet ran as straight as a gun barrel, with unwavering resoluteness. There are those who thought that he wobbled, but he was in perfect alignment with his strings.' David A. Jamieson, co-editor of the jubilee history of the Scottish AAA in 1933, in a personal note to the author, wrote that 'Much has been said of his style of running, but the only noticeable fault – if it could be termed as such – was that of throwing his head back in the closing stages of his race. Incidentally his finish was cyclonic in its fury, and that broad torso of his invariably caught the judges' eyes.' By some writers Eric Liddell was described as 'skinny' and 'spindle-legged'.[2] Though he was not a big man, at five foot nine inches

'His style is splendid.'

(1.75m) tall and weighing in at 155 lbs, he had a powerful enough build. There is an extant photograph taken at Craiglockhart, probably at the Edinburgh University Sports of 1925, which shows his impressive athletic physique to full effect.

On the matter of style, an examination of contemporary photographs invariably indicates a style by no means bad. Take the finals of the 200 metres and 400 metres at Paris. As one glances over all the competitors, the one who catches the eye for style and sheer energy is Eric Liddell's vigorous arm action, excellent leg extension and high knee lift. The fact is that he was a well-balanced athlete who ran with rare energy and vigour. I believe it can be

'That broad torso of his invariably caught the judges' eyes.'

said that any changes to his style would have had only a marginal impact on his achievements. He was a wonderful sight to behold on the track. He must have had a good pair of lungs and a great heart – in more ways than one. That in a sense was the secret of his power. He ran with such conviction, determination – with spirit. Winning was not the be-all and end-all, but he always ran to win. He took literally – and also for his life as a Christian – the exhortation of the apostle Paul: 'Know ye not that they which run in a race run all, but one receiveth the prize? So run, that ye may obtain' (1 Cor. 9:24). That God-honouring race, with no mere temporal prize, Eric would go on to run in China.

13.

LIFE IS MORE THAN SPORT

The year after his Olympic triumph was one of campaigning for Eric Liddell, with his friend D. P. Thomson being the organising influence. Their evangelistic work was very intensive, covering many parts of Scotland, and sometimes further afield. Just how peripatetic Eric Liddell was is indicated by a letter that he sent to a young lady named Elsa McKechnie, who had formed an 'Eric Liddell Club' in Edinburgh. Writing from London on 22 April 1925, Eric said this:

> As you see from my address I am in that 'little village' known as London. I am here until the beginning of May when I return to Edinburgh. My holiday has been most enjoyable. Our term [at the Congregational College in Edinburgh] closed at the beginning of April. After that I went up to Barrhead with eight or nine students and had a campaign there. We slept in one of the church Halls and looked after some of our meals ourselves, although we always went out for dinner. It was strenuous but worthwhile, and I enjoyed every minute. After that I went to Aberdeen for four days, Dundee for one and now I am here...[1]

D. P. Thomson records that Eric made great strides as a chairman, leader and speaker at these various meetings. They spoke in theatres, in music halls, in churches and in all sorts and shapes of public buildings, schools and colleges. In his addresses Eric gave straightforward Bible messages, well illustrated by experiences from the running track, the rugby field and the chemistry laboratory. He combined these evangelistic activities with some courses at the Scottish Congregational College at Hope Terrace, Edinburgh. He considered that some theological studies would be helpful in his forthcoming work in China. All the while he kept in training, as his performances in the 1925 season abundantly demonstrate.

Many of the meetings held as part of this evangelistic work were very well attended. Sometimes there were huge crowds. The situation then was different from that today. There was still a fairly widespread respect for church, and services were still well attended. It is true that evangelicalism was on the decline and the Scottish ecclesiastical malady of nominal religion was fairly well advanced, yet people did respond to such campaign meetings. Society had not then been atrophied and secularised by 24/7 television. It may be that many attended such meetings out of curiosity, given Eric Liddell's celebrity status as a great Olympic hero. Eric, however, was far more concerned to speak to the crowds about Christianity and Christ than about himself. No doubt many of those who came to hear him were touched by the simple message heard from the Olympic champion. It was the 'simple gospel'. The need of the sinner to submit heart and life to Jesus Christ was pressed on the hearers. The sinner was invited to confess sin and commit his/her life to Jesus as Saviour and Lord.

The schedule that D. P. Thomson and Eric Liddell took upon themselves was hectic, to say the least. Often meetings were arranged in connection with the athletics meetings, either on the Saturday evening or the Sunday following, and sometimes even on the Monday.[2]

Eric Liddell did not confine his speaking to meetings or campaigns arranged by D. P. Thomson. He often spoke by invitation on other platforms. In connection with the Fellowship of Bible Reading and Prayer he spoke at a meeting held in Palmerston Place United Free Church on Saturday, 17 January 1925. This was obviously something close to his heart. It is important to recognise the place of the Bible in Eric's life. It was crucial. This is clear from what he said at that meeting, which was reported as follows: '...men and women should study the word of God, working at it, in order that they might find the specific message it had for them.'[3] The Bible was central to his Christian faith. In a book produced during his evangelistic fieldwork in North China (1937–1941) and published in recent years, he was to write this:

I would suggest the discipline of rising half an hour earlier than usual and giving the time to prayer, meditation, and Bible study. Be careful, however, not to fall into the habit of thinking God can only guide you at this one special time. Be careful, too, about your attitude to others who differ from you regarding the time they find most helpful. Be prepared to change the time of your prayer if the circumstances of your life lead you to feel it necessary or advisable.[4]

He makes his position clear in another place:

> The Christian rule of right and wrong is the Word of God. It is a light for his path and an instructor to educate his conscience. The Word of God is profitable:
> 'for doctrine', to teach God's will;
> 'for reproof', to challenge all contrary to that will;
> 'for correction', to correct errors in basic thinking;
> 'for instruction', to train the conscience to lead us in the paths of righteousness (2 Tim. 3.16).[5]

Another cause with which he readily associated was that of total abstinence. In this connection he spoke at a 'No-Licence' demonstration held at the Music Hall in George Street, Edinburgh, on Wednesday, 4 February 1925. This meeting was held under the auspices of the Edinburgh Citizens No-Licence Council. Eric was one of the principal speakers. He strongly urged that the temperance movement should proclaim its message somewhat more forcefully. He considered alcohol to be a social blight and spoke of temperance in relation to fitness. At one point he gave a personal family reminiscence: 'He stood there as either the third or fourth generation of non-smokers and teetotallers. (Applause). He would never be able to say what contribution his forefathers had given to any success he had, but he knew this, that they had given their contribution. (Applause).'[6] Not all professing Christians were total abstainers. However, Eric Liddell certainly saw it as perfectly consistent with the 'sober-mindedness' exhorted in the Bible.

Also close to his heart, as one can imagine, was the question of Lord's day observance. In 1925 he added his support to a protest against the increased facilities and inducements offered by the London Midland

and Scottish Railway Company for pleasure travel on Sundays. Again in this area, in contrast to our present day, there was considerable concern to keep Sunday special and free from unnecessary activities which tended to impinge on the rest of others, and there were many prominent civic and ecclesiastical personalities who lent their weight to such an issue. On Monday, 18 May 1925 there was a well-attended meeting at St George's United Free Church in Edinburgh's West End at which Eric Liddell spoke. He made a very telling point for those days, namely that if the church were to be united on the question of its attitude to the Sabbath it would be able to carry before it anything it liked. He is reported as saying that 'Their difficulty today was that inside the Church there were those who thought very little of it.'[7]

It is certainly true to say that the prevarication and ambiguity of the churches on this 'Sabbath question' since that time have not encouraged a more careful and restful use of the Lord's day in Britain. Now Sundays are sadly scarcely distinguishable from any other days, except that there seems to be as much, if not more, shopping and sport on Sundays as on any weekday! Nowadays in urban areas sport and shopping are like a new social Sunday 'religion'. The early twenty-first-century experience would have been unimaginable to these men in the 1920s. All such additional activities have their serious spin-offs in terms of social disruption, lack of bodily rest and the inevitable employment of more and more people to serve or police those determined to travel, shop and pursue sports and recreational activities. Whether we are better off for the 24/7 restlessness is a big question. Eric Liddell, for one, would have joined in a resounding chorus of 'No!' to any such notion. Whether or not there will be a return even to the way it was in 1925 will very much depend on the success of the churches in recovering the biblical message and a degree of consensus among them on specific issues like Lord's day observance.

Eric Liddell's continuing interest in Lord's day observance was again evident during his first furlough home in 1932. At the annual meeting of the Lord's Day Association of Scotland at St Andrew's Church, George Street, Edinburgh, on Tuesday, 8 March, that year there were several motions carried, including one by Eric Liddell on 'Sunday Games':

That this meeting is of the opinion that the increasing use of the Lord's Day for games and recreations, however harmless in themselves, is detrimental to the highest interests of the youth of the country, as well as adding to the amount of unnecessary labour of other people; and calls on all young people's organizations to give full consideration to this aspect of the question.[8]

It would be a great mistake to think that Eric and the other supporters of Lord's day observance were simply 'kill-joys'. No one was happier to see young people involved in healthy sports and recreational activities than Eric Liddell. As he saw it, however, God's Word was to be respected. A quiet Sabbath could not but be for the overall advantage of young and old – all the more so if it was motivated by a concern for Christian public worship. But there were benefits from the point of view of physical rest besides any religious involvement. And these men, such as Eric Liddell, could see that once there was a 'thin end of the wedge' allowed, it would be very difficult to envisage retaining much, if anything, of a common 'day of rest', with a consequential deterioration of family life. This is exactly what has happened in our 'modern' society. These were issues clearly close to Eric Liddell's heart. To him matters of Sunday observance and temperance were at the heart of a good, well-ordered and God-honouring society and could only be for the good of the rising generation. His public speaking was always positive.

At the beginning of May 1925 he was again at St George's United Free Church.[9] Eric was Convener of the Edinburgh Young Life Campaign. On Tuesday, 5 May, they held the first of twelve special evangelistic services, arranged under the auspices of the Edinburgh Evangelistic Union. D. P. Thomson was also involved in these meetings. There was an interesting report of proceedings in the *Scotsman*, which stated that Eric Liddell and D. P. Thomson both gave short addresses. 'Both men,' said the report, 'in spite of their comparative youth, appeared to exercise a great effect upon their listeners, a tense silence prevailing throughout the body of the church during the addresses. No two speakers could have been more the complement of one another – the one, Mr Liddell, quiet and restrained, speaking slowly and sometimes in scarcely more than a whisper, although always distinctly audible; the

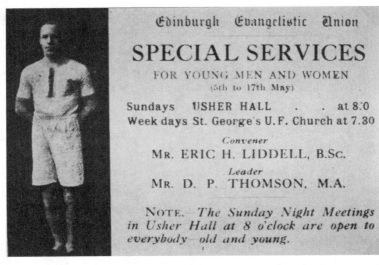

Invitation leaflet advertising a series of meetings in May 1925 under the auspices of the Edinburgh Evangelistic Union.

other, Mr Thomson, impassioned, delivering his words with great force and speed, and gesticulating freely.'[10]

Eric said in his address that they did not need to have a vast experience to give the message of Jesus Christ. They realised that those who tried to proclaim such a message must have passed through some intimate experience themselves before giving it. Many today, he continued, were missing something in life, because they were content with second-best. The best in their experience was having Jesus Christ as Saviour and Lord:

> Young, inexperienced, and without eloquence, we have come before you because we feel that we have a message for you... We feel youth has an appeal to youth, and we want to give you our experience. We are placing before you during these few days the thing we have found to be best. We are setting before you one who is worthy of all our devotion – Christ. He is the Saviour for the young as well as the old, and He is the one who can bring out what is best in us...
>
> Are you living up to the standards of Jesus Christ? We are looking for men and women who are willing to answer the challenge Christ is sending out... Have you sought a leader in everyday life? In Jesus

Christ you will find a leader worthy of your devotion and mine. I looked for one I could admire, and I found Christ. I am a debtor, and no wonder I am a debtor, for He has given me a message which can only be experienced. If this audience was out-and-out for Christ, the whole of Edinburgh would be changed. If the whole of this audience was out for Christ, it would go far past Edinburgh and through all Scotland. The last time Edinburgh was swept, all Scotland was flooded. What are you going to do tonight?[11]

D. P. Thomson gives an interesting account of the closing meeting of this series:

At the opening meeting there were about 1100 present – a capacity audience. Night by night the numbers dropped, until on the Friday we were down to about 500. Dr Black came to us that evening with a very long face. It was at my suggestion that the Committee responsible for the Mission had taken the Usher Hall, the largest available auditorium in the city, for the Sunday evening meetings. 'Thomson,' he said, 'you've made a big mistake. You'll be lost there.' Then he made a very generous offer. He would cut his own evening service short and march up Lothian Road at the head of his congregation, to help fill our vacant seats! What could we do but thank him?

That Sunday evening I passed down Lothian Road on a tramway car about ten minutes past six. There was a queue more than fifty yards long waiting to get into the Usher Hall for our meeting, which was due to begin at eight. At twenty past seven the queue had begun to form outside Lothian Road Church for an overflow meeting which had been hurriedly arranged there. When Dr Black and his congregation arrived on the stroke of eight, it was to find hundreds of people being turned away from the overflow meeting after Lothian Road and the Usher Hall had been as tightly packed as we dared. It was striking evidence of the immense hold Eric Liddell had on the Edinburgh public and a great sight to see the huge gallery of the Usher Hall packed with students of many nationalities. The fruits of that fortnight's work were many.[12]

Before Eric Liddell set out for China on 3 July 1925, several valedictory services were held for him in the east and west of Scotland. The Glasgow Students' Evangelistic Union held a meeting in Renfield Street United Free Church in Glasgow on 22 June. D. P. Thomson thought this meeting the most impressive of the farewell meetings:

> When Eric Liddell left for China in the early summer of 1925, crowded and enthusiastic valedictory meetings were held in both Glasgow and Edinburgh, the former being especially memorable. It was held on a Monday night near the end of June – not the time of year when one expects a crowd at a religious gathering of this kind. Dr George H. Morrison, of Wellington Church, Glasgow…occupied the chair, and the speakers in the Renfield Street Church that night included several well-known athletes. After nearly 1000 people had been turned away from a building already uncomfortably crowded, we managed to secure entry to the nearby St John's Methodist Church for an overflow meeting, into which hundreds poured. No valedictory meeting like it had ever been seen in Scotland before. That night, I am convinced, many got their call to missionary service overseas.[13]

An auspicious send-off. Eric is taken by carriage from the Congregational College to the railway station for the first part of his journey to China.

A farewell meeting was also held in the YMCA in Edinburgh. It was a smaller, 'select' meeting attended by several prominent Edinburgh citizens. Praise was heaped on Eric, some of which must have made him squirm. In reply he spoke very well. He said that up to two years before he had always refused invitations to speak. Then he had accepted the invitation to speak at Armadale. It had been a tremendous struggle, and yet he wanted to bear testimony to the faith that was in him, and he was given the ability. He said that it was not difficult for him to refuse to run on Sunday, but it was difficult to answer the call of his country to stay there and give a year to speaking. But again he had been given strength. He now felt it difficult to go from Scotland because he was Scottish, because of the friendships he had made in the university, in the rugby field, and through the evangelistic work he had been doing in the last year or two. Yet there was a work waiting to be done in China, and he was perfectly sure he went to the work God had for him to do.

There was also a more 'ecclesiastical' farewell service for Eric on the day following the Scottish Championships – 28 June – in the Augustine Congregational Church on George IV Bridge. Again, so large was the crowd that an overflow meeting had to be hurriedly arranged in the Martyrs' and St John's United Free Church across the road. In speaking Eric took as his theme 'rededication'. It appears that after the meeting there was such a crowd of well-wishers pressing round him that he found extreme difficulty in getting away. 'Liddell "Mobbed"' was the way one newspaper headline described it the next day.

The day for his departure finally arrived. He was due to leave Edinburgh from Waverley Station on Monday, 29 June. The first stage of the departure was from the Congregational College at 29 Hope Terrace. Some of the students obtained a carriage festooned with decorations and pulled it from the Grange area to Waverley Station. He was due to leave on the 10.15 a.m. train from Waverley to Berwick-upon-Tweed.

All along the route to Waverley Station there were enthusiastic crowds cheering him on his way. Large numbers of people had gathered at the station to give him a send-off. On the platform, surrounded by cheering crowds, Eric was compelled to give a few words as he left. He said he was going out as an ambassador to another country. Their motto should always be: 'Christ for the world, for the world needs Christ.' Entering the carriage, he leaned out of the carriage window and spontaneously sang two verses of the great missionary hymn by Isaac Watts:

Jesus shall reign where'er the sun
Doth her successive journeys run;
His kingdom stretch from shore to shore,
Till moons shall wax and wane no more.
For him shall endless prayer be made,
And praises throng to crown his head;
His name, like sweet perfume, shall rise
With every morning sacrifice.

Slowly but surely, the train pulled away and he was soon out of their sight.

Taking the east-coast route from Edinburgh, Eric travelled to Berwick-upon-Tweed, where he spent a night with his mother's relatives before taking the overnight sleeper train to London. Eric left for his long journey from Victoria Station in London on Saturday, 4 July. This took him to Folkestone, where he picked up the ferry to Flushing (Vlissingen) in the Netherlands. From there his railway journey took him to Berlin. 'There was a ten hours' wait there,' he was to write later, 'before the train for Riga [Latvia] came.' After four hours in Riga the train went on to Moscow, where the Trans-Siberian railway was picked up to the East. 'The next week on my way was the best part of the journey, as there was no change from Moscow to China (Just the other side of Lake Baikal [in Siberia]).' From there a further sixteen hours were spent in the train before he changed, presumably at Harbin, for connections with Pei-tai-ho [Beidaihe] to the south on the Bohai Gulf, where he arrived at 11 p.m. on Saturday, 18 July.

Eric's first six weeks were spent with his family before his work at the Tientsin Anglo-Chinese College began. 'The first fortnight I was there,' he wrote later, 'I seemed to do nothing but eat and sleep and bathe... I enjoyed this holiday immensely.'[14] In all he had completed a journey covering two weeks and not far short of 6,000 miles! It constituted an adventurous start to his missionary life.

14.
MISSIONARY LIFE IN CHINA

No doubt to many people the vocation which Eric Liddell followed was a strange choice. For a great sportsman it was unusual, to say the least. Was he not turning his back on fame and fortune? No doubt that was something greatly admired by many. In those days there was still an admiration for missionary work. It showed conviction, principle and a readiness to sacrifice a potentially comfortable life back home, especially for a university graduate, since graduates were a rarity and they could expect well-paid jobs. Then there was the possibility of further achievements on the sports field.

In 1932, when he was passing through Canada on his way back from his first furlough[1] in the United Kingdom, Eric Liddell was interviewed by a journalist named R. E. Knowles. Their interview went something like this:

> Are you glad you gave your life to missionary work? Don't you miss the limelight, the rush, the frenzy, the cheers, the rich red wine of victory?

To this came the astute reply:

> Oh well, of course it's natural for a chap to think over all that sometimes, but I'm glad I'm in the work I'm engaged in now. A fellow's life counts for far more at this than the other. Not a corruptible crown, but an incorruptible, you know.[2]

As one person put it accurately, 'Eric Liddell, rugby international and Olympic gold medallist, universally admired for his high character, happy humour and for his Christianity, brushed fame calmly aside to return as a missionary to China, where he had been born.'[3]

It was a challenging situation which he faced in China. There were all sorts of unrest in the Far East, and within China itself. In a report submitted in 1925, James Liddell, Eric's father (who had been moved to Tientsin as the area of his work after return from furlough in 1922, and whose labours in China were to come to a close in the middle of 1929) wrote that, 'So complex is the situation, so varied are the views expressed, so opposite the conclusions reached, so many the solutions suggested, that one staggers beneath the crushing load. A nation is in travail, seeking to reproduce that which will meet all its aspirations. Whether it will do so or not is another question.'[4] Eric was going to a country in some turmoil and one where civil unrest was not uncommon.

Eric, however, was bound for the Anglo-Chinese College of the London Missionary Society in Tientsin (Tianjin). This had been the brainchild of educational missionary Dr Samuel Lavington Hart (1858-1951). Dr Hart had founded the College in 1902 with the purpose of

Liddell family in China, 1927.
Back row, from the left: Eric, Jenny and Ernest.
Seated: Rob, Mary (with Rob and Ria's daughter, Peggy), James and Ria.

taking Christianity to the sons of Chinese businessmen and government officials. His thinking was that, if the future leaders were taught about Christian things, national life might eventually be influenced for the Christian faith. That was the idea, at any rate. However, any such hopes were to be dashed, firstly by the Sino-Japanese War (1937–1945) and then, after 1945, by the Communist Revolution led by Mao Tse-Tung. That movement was entirely inhospitable to Christianity.

Tientsin was a city in the Hopei region of Northern China. In those days it was divided into two unequal parts, the smaller, densely crowded,

Tientsin and surrounding area.
(Taken, with minor amendments, from David McCasland's Eric Liddell: Pure Gold, *© 2001. Used by permission of Discovery House Publishers, Box 3566, Grand Rapids, MI 49502. All rights reserved.)*

Chinese section, and the more spacious 'foreign concessions' in which there were British, French and Italian districts. The LMS operation in the British concession in Tientsin was known as London Mission. That was where the college was. The students were predominantly Chinese, though the teaching medium was English. The aim of the college, said one of Eric's colleagues, was 'upbuilding of Christian character and the formation of habits of mind and will and thought'.

The Anglo-Chinese College catered for about 500 boys between the ages of eight and eighteen. For twelve years Eric taught science and athletics, 'his Christian teaching and character deeply influencing the lives of the students'.[5] One of Eric's flatmates at Tientsin in the early 1930s, David McGavin, was to say that, 'In his teaching in College the same high standard was maintained, and we know that his influence among the boys was very great. His Bible Classes, out of school hours, were very well attended. I remember the joy with which he would tell us of boys who had committed their lives to Christ.'[6] Eric, however, never thought himself a great teacher. In his first circular letter home after starting his work at the college, Eric gives a good account of various aspects of college life:

> In the working of the school, they have two rather good ideas. One is a short spell of drill each day from 9.50 – 10.5, when the whole school collects in the quadrangle... after this short exercise is over half of the school go to the small church for prayers and the senior half go to the Yuan Shih K'ai Hall for prayers, mostly in English although the reading is taken in both English and Chinese and the prayer is in English and Chinese on alternate days.

The Principal of the College, Dr Lavington Hart, usually took the reading. Eric was impressed by the explanations he gave of passages and gives one striking fruit of this: 'In fact one of the teachers last term gave his life to Christ and he said that what had made him think most about it was the half hours at prayers each day.' Eric was also clearly encouraged by the positive Christian contact with the students in spiritual things:

The Anglo-Chinese College, Tientsin, where Eric Liddell began his missionary work as a teacher in 1925. (The College was taken over by the Communist authorities in 1950 and the buildings were destroyed as a result of the Great Tangshan Earthquake of July 1976).

There are five of us foreigners here, and on Sunday mornings we take turn about at the service for the students. Then we also have a Bible circle on Tuesday where we can get in a certain amount of consecutive teaching. And on Tuesday night we have a meeting open to all which the teachers take in turn. Thus we keep before us the main object of the School, to build up a definite Christian character...to work for all that is noblest and best, for what Christ would have them work.

He was under no illusion: '...there are large problems which really none but Christ can put right.'[7]

Eric reported in a letter written home three years later (1928) the encouragement that 'several members of the senior class took their stand for Jesus Christ. It was also interesting to note,' he goes on, 'that although some of the senior class did not take the step yet they came to the meeting. Oh how I covet those men "not far from the Kingdom of God" – but not in it.'[8]

In a letter written in 1930, not long before his first furlough, he speaks of the joy of seeing twenty of their students coming forward to profess Christ and receive baptism: 'This year these boys were willing to stand out and confess Christ before their fellow students.'

Eric was always actively involved in the sports activities of the college, as a master particularly concerned with, and equipped for, the sporting side of college life. However, his involvement in athletics ranged wider, not least through his contact with one Zhang Boling (1876–1951), who was so influential in developing competitive sports in China. Eric met with Boling at the Tientsin YMCA. Boling professed to be a convert to Christianity.[9] He was then President of Nankai University, Tientsin (which he had founded and which was raised to university status in 1919). Boling enlisted Eric's expertise to teach his students some of the rudiments of track running. In March 1926 and again in April 1931 he had Eric over to Nankai to teach and demonstrate the rudiments of sprints and middle-distance running.

On 14 April 1931, in the hall of the Nankai Middle School, Eric addressed two hundred athletes from Nankai University, Nankai Middle School, Nankai Primary School, and nearly one hundred track and field athletes from the Tientsin Post Office, about the techniques of sprinting and middle-distance running. Eric apparently 'explained the whole process of running in detail, from the movements, training methods, in getting off the mark and crouched starts'. It seems that Eric co-operated with Zhang Boling many times after this. It was said that 'he helped in selecting the Chinese track and field team as well as the Chinese soccer team members for the Olympic Games [i.e. of 1932], Far Eastern Championship Games and the National Games.'[10]

In his first few years in China he took part in athletics events from time to time. He clearly kept himself fit. In September 1928, Eric was invited to take part in a track meeting at Dairen [Dalian] in Manchuria. This was the South Manchurian Railway celebration meeting for the coronation of the Emperor of Japan. The meeting featured a contest between Japanese and French Olympic athletes. Eric Liddell ran in 200 metre and 400 metre invitation events. 'The Japanese and French Olympic Teams were there, with their Olympic laurels, fresh from Amsterdam,' he wrote, 'and it happened, somehow, that I won the

200 and the 400 metres.' He gave his own account of one particular incident in this meeting:

> My race was just half-an-hour before my boat. I tried to have the boat held, but failed. It was 20 minutes by taxi from the race track to the boat. I ran the race, and was starting to beat it to the taxi when something happened; you'd never guess what? The band struck up 'God save the King'. So, of course, I had to stand still as a post till they got through. Then, of course, I was just about to leg it for the taxi but, what do you think happened then? Well, you'd hardly believe it, but the fellow who came in second to me was a Frenchman, so, of course, they had to start the Marseillaise, and there I was, tied like a post again! The taxi made it in great time. I took a healthy hop, step, and leap, and was on the edge of the wharf before it stopped. The boat was steadily moving out too far to jump. But a bit of a tidal wave threw it back a little. Then I flung my bags on to the wharf and jumped. I remember I tried to remember in the very act how a gazelle jumps. I felt like one, and I made it; just made it.[11]

A newspaper correspondent who was in the car had said that the leap was fifteen feet, though Eric doubted that. The meeting was held on 24 September 1928. It seems that in the 400 metres Eric's time was 'a fraction over 51 secs.' (51.2?) – an excellent run considering that it was apparently a very windy day.

Occasionally Eric ran in special races against visiting international athletes, most notably Dr Otto Peltzer, German world-record holder at 880 yards, whom he defeated over 400 metres (with a time of 49.1 to 49.3) in Tientsin on 25 November 1929. It is to this event that Ross and Norris McWhirter referred in their book *Get To Your Marks!* (published in 1951), when they said, '...some way down on a 1929 world's ranking list, there

Eric Liddell (left) at the start of his 800 metres race against Otto Peltzer.

appeared a curious entry "Liddell E., 49.0 seconds. Date not known. Somewhere in China".'[12] Liddell and Peltzer also ran over 800 metres, but this time the world-record holder just got the better of the Scot (with a time of 2 minutes 2.3 seconds to Liddell's 2 minutes 3.1). A Scottish soldier who was out in the Far East at the time, left a memory of that meeting:

> In the pavilion afterwards, Otto said in broken English, that Eric would represent Britain in the next Olympic Games, but Eric replied. 'No, I am too old.' Otto asked how old he was. '28' was the answer. Otto roared with laughter, and said, 'Too old? I am 32, and I will represent Germany at the next Games in 1932'; and he did.
>
> I will always remember what he told Eric that day. 'You train for 800 metres, and you are the greatest man in the world at that distance.' What greater praise could any sportsman wish for when he who gave it was world record holder for that same distance?[13]

Eric Liddell's last competitive 'public' race was in the North China Championship of 1930. Though dissuaded from competing in Scotland when he returned on his first furlough in 1931, he did act as an official at the Edinburgh University Annual Sports at Craiglockhart

Eric (right) with members of a Bible Class at Union Church, Tientsin.

on Wednesday, 9 March 1932. Interestingly, this brought him together again with his old trainer Tom McKerchar, who was the official starter at the sports that day. However, his mind and heart were set on an altogether different race, the one described by the apostle Paul when he said, 'Brethren, I count not myself to have apprehended: but this one thing I do, forgetting those things which are behind, and reaching forth unto those things which are before, I press toward the mark for the prize of the high calling of God in Christ Jesus' (Phil. 3:13-14). In that furlough in 1931–32, besides a heavy programme of speaking engagements,[14] he engaged in further theological studies and was ordained to the ministry of the Scottish Congregational Church in the chapel of their college on Wednesday, 22 June 1932.

When he returned to China later that year he found himself with a considerable workload. Apart from teaching, he was superintendent of the Sunday school in the Union Church, he became secretary of the college, chairman of the games committee, and was put in charge of all the religious activities of the college. Meanwhile, other factors were working in his life.

In 1929 he had started courting Florence Mackenzie, the daughter of a Canadian missionary family, Dr and Mrs Hugh Mackenzie. She was only seventeen at the time and their courtship was a lengthy one. In relation to their engagement Florence was to say, 'I was naïve. Eric had become such a part of the family that I just didn't notice anything. Of course I was desperately in love with him, but I just couldn't get over the fact that he wanted to marry me.' Nevertheless, she accepted his proposal immediately! Eric told the story of the formal engagement in a letter to friends:

> On May 12th [1930] there was a large gathering at Mr & Mrs MacKenzie's house. There were about 40 people present from the L.M.S. and the United Church of Canada. Just after tea had been served Mr MacKenzie announced the engagement of their eldest daughter Florence – to ME. It was a very happy day indeed. After the announcement we adjourned to the tennis court where we watched and participated in several sets. Florence and I had to play one of the sets and we fortunately won. I think the other side must have arranged

it like that as they thought we ought to win. Florence left for Canada a month later, via England.[15]

What was not so well known was that when Florence first accepted his proposal of marriage he immediately wrote to his mother and sister in Edinburgh asking them to get him a diamond ring with five diamonds. They promptly went to an Edinburgh jeweller, purchased a suitable ring and sent it out post haste to China. It was when it arrived that the formal official engagement party took place on 12 May! In July Florence left for her nursing training in Toronto. She would not return to China until early in March 1934.

Eric and Florence's wedding at Tientsin, March 1934.

Eric and Florence were finally married at the Union Church, Tientsin, on Tuesday, 27 March, 1934. A report of the wedding occupied the front page of the local Tientsin and Peking Times and North China News. A civil ceremony took place in the morning and then in the afternoon a service at the Union Church. After the ceremony a reception was held in the bride's parents' house and attended by a large number of guests. None of Eric's family could be present. His father had finished his course on earth just a few months before – in November 1933. He was now with the Lord he had served faithfully, and his earthly remains had been laid to rest near those of his father in the Drymen cemetery.

After the wedding celebrations Eric and Florence went on honeymoon to Western Hills, Peiping (Beijing). Life would not be the same again for them as they settled down to life as husband and wife in Tientsin. It was a time of wonderful happiness for them both, and the beginning of a loving and fruitful married life. From this happy marriage there were three daughters born: Patricia in 1935, Heather in 1937 and Maureen in 1941. Patricia and Heather were born in China, but Maureen was born in Toronto, where Florence and the other girls had been sent when the Sino-Japanese conflict worsened in the spring of 1941. Consequently, Eric never lived to see his youngest daughter.

By the time Heather was born in January 1937, however, Eric Liddell's work was already set on a new course. As early as 1935 his thoughts were turning to more specifically Christian work carrying out evangelism in the countryside districts around Siaochang (Zaoqiang). There had been a growing shortage of missionaries in the countryside. In 1937 he finally decided that it was his duty to go to that work. This

Eric in the country work in winter near Siaochang.

involved giving up the college teaching for good, and also being away from his family for greater or lesser periods of time, because he could not take them with him. This was not easy work. There were all sorts of tensions arising from civil war between the Russian-backed Communist Red Army and the Western-backed Nationalists under Chiang Kai-shek.

Siaochang was a small village in the heart of the North China plain. The district to be covered was, however, the size of Wales. It was a great wrench to leave the college and Eric was greatly missed. The move did, however, bring him more into contact with his brother Rob, who was working as a doctor in that area as Superintendent of Siaochang Hospital. It was remarkable that in the providence of God the two brothers were now both working in an area in which their father had worked earlier. Annie Buchan, a Scottish nurse at the Siaochang Hospital, later asked Eric if he regretted the step of taking up the country work. He replied: 'Never! I have more joy and freedom in this work than I have ever experienced before.'[16] Annie Buchan explains what Eric did in his work:

> Eric's methods, in systematically visiting the churches, preparing plans, drawing maps, and holding regular conferences with the Chinese preachers, were never complicated, but simple, clear and direct, like his

own character. In preaching he never expounded elaborate theories, but suggested the possibility of a 'way of life', lived on a higher plane – to use his favourite expression – 'A God-controlled life'. In Siaochang our preachers, nurses and students hung on his words, and 'the common people heard him gladly'.[17]

It was hard and dangerous work, intensified by the escalation of the Sino-Japanese conflict at that time. The Japanese had not been at war with Britain, but once they were in 1941, the situation became extremely dangerous for British nationals. Eric, however, was untiring in his cheerfulness and he travelled around the area with apparently boundless energy and good spirits. 'Looking back on that time,' said a colleague of those days, 'one can realise how very much we owed to his unconquerable spirit. Our own tempers and nerves were strained by constant alarms and excursions, and by unexpected responsibilities and decisions, but it is possible to realise more fully now how much more his faith and confidence meant to us all.'

There is a striking example of the sort of danger faced in those days, after the escalation of hostilities between Japan and China. When hostilities broke out in earnest in 1937 Eric and his brother, Rob (then Superintendent of the Mission Hospital in Siaochang), were on holiday at the coast. Communication by the late Autumn had been lost between Tientsin and Siaochang. It appears that there was at that point only one male European missionary remaining in Siaochang, the Rev. W. F. Rowlands. Despite the dangers, Eric and Rob determined in November 1937 to venture forth to resume their work at Siaochang and relieve Rowlands. They travelled largely by river and experienced a series of dangers. What great courage and devotion these men were to show! They were constantly in danger from armed bandits and at one point were only allowed to continue their journey after they had handed over some money. For some days they were without food, and when they finally reached their destination after a 10-day journey, they were both hungry and unkempt! As one recent biographer commented, their story was like a chapter from a John Buchan adventure war and spy novel.[18]

Early in 1938 Eric was again involved in a remarkable incident. He told the story himself, and during his furlough copies of it were widely distributed, along with a lithograph of the flower picture mentioned in it as a means of raising funds for the mission work. This account provides a flavour of the sort of things he was involved in during that dangerous time:

When journeying back from Tientsin to our Mission Station of Siao Chang, my colleagues and I heard of a wounded man, lying in a temple, 20 miles from our Mission Hospital. No carter would take the risk of taking wounded men, for fear of meeting the Japanese troops on the way. However, one Chinese carter said he would go, if I accompanied him. They have a wonderful confidence in us!!! It would be quite dangerous for him, but, I think, there was no danger as far as I was concerned.

On Saturday February 18th, the carter started on the journey and some hours later I cycled after him. By evening the carter reached Huo Chu, 18 miles from Siao Chang, where we have our Mission premises. I cycled on to Pei Lin Tyu, 3 miles further on, to see the Head man of the village and make arrangements for the wounded man 'to be removed'. He lay in the temple about 100 yards outside the village. The temple is a filthy place open to the wind and dust. No one ever comes along to clean it.

No home was open to the wounded man, for if the Japanese descended on them and found that a home had anything to do with the military it would be destroyed at once, and the lives of those in it would be in danger. For 5 days the man had lain in the temple. A friend came daily to the temple to feed the wounded man. He lay on a thin mattress on the ground. When we remember that the nights and days are cold and every night the temperature would be at freezing if not well below it, we marvel that he was still alive. The Japanese (a tank and 10 motor lorries) were at the next village a mile away. I told the wounded man we would be back early the next day and then I returned to Huo Chu. That night, as I lay down, wrapped in my old sheepskin coat; my thoughts turned to the next day. Suppose I met the Japanese, what would I say? I felt for my Chinese New Testament, a book I constantly carried about with me. It fell open at St Luke 16. I read until I came to verse 10 and this seemed to me to bring me my answer. 'He that is faithful in that which is least is faithful also in much and he that is unjust in the least is unjust also in much.' It was as if God had said to me, 'Be honest and straight'; I turned and went to sleep. We started early next morning. As we approached the first village, there was a man standing in the entrance to it, beckoning us in. We entered the village and as we passed through it the Japanese mechanized troops went round it. We fortunately missed each other.

Many of the roads had been dug up, and were like enlarged trenches, and in clambering out our cart overturned.

We reached Pei Lin Fyu early in the day and went to the temple. It was Chinese New Year's Day. People were in the temple burning incense. They were even burning it at the side of the wounded man. I asked the people to come out. I gave them a talk on fresh air being of more value to sick or wounded, than air laden with incense smoke. Then I turned to those great words in Micah: 'Wherewith shall I come before the Lord? Shall I come before Him with burnt offerings? – He hath showed thee, O man, what is good; and what doth the Lord require of thee but to do justly, and to love mercy, and to walk humbly with thy God?' Sir George Adam Smith in his classic on 'The Twelve Minor Prophets', when he comes to this passage writes it in large letters, then says, 'This is the greatest saying in the Old Testament, and in the New there is only one greater: "Come unto ME, all ye that labour and are heavy laden and I will give you rest."'

We laid the man in the cart and left.

On reaching Huo Chu, we heard of another wounded man whom we could pick up by going out of our way a short distance. We decided to go and see. When we reached Pang Chuang we went to see the Headman. He and some others led us to one of the outhouses. Several men went in first to warn the wounded man that a foreigner was coming in to see him but that he need not be afraid. On entering I could see, in the dim light, a man reclining on a bed; dirty rags were wrapped round his neck. He was one of six men who had been surrounded by the Japanese. They were told to kneel for execution. Five knelt but the sixth remained standing; when the officer came to him, he drew his sword and slashed at him making a gash from the back of his neck round to his mouth. He fell as dead. After the Japanese left the villagers came out and finding him still alive had taken him to this outhouse where he had lain for several days. I told him my cart was only a small one, made for carrying one person, but, that if he was willing to sit on the shafts for 18 miles (5 hours) I would take him to Siao Chang hospital. I could not guarantee his safety if we met the Japanese; he would have to take his chance. He took it. For the first few miles a Japanese aeroplane was circling round slightly south of us. It indicated that the Japanese troops were moving almost parallel to us a mile or two away.

At 4 p.m. we reached S. C. Hospital. Two days later the first man died, but the second man lived.

Treated first by Dr Graham then by Dr McAll, he soon recovered. His mind turned towards the Christian life and teaching and within a couple of months he made the first steps in Christian living.

In gratitude he painted a number of pictures for me. They show the painter and also the poet.

One I had lithographed. The saying on it runs 'She (the peony) is the most beautiful in the city (China); her modesty and manner come from God.'[19]

Later the same year Eric wrote a circular to his family 'back home', in which once again vivid descriptions are given of the sort of work he did at Siaochang and the dangers that he faced:

I am writing this after an eventful few days. Last Sunday we had planned to hold a big baptismal service for several nearby villages but, already the day before, we heard heavy gunfire in the distance and by breakfast time a scouting plane was circling overhead, so many from the outlying villages didn't turn up, rightly fearing that an attack was about to start. As I addressed those receiving baptism two shells exploded outside with a terrific noise and there was silence for a moment before we were able to continue. I don't think any who were baptized that day will easily forget what happened. No one left after the service was over, so we just continued with hymns and witness to keep up our spirits. As there were no opposition forces here, truckloads of Japanese soldiers soon hurtled through the village gates and they searched every building in the place. Though they came into the church they left without causing any real damage, but in the evening, when everyone had gone home and was too frightened to come to evening service, the church door opened and in came the man who used to be the local opium-addict, thanking and praising God. It seems that, having reached a living faith in Christ, he had then been arrested on a trumped-up charge but, unlike many others, he had been acquitted. Hurrying home he came to church straight away to give thanks for his deliverance, unaware of the terror we had all known earlier in the day. Feeling I had been given a congregation, I got on with the service!

In the same circular Eric describes a remarkable incident involving confrontation with a Japanese soldier: 'It makes me feel less strange when I hear people giving me father's old title – Li-Mu-Shi – Pastor Liddell – if I am doing something positive to help them. And certainly the way they respond to hearing about Jesus is encouraging – even among the Japanese! Not long ago I was stopped by a Japanese soldier who, on seeing my Bible, asked if I was a Christian. I replied that, yes, I

Eric and Florence with Heather (left) and Patricia (right) during a furlough in Scotland in 1940.

was, and he shook me firmly by the hand and let me go. I assure you I sent up an immediate prayer of thankfulness – and heaved a great sigh of relief!'[20] This shows both the potential dangers he faced at that time (1937-38) and the faithfulness and winsomeness he showed both to the Chinese and the Japanese.

It was clear from that same letter that Eric was still involved in athletics events, helping to run sports when occasion allowed. In commenting on his involvement in the North

China Championships at Tientsin early in 1938, he refers to points in which he had to act and show tact. 'I was very conscious throughout,' he writes, 'of God's power to help in the clarity of thinking. It was like the 400 metres in the Paris Olympics – now amazingly 14 years ago – running the first 200 metres as hard as I could and then, with God's help, running the second 200 metres even harder!' With a touch of nostalgia he adds: 'I wonder where all those other athletes are now – Harold Abrahams and Guy Butler, and old Tom McKerchar my trainer?'[21]

Eric had his second furlough in 1939. It goes without saying that this was a time full of all sorts of international tensions as the world stood on the brink of another world war. In Europe war would soon break out between Britain and Germany. In the Far East the Japanese were intensifying their aggression against China. And in a way Eric Liddell was caught in the middle of it. Again during his furlough he undertook deputation work on behalf of the mission and a number of other speaking engagements.

In March 1940 Florence and the two girls crossed the Atlantic to join Eric in Scotland. Five months later they started the return voyage to China via Canada. By that time, however, they were in a convoy of fifty ships and faced all sorts of potential dangers. Several of the ships in the convoy were torpedoed and sunk. On the Sunday during the crossing Eric conducted a service which, he said, 'was in the form of a thanksgiving for our escape'. These were indeed perilous times! After ten days' break in Canada, they continued their return journey to Tientsin, arriving before the end of October.

The next crisis related to the escalation of the Sino-Japanese War. Siaochang became increasingly difficult to work in. The sort of situation he faced was well described in one of Eric's letters. It involved what happened following a wedding at a weekend:

> I stayed over on Sunday, taking the service and chatting with the people. I should have returned that day, but the cart I was expecting did not arrive till nightfall. It had been delayed by the 8th Army [Communist Chinese], who were stopping the moving of all the carts. On our return journey today [Monday] there was little of incident

except at one point. The enemy [Japanese] must have taken us for the 8th Army and fired two shots. We just got off our bikes and stayed still till they realized their mistake, and then we went on.

My work will be going round the various churches. I now go out to the south-west to a part I have never visited before. When I am out it is giving, giving, all the time, and trying to get to know the people, and trying to leave them a message of encouragement and peace in a time when there is no external peace at all.[22]

Things worsened. In February 1941 the Japanese closed down the hospital and foreign residences, sealed the properties and took all the keys of the various buildings from the superintendent. The Compound at Siaochang was thus closed, and the missionaries were finally forced to abandon the work there. Eric cycled alongside the last cart that drew out of the compound. It was a sad moment for him. He had such happy memories of that place – memories of early happy childhood days, days of youthful innocence. He had memories of his father's work there, and then, more recently, his own together with his brother, Rob. Yet the Lord had his purpose in this, and Eric believed that there would yet be fruit from the work and prayers of those who had so faithfully laboured for Jesus and the gospel in Siaochang. By 18 February everyone was back in Tientsin. A cable was sent to London: 'Siaochang safely evacuated.'

After Eric arrived back in Tientsin it seemed prudent and necessary in the interests of safety for Florence, who was then expecting their third child, and the two girls to head for safety in Canada. In June 1941 the whole family set off for Japan with a view to Florence and the girls catching a boat from there across the Pacific. The family had four precious days in Japan before Florence and the girls boarded the *Nita Maru*. This was, as it happened, the last sight they were to have of their husband and father. Eric committed them to the Lord and, after many hugs and kisses, there only remained the sweet sorrow of parting. Their third daughter, Nancy Maureen, was born on 17 September 1941 in Toronto. Eric was naturally elated by the news, but in the event, sadly, he was never to see her.

Returning to Tientsin, Eric continued to live and do what he could in the interests of the gospel of Christ as long as it was possible. At first he shared a flat with an old colleague at the Anglo-Chinese College, A. P. Cullen. Cullen had been a tutor at Eltham College in the days when Eric had been a student there thirty years earlier. It was a happy arrangement, and the two men enjoyed good fellowship in trying circumstances until the college was closed by the Japanese.

The Japanese bombed Pearl Harbor in December 1941. This brought America into the war. As a consequence, the position of the 'enemy aliens' in Japanese-occupied China became vulnerable, to say the least. The Tientsin College was closed and sealed by the Japanese in January 1942, and Eric and Gus Cullen had to find other accommodation. This they managed to do in Tientsin through the kind offices of members of the English Methodist Mission. They were very restricted in the work they could do, however, and it seemed to be only a matter of time before they were interned by the Japanese. That in fact happened fourteen months later, in March 1943.

In the period before being interned at Weihsien [Weifang] in March 1943, among other things, Eric published *Prayers for Daily Use* for the Union Church in Tientsin. In the preface he tells readers, 'I have tried to bring before you certain thoughts that I have found helpful in the Christian life. The aim is that we should be like Jesus; thoughtful, kind, generous, true, pure and dependent entirely upon God's help, seeking to be the kind of man or woman He desires us to be; seeking in all things to do His Will and to please Him.' 'The prayers,' he adds, 'are not intended to take the place of your private devotions.' A section entitled 'The Key to Knowing God' provides insight into Eric Liddell's own approach in his Christian faith:

> One word stands out above all others as the key to knowing God, to having His peace and assurance in your heart; it is OBEDIENCE.
>
> To OBEY God's Will was like food to Jesus, refreshing His mind, body and spirit. 'My meat is to do the Will of Him that sent me.'
>
> OBEDIENCE to God's Will is the secret of spiritual knowledge and insight. It is not willingness to know, but willingness to DO (obey) God's Will that brings certainty. 'If any man will do (obey) His Will,

he shall know of the doctrine, whether it be of God, or, whether I speak of Myself' [John 7:17].

OBEDIENCE IS THE SECRET OF GUIDANCE. Every Christian should live a God-guided life. If you are not guided by God you will be guided by something else.

The Christian who doesn't know this sense of guidance in his life is missing something vital. Take OBEDIENCE with you into your prayer hour, for you will know as much of God, and only as much of God, as you are willing to put into practice.

When we walk with the Lord,
In the light of His Word,
What a glory He sheds on our way!
While WE DO HIS GOOD WILL,
He abides with us still,
And with all who will TRUST AND OBEY.[23]

Also, in the year before his internment Eric worked on a manual of Christian discipleship. This is the work that was published by Abingdon Press (USA) and Triangle/SPCK (UK) in 1985 under the title, *The Disciplines of the Christian Life*.

The next step, however, would lead to his final days in this world.

15.

INTERNMENT

7 December 1941 was a turning point for the mission work in north China. That was the day the Japanese bombed Pearl Harbor and the Americans declared war against Japan. Eric Liddell, among others, was effectively under house arrest in Tientsin from that time until he was rounded up with other 'enemy nationals' – British, American and other 'non-Orientals' – in March 1943 for internment at the 'Weihsien Civilian Assembly Centre', housed in a facility built by the American Presbyterian Missions Board. The internees were only allowed to take four pieces of luggage each. One had to be a bed, or bedding, and the other three trunks or boxes. Two suitcases could also be carried as hand luggage on the journey.

Eric was captain in charge of the third contingent that was to make its way to the internment camp at Weihsien. The third group of men, women and children of various nationalities assembled in Tientsin at 7.30 in the evening of 30 March 1943 and, under Japanese guard, set off at 9 o'clock for the station. The streets were lined with sympathetic silent crowds, mostly Chinese. When they reached the train the internees took their allotted places and the train moved off a little before midnight.

It was an arduous journey. Few slept. At 10.30 the next morning there was a change of trains at Tsinan [Jinan] (capital of Shantung [Shandong] Province). The group finally arrived at Weihsien at 3.40 in the afternoon. A tired group of rather bedraggled folk made their weary way by an assortment of trucks and buses to the 'Civil Assembly Centre' at the former American Presbyterian Mission compound. There they gathered in the Athletic Ground for directions about accommodation quarters.

In 1943 the Weihsien Camp reached its full complement of 1,800 internees. It was a crowded compound, though there was a hospital and a field suitable for games and sports. There was a real mixture of ages and skills in the camp, and various committees were soon organised to oversee activities, education, sports and discipline. Eric shared a small dormitory room on the top floor of the camp hospital, at first with two other missionary colleagues. It was only nine feet (2.75m) by twelve (3.65m), and it was later to accommodate a fourth internee![1]

The room in the Weihsien camp which Eric shared with two, and later three, other internees.

Among the internees were some aged missionary workers, including Herbert Hudson Taylor, son of the founder of the China Inland Mission, J. Hudson Taylor. Herbert was in his early eighties at the time. Also with him was his son William Taylor, together with his wife and four children. William was the third generation of the Hudson Taylor family involved in mission work in China. One of William's sons, James

Hudson Taylor III, was later to enter missionary service in the Far East. Another internee was the Rev. John Parker. He was eighty-two when Eric arrived at the camp. Parker had been Eric's father's predecessor in the work in Mongolia with the London Missionary Society. Sadly, he died in the camp in June 1944. Herbert Taylor, though, survived the camp and lived on until 1950.

In his first five months in the camp Eric taught mathematics for half a day and oversaw the sports for the other half. The input by so many missionaries ensured, as one biographer put it, that 'the internment would be turned from a tribulation into an opportunity'.[2] Nothing, however, could conceal the truth that life was hard in the camp.

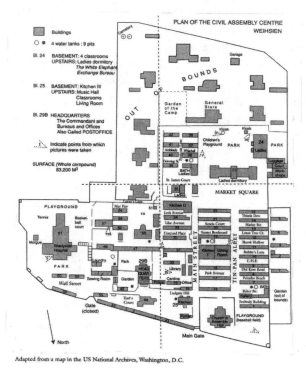

Map of the Weihsien Camp.
(Taken from David McCasland's Eric Liddell: Pure Gold, ©
2001. Used by permission of Discovery House Publishers, Box
3566, Grand Rapids, MI 49502. All rights reserved.)

Conditions were cramped, nutrition was limited, and facilities were spartan. Also, the presence of Japanese soldiers on guard, barbed wire, guard towers, searchlights and a roll-call at 7.30 each morning were hardly conducive to a relaxed atmosphere! It was a life to be endured, hardly enjoyed, although the Christian missionaries and workers like Eric Liddell did seek to encourage the others to cast their burdens on the Lord. There was a church building in the compound, shared by Roman Catholics and Protestants. It was in use throughout the day every Sunday. Eric was heavily involved in taking Protestant services, prayer meetings, Bible classes and Sunday schools.

In the camp Eric steadfastly refused to organise sports on Sundays, though he did relent to the extent of refereeing impromptu games on Sunday after the children fought during a game they had organised by themselves. This was the sort of tension that developed in the camp, when there were some parents who allowed their children to participate in such activities on a Sunday. No doubt it was a dilemma for Eric. True enough, it was hard for all these young people unnaturally cooped up in the camp. One Irish missionary described what happened:

> I think one of Eric's hardest decisions must have been about Sunday games. At first the policy was to have none. But the teenagers, cooped up in the Camp, some from non-Christian homes, protested against this, and themselves organised a hockey game, the boys versus the girls. It ended in a free fight, because there was no referee. As the responsible official, he did the right thing in these conditions. The world knows his personal position from his great testimony at the Olympic Games.[3]

Eric was no doubt concerned to preserve a more ordered Lord's day for those who desired it, by exercising an element of order in that quite exceptional situation, rather than pretend that nothing was happening and endure untoward noise and fighting on the part of those involved. His own Sundays in the camp were, however, largely spent in Christian worship and service, devotions and teaching. His regard for the Lord's day and what it offered remained undiminished, notwithstanding this concession in a rather inhumane situation.

One internee, then just a young boy but later to become a missionary with the Overseas Missionary Fellowship, has left a record of some of his memories of Eric Liddell in the camp:

> Eric ran a Friday-evening youth club, and it was on these occasions, as well as the Sunday afternoon services, that he loved to speak on such passages as Matthew 5 or 1 Corinthians 13. The manuscript of his devotional book, *A Manual of Christian Discipleship*, was circulated to much profit among quite a number of people in the camp...
>
> Many recall a series of messages Eric Liddell gave on the topic of the Holy Spirit.[4]

Another internee asked the question: 'What was his secret?' Tellingly she provides the following answer:

> Once I asked him, but I really knew already, for my husband was in his dormitory and shared the secret with him. Every morning about 6 a.m., with curtains tightly drawn to keep in the shining of our peanut-oil lamp, lest the prowling sentries should think someone was trying to escape, he used to climb out of his top bunk, past the sleeping forms of his dormitory mates. Then, at the small Chinese table, the two men would sit close together with the light just enough to illumine their Bibles and notebooks. Silently they read, prayed, thought about the day's duties, noted what should be done. Eric was a man of prayer not only at set times – though he did not like to miss a Prayer Meeting or Communion Service when such could be arranged. He talked to God all the time, naturally, as one can who enters the 'School of Prayer' to learn this way of inner discipline. He seemed to have no weighty mental problems: his life was grounded in God, in faith, and in trust.[5]

There were the memories of his athletic prowess too. For, notwithstanding the rigours of the years up to the internment, he had retained a good level of physical fitness.

By the end of 1944, however, he had slowed down and there was clearly something wrong. In December of that year he began to suffer headaches. A brain tumour was suspected, especially after he experienced a slight stroke on Sunday, 11 February 1945. The end came on 21 February. 'I was with him when he died,' wrote Annie Buchan afterwards. 'The last words he said to me were, "Annie, it is surrender." He then lapsed into a coma, and about half past nine that evening he went peacefully home.'[6] An autopsy was carried out. It showed that in fact he had an inoperable tumour deep in the left side of his brain. He passed from this life into the presence of his Lord at 9.20 p.m. on the evening of 21 February 1945, aged forty-three.

That same day Eric had written a letter to his dear wife in Toronto. She did not receive it until 4 May, two days after she first learned of his passing. The Bible says that 'Blessed are the dead which die in the Lord from henceforth: Yea, saith the Spirit, that they may rest from their labours; and their works do follow them' (Rev. 14:13). Nevertheless, such a loss is felt with sorrow, for those closest to the one who has gone, and for all, too, whose lives have been touched in one way or another by the person concerned. And Eric Liddell's life and example touched many lives, and continue to do so. Like the faithful in Hebrews 11, 'he being dead yet speaketh' (v. 4). His example also touched me personally. When I read the story of Eric Liddell as a nineteen-year-old in 1966 it made such a profound impression on me that I seriously sought the Lord whom Eric had served, and soon came to enjoy the peace of God that passes all understanding.

Needless to say, when the news of Eric's death became known in the camp there was universal mourning among the internees. What a great loss Eric Liddell was to the life of the camp! Three days after Eric's passing a short service was held. It was Saturday, 24 February, and a huge crowd pressed in and around the Assembly Hall of the camp. The service was conducted by a senior LMS missionary, the Rev. Arnold Bryson. It was a solemn occasion, and yet not unmixed with joy at the passing of a saint of God. Among other things, Mr Bryson was to say:

> Yesterday a man said to me, 'Of all the men I have known, Eric Liddell was one in whose character and life the spirit of Jesus Christ was pre-eminently manifested.'...What was the secret of his consecrated life and far-reaching influence? Absolute surrender to God's will as revealed in Jesus Christ. His was a God-controlled life and he followed his Master and Lord with a devotion that never flagged and with an

intensity of purpose that made men see both the reality and power of true religion. With St Paul, Eric could say, 'I live, yet not I, but Christ liveth in me.'[7]

His mortal remains were then interred in the Japanese part of the camp, alongside some thirty or so others who had died in the camp since internment. A simple wooden cross with his name written in shoe-blacking was erected on the spot.

In 1985 David Michell and some other former internees returned to Weifang, as it was now called, to visit the site of their internment forty years earlier. 'I looked in vain,' he wrote, 'for any sign of the little camp graveyard. The humble mound of earth and simple wooden cross with Eric H. Liddell written with shoe-blacking on the cross piece had long since gone. Large blocks of apartments now obscure the site. But in my searching I found a lovely garden with an ornamental gate behind it. I envisaged that this was where the wasted pallbearers had stopped in their solemn task as we had watched them bear the simple coffin from camp.'[8]

Sadly, Eric's mother had passed away in September 1944, eleven years after the death of his father. It is almost certain that news of her passing never reached Eric at the camp. Eric's parents' mortal remains were buried in the Drymen cemetery, awaiting the resurrection of the last day. Carved on their gravestone is the inscription:

AND IN MEMORY OF THEIR SON

ERIC HENRY LIDDELL B.SC.

WHO DIED IN WEIHSIEN INTERNMENT CAMP

21ST FEBRUARY 1945 AGED 43 YEARS.

The text at the foot reads:

IN HIS PRESENCE IS FULNESS OF JOY.

16.
A LIFE WELL LIVED

One of the finest tributes paid to Eric Liddell, from one who knew him well, was from David McGavin, who worked in China as an agent, and later General Secretary, of the National Bible Society of Scotland during the time Eric was working there. McGavin said this of Eric Liddell:

> Eric was not only one of nature's gentlemen, he was a perfect Christian gentleman, and therein is the secret of all that he was and did. His life was centred in Christ, and everything was done as to the Lord. It is said that to really know a person one must live in the same house with them. This was my privilege when Eric and his two colleagues invited me to share their flat in Tientsin, and I found that, at home, as elsewhere, Eric's life glorified God…Eric Liddell was the most Christlike man I ever knew, and there are many who, like me, thank God upon every remembrance of him.[1]

This is a view of Eric Liddell such as we might expect from colleagues and friends within the Christian circles in which Eric moved in China. It was a view widely expressed. One of the most perceptive tributes to Eric came from a diary kept by an internee to record impressions of camp life. This is what the diarist was to write on the day of Eric's funeral:

> He was not particularly clever, and not conspicuously able, but he was good. He was naturally reserved and tended to live in a world of his own, but he gave of himself unstintedly. His reserve did not prevent him from mixing with everybody and being known by everybody, but

he always shrank from revealing his deepest needs and distresses, so that whilst he bore the burdens of many, very few could help bear his. His fame as an athlete helped him a good deal. He certainly didn't look like a great runner, but the fact that he had been one gave him a self-confidence that men of his type don't often have. He wasn't a great leader, or an inspired thinker, but he knew what he ought to do, and he did it. He was a true disciple of the Master and worthy of the highest of places amongst the saints gathered in the Church triumphant. We have lost of our best, but we have gained a fragrant memory.[2]

This was not written for public consumption and it has the virtue of real honesty. Eric was a saint in the sense that he was a true Christian believer. However, like all true believers, he had to contend with limitations. But he made the best of what the Lord had given him by way of talents and opportunities. In this Eric was, and will ever remain, a good role model for all who would be faithful to the Lord Jesus Christ in this present world and have a living hope of heavenly glory.

Eric Liddell in his later years (1940).

Such testimonies could be multiplied. Perhaps this language sounds strange in the ears of our secular age in which so little is seen of the power of true personal Christian religion. The fact is that he was a man who took God's Word seriously. If a man or woman reads the Bible seriously and prayerfully and seeks to order his/her life by its clear teachings, as Eric Liddell did, then that person will surely show the fruits of it in a God-honouring and Spirit-controlled life. Certainly, that was exemplified in the life of Eric Liddell, according to the consistent testimony of those who knew him.

After news of Eric Liddell's death became known, there were memorial services held in various centres, most notably in Toronto,

Edinburgh and Glasgow. The service in Toronto was held at the Carlton Street United Church on 5 May. Eric's widow, Florence, and their children were present. His death was naturally a great loss to Florence and their daughters. In a letter dated 11 May 1945, written to Thomas Cocker-Brown of the London Missionary Society in London, Florence Liddell said of the death of her dear husband: 'It was a stunning blow and I can hardly believe it, but I have been very conscious of the prayers and thoughts of countless friends over in England and here too.'

> At times [she went on], I have been numbed and overwhelmed by a sense of unreality – of pain – of fear for the future and then there has come welling up from within that power of faith which has carried me through. My faith has been wonderfully strengthened. In looking back I have so much to be thankful for. God has provided so wonderfully – we have been so happy and I know that He is working out His purpose and that good can come out of even this...My heart aches for Jenny, Rob and Ernest. I wish they had been at the Memorial service we had here last Saturday...I feel that Eric and I had as much happiness in our few short years together as many couples have in a whole lifetime and I thank God for the privilege of being Eric's wife.[3]

Florence lived on in Canada. She was married again in 1951, to Murray Hall, a widower, who died in 1969. It was my privilege and delight to

Florence Liddell with her three daughters (from the left) Maureen, Heather and Patricia, in 1981.

meet Florence Liddell Hall in the home of Eric's sister Jenny Somerville at Liberton, Edinburgh, during the summer of 1983. This was just a year before her passing away on 14 June 1984.

Eric's sister, Jenny, was a delightful lady. She married a missionary doctor, Charles W. Somerville (1877–1966), and they lived latterly in Edinburgh. They had two daughters. I had several conversations with Jenny Somerville. She possessed a considerable collection of old Liddell family photographs. Both the conversations with her and the access to the family memorabilia helped to bring alive the character of her worthy brother. Jenny passed away in her ninety-first year on 8 June 1994.

As for Rob, he returned to Britain on furlough in mid-1939. His wife Ria and the children had preceded him on account of an illness suffered by their seven-year-old son. James had been diagnosed with tuberculosis in his spine and there was not any adequate treatment to be had for that condition in China. Therefore Ria, with Peggy and Jim, had returned home a couple of years earlier. After his furlough in 1939 Rob never went back to China. He regretfully resigned from the Missionary Society in 1940 on account of the prospect of a lengthy convalescence for Jim, and in view of the outbreak of war which had overtaken them. He became a well-respected surgeon in Scotland and a Fellow of the Royal College of Surgeons of Edinburgh. It was said that he never began an operation without first engaging in prayer. He emigrated to Whyalla in South Australia, where he joined his son Jim in pioneer medical work. Rob and Ria's children, Jim and Peggy, both became doctors. Rob passed away on 30 May 1973, trusting in Jesus. His wife Ria survived him by nine years.

Ernest was the least known of the Liddell family. He returned to Scotland from China with his parents in 1929. During the war he suffered a serious brain haemorrhage which left its mark on him for the rest of his life. He did, however, pursue a career in banking in Edinburgh. Ernest had a great love and admiration for his siblings, though he made no open Christian profession. He died in Edinburgh on 11 February 1975, aged sixty-two.

Ernest was married to Alice Anderson. I was to meet Alice in unusual circumstances in 1982. I was on a train – from London to Edinburgh, I think – and was checking over proofs of my book on *Scottish Athletics*, which was shortly due for publication. An elderly lady sitting nearby spotted the mock-up of the dust jacket. It contained pictures of four great Scottish athletes, including Eric Liddell. She then told me that her brother-in-law had been a great athlete and had won an Olympic gold medal. It turned out that this was Alice Liddell, the widow of Eric's brother Ernest, and she lived in Edinburgh! We went together the next year to Jenny Somerville's house at Liberton in the southern suburbs of Edinburgh. Jenny had with her Eric's widow, Florence, and one of her daughters, Heather. Alice passed away in Edinburgh in February 1997, aged eighty-five.

The memorial service in Edinburgh was held on Sunday, 27 May 1945, in Eric Liddell's own church during his student days, Morningside Congregational at Holy Corner. The service was held at 8 o'clock in the evening, and apparently there were nearly 1,000 people present, including his brothers Robert and Ernest and his sister Jenny Somerville. The Glasgow service was held in the Dundas Street Congregational Church on Monday, 28 May. Many well-known ministers and sportsmen took part in the service, as did his brother Rob. D. P. Thomson has left a fine account of this meeting in his biography of Eric published in 1971.[4] In reporting the service on the Tuesday, the Glasgow *Evening News* wrote that 'Scotland has lost a son who did her proud every hour of his life.' Edinburgh's *Evening News* stated that he was 'one of the best known and admired men who ever took part in sport, whose devotion to his principles won him esteem everywhere'. There was special interest created by the fact that among those who gave a tribute at the Glasgow service was the famous manager of Glasgow Rangers Football Club, William Struth. His words struck a chord, especially coming from one who was not associated with the clergy or the missionary fraternity. He said:

> On looking round this wonderful gathering tonight I feel privileged to be here to pay tribute to the late Rev. Eric Liddell. It is usual to associate a champion with some brilliant performance, such as an

Olympic victory, a Record, or a Championship success. Eric Liddell's remarkable career provides a wealth of such successes, and yet, I suppose, no one in sport automatically thinks of these great triumphs when Eric Liddell's name comes to mind. Rather, we immediately think of Eric Liddell, the man whose deep moral courage matched the splendid physical courage which showed itself in his athletic career, and later in the particular calling which he chose as his life's work.

He deliberately sacrificed a fine chance of one Olympic title because of his religious convictions. He just as certainly put aside a career of brilliance and affluence to serve his Master in the most practical of all forms of Christianity. In his work in China he created an opportunity for the talents with which he was so richly endowed, courage, determination, skill, endurance, and self-sacrifice, to be utilised to the full.

Sport gave to Eric Liddell its highest honours; nevertheless, it is true to say that he honoured sport rather than sport honouring him.

The details of the last few years of his life are not yet known to us, but we can be certain that under the most severe of all trials, he exhibited just those qualities which he showed in his sporting life. His life was perhaps a short one; but his work, as he clearly saw it, and, as we believe, divinely inspired, carried out away from the applause of the crowd, will remain a source of inspiration to many.

In these days of exaggerated hero worship and publicity for sports champions, Eric Liddell's example reminds us to put things in their proper perspective. Sport to him was sport – not the be-all and end-all – and success in it did not prevent him from picking out the things spiritual from the things temporal. His was an example which must have helped others to make a similar choice.

Athletics are proud of him, and are grateful for the example of this Christian gentleman. He surely is one of those saints 'who from their labours rest; who Thee by faith before the world confessed'.[5]

This comment of Struth's constitutes a wonderful summary of Eric Liddell's whole life. His was indeed a life well lived. Eric Liddell achieved an enviable balance between the things temporal and the things spiritual. Sport was a great passion for him, but was never out of perspective.

MEMORIAL SERVICE
FOR
The Rev. ERIC H. LIDDELL, B.Sc.

DUNDAS STREET CONGREGATIONAL
CHURCH, GLASGOW
ON
Monday, 28th May, 1945, at 7.30 p.m.

Presiding: Rev. JAMES M. CALDER
President, Congregational Union of Scotland

Organist: Miss HARRIET WHITELAW
Elderwork Street Congregational Church, Glasgow

The Offering will be devoted to the work of the
London Missionary Society in North China with
which Mr. Liddell was associated

*Memorial Services were held after
Eric's passing in 1945.*

It was a source of challenge and joy for him. He saw it as something that taught powerful lessons for life, even though in itself it would remain an avocation. It never became an all-consuming interest. What was his all-consuming interest was his service for Christ. His paramount concern was to be a faithful servant of His and to live his life to help others to believe and follow Christ.

D. P. Thomson suggests that fellowship with God was the nerve-centre of Eric's life. He paid this moving tribute to his old friend and colleague in his *Personal Encounters*, published in 1967:

Never in the years we worked together – in shadow or in sunshine, in times of testing and difficulty, in hours of exhilarating triumph – did I hear him say or know him do anything of which I can imagine Christ would have disapproved. His was the most consistent Christian character, as well as one of the most attractive and winning of personalities of any man I have ever known intimately.

With it all went his unfailing sense of humour – 'that smiling face, with the twinkling blue eyes,' as the one who knew him best described it – his character, his readiness to help personally at the cost of any inconvenience or self-sacrifice, his wish that others and not he should have the glory when success crowned his efforts, and his intense desire to be ever in the path of obedience to Him to whom he had given his all.

Athlete, evangelist, missionary-friend, husband and father – he has been missed as few men of his generation have been. By multitudes he is remembered with affection and gratitude as one in whose life they saw so much of the strength and beauty of Christ.[6]

The secular world, too, was ready to give due tribute to Eric Liddell's worth as an athlete and as a Christian. An obituary notice in the *Edinburgh Evening Dispatch* of 4 May 1945 expressed a widespread view that Liddell was 'one of the best-loved and most warmly admired men who ever took part in sport. His devotion to his principles won him the highest esteem everywhere, particularly as he was free from the slightest hint of "gush" or Pharisaism.'

To the same effect, Harold Abrahams, in an article in *World Sports*, said of Eric Liddell:

> His name will forever remain as perhaps the most famous and most respected and loved athlete Scotland has ever produced. His style was about as unorthodox as it could be, but the main thing is that he always displayed the greatest courage, and he will be remembered as one of the finest sportsmen who ever donned a running shoe.[7]

In *The story of Edinburgh University Athletic Club*, published in 1966, Dr Neil Campbell stated his opinion that 'No athlete has ever made a bigger impact on people all over the world, and the description of him as "the most popular, and best loved athlete Scotland has ever produced" is no exaggeration.'[8] When one takes into account the fact that there have appeared a multiplicity of works on the life of Eric Liddell, such statements do not seem to be excessive.

In more recent times there has been a proliferation of biographies and autobiographies published on sporting celebrities. There have, however, never been as many biographies produced of one Scottish sportsman as there have been for Eric Liddell. His life and achievements and Christian witness live on. This has been in many ways strengthened by the 1981 Oscar-winning movie *Chariots of Fire*, which succeeded, perhaps as no book could, in bringing alive the character of the great Olympic hero.

As far as the biographies are concerned, the one written and published by D. P. Thomson, first in a paperback form in 1970 and a year later in a hardback illustrated format, is indispensable. It is thorough, personal and, as one might expect, thoroughly sympathetic with Eric Liddell's Christian position. All other biographers have stood on Thomson's shoulders. Sally Magnusson produced a well-written biography, *The Flying Scotsman*, in 1981 on the back of the release of *Chariots of Fire*. It produced little new material but did include contemporary comment, which is, frankly, of a mixed quality. Russell W. Ramsey produced a family-authorized biography in 1987, *God's Joyful Runner*. Needless to say, it is sympathetically written. Of the more recent works the most capable is that by David McCasland, who produced *Eric Liddell – Pure Gold* in 2001, along with an excellent documentary in the form of a three-part television production from Day of Discovery entitled simply *The Story of Eric Liddell*. One of the features of this documentary is film of virtually the whole of the Olympic 400 metres final in Paris. This is undoubtedly a superior production to the television documentary produced by the BBC in 1983. Entitled *The Flying Scotsman*, the BBC production was superficial, overly anecdotal in style and somewhat short on sporting detail. The same could be said about the ITV documentary entitled *The Real Chariots of Fire*, produced in 2012 to coincide with the London Olympics that year. These biographies, and others of varying quality, have, however, served to keep alive the memory and the principles of Eric Liddell for our modern, more sceptical, generation, which has little understanding of a man like Eric Liddell.

Several other things have kept alive his life and witness. An 'Eric Liddell Memorial Fund' was set up in 1945 under the chairmanship of Sir Iain Colquhoun of Luss. The fund was managed by a huge committee of all sorts of prominent personalities from aristocratic, business, ecclesiastical and sporting fraternities. The purpose was fourfold:

1. To provide in some measure for the education and nurture of Eric Liddell's daughters;
2. To endow a missionary scholarship at Edinburgh University;
3. To institute a challenge trophy for amateur athletics in Scotland; and
4. To set up a suitable memorial in North China.

The appeal was made in the sum of £10,000. Of these aims only two were secured: help for the education of the Liddell girls, and the institution of an Eric Liddell Trophy to be presented annually for what was adjudged to be the most meritorious performance at the Scottish Schools Athletic Association Championships.

As far as a memorial in North China was concerned, this was achieved later, when in 1985 former Overseas Missionary Fellowship missionary David Michell returned to the Weihsien Camp with other former internees and took with them a plaque. The inscription read:

> This plaque is presented by the CIM Chefoo Schools Association
>
> To Commemorate with deep gratitude the 40th anniversary of the liberation of 1400 prisoners, including some 500 children, from the Weihsien Internment Camp by 7 American GIs on August 17, 1945, at the end of World War II.
>
> The last resting place of Eric Liddell, Olympic hero of 'Chariots of Fire,' who died in the Camp February 21, 1945.

Below the inscription was an embossed picture of Eric Liddell together with the names of those who presented the plaque.[9]

An unusual event took place at Weifang on Sunday, 9 June 1991. It was a celebration at the garden of remembrance on the site of the internment camp, where David Michell had been in 1985. This time there was a ceremony to mark the setting up of the *Eric Liddell Foundation*, a trust formed to bring together Chinese, Hong Kong and British athletes for sports and 'character-building education'. In that quiet corner of the Number Two Middle School grounds where the garden had been built, 'a seven-foot-high slab of red granite from the Isle of Mull was unveiled...Gold characters on the front of the stone told the bare details of Liddell's life in English and Chinese. On the back

A Memorial Fund was set up shortly after Eric's passing.

A Memorial stone provided by Edinburgh University was set up by the Eric Liddell
Foundation at Weifang in 1991.
David Michell (OMF) is addressing the gathering.

was a text…"They shall mount up with wings as eagles. They shall run
and not be weary."'[10]

In point of fact on the front of the stone was the inscription:

ERIC H. LIDDELL SPORTS GROUND

'THEY SHALL MOUNT UP

WITH WINGS AS EAGLES

THEY SHALL RUN

AND NOT BE WEARY'[11]

On the reverse was inscribed this, in English and Chinese:

ERIC LIDDELL

Eric H. Liddell was born in Tianjin of Scottish parents in
1902. His athletic career reached its peak with his gold medal
victory in the 400-metre event at the 1924 Olympic Games.
He returned to China to work at Tianjin as a teacher. Eric

Liddell was interned in a camp at the present site of the
Weifang Second Middle School and died in this camp shortly
before the Japanese were defeated in 1945.
Eric Liddell embodied fraternal values, and his whole life
was spent encouraging young people to make their best
contributions to the betterment of mankind.

The last paragraph of the inscription is somewhat ambiguous. The absence of any reference to his Christian faith and witness may in this case have been dictated by what the Chinese authorities would allow. Quite a few organisations and facilities have adopted the name of Eric Liddell for predominantly social or sporting reasons. The truth is, however, that it was his Christian faith that informed and motivated all Eric's sporting and social activities. In connection with that poignant dedication ceremony David Michell, who was present, left a moving account of the events of that Sunday:

Sunday morning, June 9, dawned with heavy clouds over Weifang city and then rain began to fall. However, by the time our group of forty assembled to take the coach to the school, the rain had stopped. One of the Chinese later remarked to Norman [Cliff] as the sun came out shining brightly, 'God in heaven is shining on you.'

Mr Lu of the Foreign Affairs Department stepped down from the bus and shook hands with Mr Wang, the Principal of the Second Middle School. To the skirl of the bagpipes and the shrill and beat of the Chinese band, with crowds of gaily dressed Chinese students and onlookers pressing round, we marched into the school. What had been the Japanese headquarters at the back of Weihsien Camp in wartime was now the front of the school. Three of the original American Presbyterian missionary homes were still there and in use as staff buildings.

We first entered the Lab building, which is the largest of the school buildings. It stands in the place where Block 23 of our Prison Camp used to be. In that building we, the youngest Prep School children, lived during Camp and Eric Liddell, Norman Cliff and others had all lived in the cramped room above us.

After speeches and an introduction of the three Weifang athletes who will be coming down to Hong Kong in September through the *Eric Liddell Foundation*, we set off for the nearby garden for the dedication ceremony.

By 9:30 a.m. the band and bagpipes were quiet and civic leaders, teachers and students stood quietly with our group of overseas visitors and reporters. In a gentle garden setting, through a moon-gate, stood the silk-draped 7-foot-high red granite rock from the Island of Mull, a gift of the University of Edinburgh. It was engraved on both sides in English and Chinese.

Eric Liddell's niece, Dr Peggy Judge of Edinburgh, and the Vice-Mayor of Weifang unveiled the stone. Then Norman Cliff and I, who had both been fellow POWs in camp with Eric Liddell, spoke of our boyhood memories of our missionary hero, who died of a brain tumour six months before the war ended.

Speaking of our hero as Uncle Eric, we recalled our moments of 'Olympic glory' as he ran to the cheers of fellow prisoners and captors alike in the shadow of the towering prison camp walls forty-five years before. Cliff, who was a pall-bearer, spoke of him as a true sportsman and ended his remarks with a prayer reminiscent of Eric Liddell's life – the prayer of St Francis, 'Lord, make me an instrument of Your peace.'

I spoke of Eric Liddell's love for sport, for children, for all people, including the Japanese soldiers, and for God. He lived at peace with God day by day. His serenity of spirit brought cheer and inspiration to all he worked with and who met him in their daily toil. Early each morning by the light of a peanut oil lamp, he and one of his roommates met for prayer and Bible reading. This was the source of his strength. To serve God and his fellowmen was his constant goal.

I concluded with the words, 'Throughout these nearly fifty years we have remembered Eric Liddell. We continue to remember him today for his sporting prowess, his life as a humanitarian and as a Christian gentleman, and also for his eager interest in young people and for his love for China.' In hushed silence we bowed our heads as the lone piper played the lament, 'On the Shores of Loch Katrina [Katrine].'

The following day our *Eric Liddell Foundation* party visited the former Anglo-Chinese College in Tianjin, where Eric Liddell taught.

I presented on behalf of Eric Liddell's three daughters in Ontario the last gold medal he won for a major race. It had taken place in Tianjin in 1929, when he defeated Dr Otto Peltzer, the 500 and 1500 metre world record holder. Also presented at both Weifang and Tianjin were Chinese translations of *Disciplines of the Christian Life*, devotional material written and assembled by Eric Liddell. We thought about the fact that the message of *Chariots of Fire* had rung true throughout the world as it depicted muscular Christianity at its best. We also reflected that today in China, in a beautifully manicured 'Garden of Inspiration', in silent vigil a stone speaks of the spirit of Eric Liddell and bears testimony:

They shall mount up with wings as eagles; they shall run and not be weary.[12]

Eric Liddell's memory was also kept alive in other ways. In 1972 Eric's younger brother, Ernest, opened an 'Eric Liddell Pavilion' in connection with Edinburgh University's new sports field at Peffermill.

Ten years later an 'Eric Liddell Fitness Training Centre' was opened as a facility of Edinburgh University by HRH Prince Philip, the Duke of Edinburgh. On the sixtieth anniversary of Eric's triumph in the Paris Olympics, the

The opening of the Eric Liddell Fitness Training Centre at Edinburgh University in 1982. Eric's sister, Jenny is seen here with HRH , the Duke of Edinburgh, who opened the facility.

Scottish Philatelic Society issued a cover in honour of Eric Liddell. It was even carried by the 'Flying Scotsman' locomotive!

Unquestionably the most prominent of the memorials has been the opening of the 'Eric Liddell Centre' at Edinburgh's Holy Corner. This started as the Holy Corner Church Centre, developed in the former North Morningside Church of Scotland, on the opposite corner to the former Morningside Congregational Church of which Eric Liddell

Eric Liddell's eldest daughter, Patricia Russell (left), with his niece, Peggy Judge (Rob's daughter), at the unveiling of Lesley Pover's sculpture of Eric at Edinburgh University in 1997.

had been a member in the 1920s. The North Morningside Church had become 'redundant' in the 1970s and the idea of a centre was launched in 1980. In 1992 the decision was taken to rename the centre the 'Eric Liddell Centre'. Funds were raised to renovate and adapt the building, which was of a considerable size. Its purpose is social and spiritual, supporting caring and educational projects, providing a coffee shop, conference facilities and other services of a broadly Christian nature.

Eltham College did not forget the athlete who was arguably their most famous son. In June 1996 they established a state-of-the art sports building called the 'Eric Liddell Sports Centre' within the college. It was opened by double Olympic 1,500 metres gold medallist, Sebastian Coe, then a Member of Parliament. At the entrance to the centre stands a bronze figure described as 'Eric Liddell, Sportsman and Evangelist', specially commissioned from sculptress Lesley Pover. The news report of this event ended by stating that 'The bronze bust that every pupil must walk past upon entering the sports centre reminds them that they are heirs to a noble tradition.'[13] An identical statue by the sculptress was unveiled at Edinburgh University by Eric's eldest daughter, Patricia Russell, in November 1997.

It is amazing how frequently references to Eric Liddell appear in the press. In *The Daily Telegraph* of Thursday, 18 August 2005, there appeared an article reporting a commemoration at Weifang the previous day marking sixty years since the liberation of the internees from the internment camp there. A fellow internee of Eric Liddell's, Stephen Metcalf (by this time aged seventy-eight), was interviewed by the reporter in the course of the celebrations. He said, 'He gave me two things. One was his worn-out running shoes…The best thing he gave me was his baton of forgiveness. He taught me to love my enemies, the Japanese, and to pray for them.'[14]

Another fellow-internee was Norman Cliff. In a talk which he gave in 1996, Dr Cliff was to say this: 'As I prepared this talk I asked myself, "After fifty-one years what would Eric Liddell say to you and me today?" He would say many things. I have chosen just two things. One: he would say at this time of broken homes, breakdown, immorality, crime, violence, neglect of the Lord's day, neglect of the Lord's house, to come back to the Sermon on the Mount and to its teaching on purity, love and reconciliation. I think that is one thing he would say. Secondly: Eric Liddell would say, "When you speak of me, give the glory to my Master, Jesus Christ." He would not want us to think solely of him. He would want us to see the Christ whom he served.'[15]

In the autumn of 1946 D. P. Thomson gave an address on Eric Liddell in a service at St Paul's Parish Church, Galashiels. The address was reported fully in a local newspaper. It sums up the challenge of the life of Eric Liddell for our day as effectively as it did in the day in which the words were spoken:

> The man in whose honour they had met had finished his athletic career at 25. By that time he had already won an assured place not only in the annals of Scottish and British sport, but in the aristocracy of character. What was his secret?
>
> *It was first of all*, he ventured to say, the home from which he came. No one who knew Liddell's father and mother, no one who had been a guest in their home, who had sensed its atmosphere and its outlook, and had become aware of the spirit which permeated it, could be in any doubt about that. Home was the first great formative influence in the making and shaping of Eric Liddell, as it was of so many. It was there that he got both his ideals and his inspirations.
>
> In what kind of homes and in what kind of atmosphere, were the youngsters under their care today growing up? Had they an outlook in any way comparable? Were the kind of things Liddell stood for being instilled into them?

Then there were the convictions for which he had learned to take his stand while still a boy at school! A little boy of seven, he would remind them, left at an English boarding-school when his parents returned to their work in China. For these convictions – of honesty, of purity, of fair play, to name only three – he had been prepared at that early age to stand up, even when it meant facing the bully of the junior school.

All through his life Eric Liddell had been characterized by the quiet concentration with which he went about any task he might have in hand. It might be a college essay or a degree examination. It might be a big match for which he was getting ready, or a track event for which he was going into special training. It might be an address or a sermon he was preparing, or a young lad he was trying to help. It was the same in every case. There was no hurry, no fuss, no sense of strain, or fret, or worry – just a quiet resoluteness and calm that were very impressive to watch...

Above and beyond all these things, however, was that by which Eric Liddell's whole life was inspired and motivated – the stand he took for Jesus Christ while still a student at the University, when just on the threshold of his greatest athletic fame. From that hour he was Christ's man, and the things for which he stood, whatever the cost might be, were the things which the Spirit of Christ impressed upon him, and which his own study of the New Testament had revealed to him. A great athlete he was, and a fine personality, but he was first and last a Christian; a loyal, devoted follower of the One to whom he had given his all.

How many of them there that afternoon had taken the same decisive step? How many of them knew beyond all shadow of doubt whose they were, and for what cause they were striving?

The thing that characterised Eric Liddell's more mature years was the quest which he pursued so resolutely to the very end, for a fuller knowledge of God and a closer approximation to His mind and will...

Such was the man whom we commemorate today, and such he remained to the end. The tributes to what he was and to what he did in the last months of his life, are, if anything, even more striking than those which I have quoted.

Let them remember this – it was his love to Christ and his utter devotion to the service of the Master that carried him through. It was that alone which made him the man he was – the man that, under God, he became. What could the same love, and the same devotion, not do for them?[16]

This is quite a tribute – a touching personal and fitting one – to the subject of this biography. No doubt the question may be asked: What is Eric's enduring testimony? It is true that the world has changed so much since his passing. Yet we would be remiss in not benefitting from this faith-driven man who saw life in terms of obedience to God and a faithful walk with Jesus Christ, with the living hope in life and death that is thus embraced. We further consider his 'legacy' in the closing chapter.

17.
'MORE THAN AN ATHLETE'

There is a continuing fascination in the story of Eric Liddell, outstanding Olympian and Christian missionary, even after so many years since the close of his life and work on earth. D. P. Thomson's biography of Eric Liddell, *Scotland's Greatest Athlete* (1970), may well have been one of the last things written on Eric had it not been for the strange providence of the making and release of the oscar-winning movie, *Chariots of Fire*, in 1981. That created a whole new interest in the 1920s Olympic champion. Since then, as may be seen from the select bibliography, numerous biographies, of varying substance and quality it must be said, have hit the book stores, as well as press articles, DVD and TV documentaries and films of various sorts, in Britain, the United States and China. One suspects that without this 'strange providence' Eric might have been remembered as little more of a footnote in sporting and missionary history.

In truth he was an 'ordinary', uncomplicated man, but a determined man of clear convictions. Yes, he won an Olympic title in unusual circumstances, to say the least. Not only so, to the eyes of the world he appeared so easily to turn his back on fame and worldly comfort in pursuit of an unpopular desire to serve the Lord Jesus Christ in missionary service in a far-flung and notoriously hard area of the world for such service. He was seemingly content to pursue a life away from a spotlight so cherished in the West. In this respect, perhaps, his life was really remarkable. For sure it has been the moving cause of a continuing fascination in the story of this 'ordinary', uncomplicated man.

It is of more than passing interest that the overall impression of Eric has consistently been one of admiration. The more one looks at it, the more one sees that this story has an attraction on the level of heroism, or even 'romance.' Heroic traits can be discerned in all his faith-driven life. And people warm to heroism. Especially is this so, one would suggest, where there are pure motives, as there undoubtedly were with Eric Liddell. Perhaps there is also a bit of nostalgia for a time when things were less 'professional' and exclusive than they are in the modern era, not least in the field of sport. He is arguably a fine example of holding the sport in proper balance and perspective. The heroism of the story carries through his life to the sad end in the Internment Camp at Weifang early in 1945, though as a convinced Christian he passed away in lively hope of the life everlasting.

The Chinese authorities have produced materials commemorating the sad events involving the Japanese Internment Camp at Weifang, both in the Museum itself, but also through a DVD (in Chinese, 2005) and a beautifully produced book entitled *Flying Peace* published by the Shandong Art & Literature Publishing House in 2005 with parallel English and Chinese texts. The book was produced 'to the memory of the 60th anniversary of the victory of the World War II and the 60th anniversary of the liberation of the former Weihsien Concentration Camp.' Eric's life is notably highlighted amongst the material in the Museum. It was quite clear that there remained in China a high regard for those foreigners – including many professing Christians like Eric Liddell – who had helped the Chinese people during the traumatic times of the Japanese offensive against China.

At any rate, interest in this fascinating 'ordinary' man has continued down the years. This was always likely with the 2008 Olympic Games being held in Beijing, and even with the 2012 Games in London. In February 2008 the first edition of this book was 'launched' with Lord Coe in Waterstones book store in Piccadilly, London. The following month it was even highlighted as a 'Book of the Week' in the sports pages of *The Independent*, very likely unprecedented for a book from a Christian publisher.[1] It was also given a considerable spread in

The author with Lord Coe at the launching of Running the Race *at Waterstones in London, in 2008.*

the sports section of the *Daily Telegraph* where it was described as an 'acclaimed' biography.[2]

In Beijing itself, in 2008, various politicians and other dignitaries from the West went the rounds of locations of interest in the Eric Liddell story. The Chinese media were all too happy to take this up as, after all, in a sense he was by birthplace at least the first Olympic champion from China! Incidentally, one unfortunate mistake, so it appears, in the first printing of this book related to the final resting place of his mortal remains. Somehow the story had got around that the bodies of internees had been moved to the Mausoleum of Martyrs at Shijiazhuang, which, however, remains unsubstantiated if not unfounded. At the same time the exact location of the Internment Camp cemetery had never really been located as it seemed to have been long built over. The memorial stone erected in 1991 in the end was located in the proximity of the Shadyside Hospital in which Eric passed away in 1945. This Hospital remains as one of the last remnants of the former facility built by the American Presbyterian Missions Board at Weifang, used as an internment compound during the Sino-Japanese conflict.

Documentary and other films continue to be made about Eric's life. In 2012 a documentary was produced in China by Tianjin TV: *Eric H. Liddell – Olympic Champion. Born in Tianjin, China.* This reproduced

Shadyside Hospital, Weifang, in 2008.

outstanding illustrations and footage from the era as well as interesting interviews with Chinese who had known Eric in their youth. One full-blown feature film has been produced, entitled *On Wings of Eagles* (2017). This has been described as an 'unofficial sequel' to *Chariots of Fire*. It focusses on Eric's experiences in China, especially during the Sino-Japanese conflict after 1937 and in the Internment camp. It was, however, strongly criticised by some for making little mention of Eric Liddell's robust Christian faith and commitment.

There have also been further biographies, not least Duncan Hamilton's major work *For the Glory* (2016). This is a well-researched and competent piece of writing focussing as it does particularly on Eric's experiences in China. Hamilton writes a gripping story. Having said this, in our view there is in large measure in the book a deficient view of Eric's real Christianity. That is not to say that the author is not sympathetic with his subject. But it means that the vibrant faith and hope and love of his subject for Christ are not warmly and understandingly displayed. Among other things Hamilton deprecates what he sees as the London Missionary Society's excessive 'pressure' on Eric to transfer to country preaching and pastoral work around Siaochang in 1937.[3] It is quite clear, however, that something of this 'calling' must have been on Eric's own mind for some time, given that he had been ordained as a minister of the Scottish Congregational Church in 1932 – he was the Reverend Eric Liddell thereafter. Furthermore, there were his own feelings, as reported by Annie Buchan, a Scottish nurse at the Siaochang Hospital and a colleague of Rob and Eric. Hamilton himself in one place states Eric's aptitude for the country work. He writes that, 'Country evangelism was Eric Liddell's forte.' He then goes on to refer to Annie Buchan's enquiry of Eric about his decision to move to that country work. Did he regret it? 'Never!' replied Eric, 'I have more joy and freedom in this work than I have ever experienced before.'[4] This makes Hamilton's earlier severe strictures about the LMS appear all the more inappropriate.

Assessing Eric Liddell as an athlete is easy and not so easy. It is easy in the sense that his record speaks for itself. He was whole-hearted, determined, and heroic, but generous in defeat. Yet his 'career' was brief and, given the opportunity, he might have competed in the Olympic Games of 1928 and 1932. His reputation was therefore based on relatively few races and records. The Paris performance in 1924 did cap it all and established him (as they say) as one of the 'legends' of the track. There is also his rugby to take into account, as well as his continuing performances in China up to 1930. However, one feature of his sporting life was that it never displaced his primary purpose of serving the Lord and engaging in His service. He was in truth, as Colonel F. A. M. Webster wrote in his obituary notice for Eric in *The Leader* (1945) magazine after his death, 'More than an Athlete.'

The whole world of athletics has moved on so much from Liddell's day, what with hi-tech facilities, scientific training methods and coaching, advanced medical support and professional performances (not to speak of diet and, dare one say it, performance-enhancing drug-taking) at a level inconceivable to the athletes of Eric Liddell's generation. For Eric this would all have been an exaggerated importance to something basically a serious pastime. One suspects that he might even have thought of it as a modern form of idolatry. However, in his own day at least, Eric had a strong claim to be the world's premier 440yards/400metres track star.

Assessing Eric as a Christian missionary is likewise not so easy, at this distance in time. For several reasons: there is so relatively little available on the *substance* of his work in China, or on his *precise* position on so many theological or doctrinal matters. However, there is *sufficient* to recognise an evangelicalism that embraced a concern for the teaching and experience of the Christian good news concerning the Lord Jesus Christ as the only Saviour and object of saving faith. There is also sufficient testimony of those close to him, and observers not so close, that he lived a life consistently with the truths of the Bible as the Word of God, as a genuinely godly man. This much is evident throughout this biography.

One issue in his outlook relates to the influence of the 'Oxford Group' (later known as 'Moral Rearmament'). This movement was launched by a Lutheran minister, Frank Buchman (1878-1961), in 1922. It was intended as a global evangelistic crusade to encourage divine guidance and individual life-changing principles. It focussed on spiritual surrender in terms of four 'absolutes': honesty, purity, love and unselfishness. It seemed to address the growing nominalism in lifeless, liberal Protestant Churches between the wars. In the process, however, it tended to create an alternative sort of nominalism or legalism and to obscure aspects of Christ's work and the objective authority of Scripture. What impact it had on Eric is hard to say, but one is inclined to believe that he simply thought it helpful in some respects for his Christian walk at the time. D. P. Thomson says very little of this in his earlier biography. Eric himself does refer to it once in his *The Disciplines of the Christian Life*: 'I find the Four Absolute Standards given by the Oxford Group very helpful in clarifying the meaning of sin and the spirit of the law as given in the Sermon on the Mount: *Absolute Honesty. Absolute Purity. Absolute Unselfishness. Absolute Love.*'[5] This seemed to strike a chord with him in his own desire to pursue a disciplined spiritual life. However, apart from that there is no reference at all to the teaching or distinctives of the Group. He did clearly have a high view of the teaching of Scripture, as witness his concern to preserve the Lord's day as the Christian Sabbath free from extraneous things like sport and recreations. He clearly saw the Lord's day in terms of the demands of the 4th commandment for the New Testament Christian. He was no legalist, but he had a proper view of the law of God as giving timeless directives for living a Christian life honourably and well.

What is his legacy? The world has changed immeasurably since Eric Liddell's day. Whether for the better in moral terms may be seriously questioned. However, there have been far-reaching changes in all aspects of social life. We are now in many respects in a 'global village' and have experienced a revolution in technology and communications, and a 'new morality (or immorality)'. Eric Liddell took two weeks to travel by the Trans-Siberian railway to China from London in 1925. It would today take him about one day by plane! In those pre-War days letters would take several weeks to reach their destination. Now it is more or less instantaneous in the age of the Internet and satellite communications. Sport has also changed radically what with professionalism (for athletes, spectators and administrators), conditioning, facilities and 'hi-tech' aids, as well as carefully controlled diets (and drugs?). Olympic Games events can now be broadcast around the world as they happen!

Does a person like Eric Liddell really speak to such a new 'modern' generation? What can we say but that the world is more than transport and communication and technology, and sport is more than money, professionalism and technology. When the changing mores and outward circumstances of any age are stripped away, the *human spirit* is essentially the same. It is simply a 'modern conceit' to think that matters of right and wrong believed in the past somehow are redundant today! There are surely considerations of character and lifestyle. There are inescapable searching issues of life and death. There is answerability to our Maker. There are also the moral and spiritual dimensions of our lives in this supposedly 'brave new world'. When all is said and done, the human spirit is the same, independently of the changing mores of any age. To Eric Liddell the teaching of the Bible and its authority were crucial as the timeless basis of truth for true Christian faith and life. This is clear from his *The Disciplines of the Christian Life*. For him the Bible was clearly God's Word for the individual and for all of human social life.

In a real sense the world needs characters like Eric Liddell more than ever. He is a prime example of someone who on the one hand was wholehearted in what he attempted among men and for God, but who on the other hand did not exaggerate the importance of mere sport in his life. He was a fine upright person, and also a God-fearing man who sought to live conscientiously by the teaching of the Scriptures. He is an example at many levels to successive generations of how to worship well, play well, live well and die well. None of these things can be separated from his faith in Jesus Christ. They are a central part of his 'legacy'.

As for the mission work, again life in China changed radically for such work after the post-War Communist revolution that effectively closed the door on any such Christian mission work. China was always rather an inhospitable environment for Christian missionary work (as the West itself has now become to a considerable extent!). In terms of policy it seemed to some that such mission in any case was one of 'imperialist arrogance.' That, however, does injustice, for example, to the sheer amount of humanitarian, educational and medical work so lovingly carried out over the years by selfless missionaries. This is not to say that there were not inexcusable instances of maltreatment of nationals or trampling over their culture. More common, however, was the martyrdom of the missionaries. In addition, the church gospel work, whilst in many places with the passage of time ill-served by the growth of a liberal and nominal Christianity which came to dominate in the West[6], was at least initially and in some degree throughout motivated by the Great Commission of the Lord Jesus Christ as charged upon the church in Matthew 28:18-20. For Christianity is not just applicable to Jerusalem, Judea or Samaria (or Europe!) but, in obedience to Christ's word: 'ye shall be witnesses unto me both in Jerusalem, and in all Judea, and in Samaria, and unto the uttermost part of the earth' (Acts 1:8). In this context the mission work of William Chalmers Burns, James Gilmour, James Hudson Taylor, followed by the Liddells and a host of others, was consciously undertaken to point to one Saviour for sinners and the one way to heaven, and by no means was it interested in any imperialist expansion. There is little doubt that it bore fruit. Even after the closure of the country to such formal work, we can believe that the sowing done by such missionaries continues to bear fruit. At any rate it appears that in China today there are millions of professing Christians, beyond even the most optimistic expectations or hopes of the men we have mentioned.[7] It reminds us that in the sovereign purpose of God no work carried out in obedience to the command of the King of kings will prove fruitless.

In the end Eric's life and work, uncommonly short as it was, challenges us in terms of the biblical injunction, fittingly likening Christian life to a crowd of spectators gathered for great athletic Games and observing athletes as they prepare to execute their races: 'Wherefore seeing we also are compassed about with so great a crowd of witnesses, let us lay aside every weight, and the sin which doth so easily beset us, and let us run with patience the race that is set before us, looking unto Jesus the author and finisher of our faith; who for the joy that was set before him endured the cross, despising the shame, and is set down at the right hand of the throne of God' (Heb. 12:1-2). We are privileged in some measure at least to witness such men as Eric Liddell running the race, looking unto Jesus, encouraging us to do likewise.

By his worthy example of faithfulness to Christ and truth, Eric Liddell, Olympic champion and missionary, speaks to succeeding generations around the world, still calling them to follow Christ, just as he sought to do faithfully in his day. We leave the last word to Eric himself:

> John the Baptist's message was 'Repent, for the kingdom of God is at hand'...It is by personal knowledge of Christ that we become citizens in this kingdom, and that privilege is open to all. The humblest and most obscure may have direct personal communion with Christ through the Holy Spirit. Indeed, every one of us must have such personal knowledge if we are to be citizens of the kingdom.[8]

CAREER HIGHLIGHTS: (1) ATHLETICS 1921-1925

1921

May 28:   Edinburgh University Athletic Club Sports, Craiglockhart, Edinburgh
           100yd: Heat 1: 2nd (Won by G. I. Stewart in 10.6; by ½ yard)
           100yd: Final: 1st (10.4)
           220yd: Final: 2nd (Won by Stewart in 23.4; by inches)
           Invitation relay race: 1st EUAC, (E. H. Liddell, J. M. Davie, T. Ritchie, G. I. Stewart) (1:38.8)

June 4:   Queen's Park Football Club Sports, Hampden Park, Glasgow
           Inter-city relay race: 1st Glasgow (H. J. Christie, J. B. Bell, G. Dallas, D. McPhee); 2nd Edinburgh (E. H. Liddell, I. M. Robertson, T. Ritchie, W. B. Ross) [*Liddell led over the first 220 yards, but Glasgow ran out easy winners*]

June 18:   Scottish Intervarsity Sports, University Park, St Andrews
           100yd: Final: 1st (10.6)
           220yd: Final: 1st (22.4)

June 25:   Scottish Amateur Athletic Association Championships (SAAA), Celtic Park, Glasgow
           100yd: Heat 3: 1st (10.6)
           100yd: Final: 1st (10.4)
           220yd: Heat 3: 1st (24.0 walkover)
           220yd: Final: 1st (22.6) (Championship best)
           One mile relay race (880 x 220 x 220 x 440): 1st EUAC (E. W. Cormack, E. H. Liddell, G. I. Stewart, J. M. Davie) (3:43.0) (Championship best)

June 29:   Edinburgh Pharmacy Athletic Club Sports, Powderhall Grounds, Edinburgh

120yd (open) handicap: Heat 10: 1st (off scratch)
120yd (open) handicap: Semi-final 2: 1st (12.2)
120yd (open) handicap: Final: 1st (12.0) (with wind)

July 2: Heart of Midlothian Football Club Sports, Tynecastle Park, Edinburgh
100yd (open) handicap: Heat 8: 1st (10.2) (off scratch)
100yd (open) handicap: Semi-final 2: 1st (10.2)
100yd (open) handicap: Final: 2nd (Won by R. G. Rintoul [Unatt., 5½yd] in 10.2; by 1 foot)
220yd (open) handicap: Heat 9: 1st (23.8) (off scratch)
220yd (open) handicap: Final: 4th (Won by G. T. Stevenson [Shettleston Harriers, 2yd] in 23.2. Nine ran.)

July 9: Triangular International, Windsor Park, Belfast
100yd: 1st (10.4)
220yd: Heat 1: 1st (23.0)
220yd: Final: 3rd (1st, W. A. Hill [E], 23.8; 2nd, F. Mawby [E], by 1½yd)

July 16: West Kilbride Athletic Club Sports, Seamill Park, West Kilbride
100yd handicap: 1st (10.0) (off scratch)
220yd handicap: 3rd (off scratch) (1st, C. Fraser [Maryhill H., 16yd], 24.2; 2nd, R. V. Liddell [Unatt., 12yd]; won on tape, inches between 2nd and 3rd)

July 23: Eglinton Harriers Sports, Victoria Park, Saltcoats
100yd handicap: 1st (10.0) (off scratch)
220yd handicap: 3rd (off scratch) (Won by R. Toole [Eglinton H., 17yd] in 23.6; won by inches, good 3rd)

July 30: Greenock Glenpark Harriers Meeting, Cappielow Park, Greenock
100yd (invitation): 3rd (off scratch) (Won by J. Ross [Greenock G. H., 4½yd] in 10.8; by inches)

August 6: Rangers Football Club Sports, Ibrox Park, Glasgow
100yd (invitation) handicap: 1st (10.0) (off 1½yd)
300yd (open) handicap: 3rd (off 4 yards) (1st, H. J. Christie [W.S.H., 10yd] [31.6], 2nd, S. Colbery [Maryhill H., 12yd]; won on tape)

August 13: Celtic Football Club Sports, Celtic Park, Glasgow
100yd handicap: 1st 10.4 (off 1yd) (2nd, H. F. V. Edward [Polytechnic Harriers, off scratch]; by inches)

220yd (open) handicap: 1st (23.6) (off scratch)

1922

May 27: Edinburgh University Athletic Club Sports, Craiglockhart, Edinburgh
100yd: 1st (10.2) (record)
220yd: 1st (21.8) (record and Scottish native record)
440yd: 1st (52.6)

June 3: Queen's Park Football Club Sports, Hampden Park, Glasgow
100yd (invitation handicap): 3rd (off scratch) (Won by J. Crawford [Shettleston H., 4½yd] in 10.2)
100yd (open) handicap: 4th (off scratch) (Won by J. Crawford [Shettleston H., 4½yd] in 10.2)
One mile inter-city relay race (220 x 220 x 440 x 880):
1st Glasgow (H. J. Christie, G. T. Stevenson, G. Dallas, D. McPhee) (3:46.4); 2nd Edinburgh (E. H. Liddell, L. J. Dunn, I. M. Robertson, C. B. Mein) (won by 2yd)

June 17: Scottish Intervarsity Sports, King's College, Aberdeen
100yd: 1st (10.4)
220yd: 1st (22.8)
One mile relay race (880 x 220 x 220 x 440): 1st EUAC (C. S. Brown, L. J. Dunn, E. H. Liddell, I. M. Robertson) (3:46.8)

June 24: SAAA Championships, Powderhall Grounds, Edinburgh
100yd: Heat 1: 1st (10.2)
100yd: Final: 1st (10.2)
220yd: Heat 2: 1st (23.4)
220yd: Final: 1st (22.6) (equals Championship best)
One mile relay race (880 x 220 x 220 x 440): 1st EUAC (C. S. Brown, L. J. Dunn, E. H Liddell, I. M. Robertson) (3:40.0) (Championship best and Scottish all-comers' record)

July 8: Triangular International, Hampden Park, Glasgow
100yd: 2nd (1st, L. C. Royle [E] [10.4]; won by inches)
220yd: Heat 1: 2nd (1st, Royle [23.8])
220yd: Final: 2nd (1st, Royle [22.4]; won by ½ yard)

July 15: Edinburgh and District Inter-Works Sports, Powderhall Grounds, Edinburgh
150yd (open) handicap: Heat 2: 1st (16.0) (off scratch)

213

150yd (open) handicap: Final: 1st (15.0) (off scratch) (equals Scottish native record)

July 26: North British Hotel Athletic Meeting, Powderhall Grounds, Edinburgh
100yd (open) handicap: Heat 3: 1st (10.4) (off scratch)
100yd (open) handicap: Final: 1st (10.1) (off scratch)
One mile relay race (440 x 220 x 220 x 880): 1st Maryhill Harriers (3:45.0); 2nd EUAC; won by 5 yards

July 29: Greenock Glenpark Harriers Meeting, Cappielow Park, Greenock
100yd (open) handicap: Heat: 1st
100yd (open) handicap: Semi-final: 1st
100yd (open) handicap: Final: 2nd (10.0) (off scratch) (equals Scottish native record); (Won by P. R. Gardner [Glasgow P.O.A.C. & Bellahouston H., 6yd] in 10.0; won on tape)

August 5: Rangers Football Club Sports, Ibrox Park, Glasgow
100yd (open) handicap: Heat: unplaced
220yd (invitation) handicap: Heat 2: 1st (22.4) (off 2yd)
220yd (invitation) handicap: Final: 1st (22.0) (off 2yd)

August 9: Hibernian Football Club Sports, Easter Road, Edinburgh
120yd (invitation) handicap: 1st (12.2) (off 1 yard) (2nd, H. F. V. Edward [Polytechnic H., scratch]; by inches)
100yd (open) handicap: Heat: unplaced

August 12: Celtic Football Club Sports, Celtic Park, Glasgow
120yd (invitation, scratch): 1st (12.2) (2nd, H. F. V. Edward [Polytechnic H.]; 3rd, W. P. Nichol [Highgate H.]; won by 1 yard)
220yd (invitation) handicap: 1st (22.4) (off 2yd) (2nd, H. F. V. Edward [scratch]; 3rd, W. P. Nichol [2yd]; won by inches)

1923

May 26: Edinburgh University Athletic Club Sports, Craiglockhart, Edinburgh
100yd: 1st (10.6)
220yd: 1st (22.8)
440yd: 1st (52.8)

June 2: Queen's Park Football Club Sports, Hampden Park, Glasgow
100yd (invitation) handicap: 2nd (off scratch) (Won by J. G. McColl [W.S.H., 4 yd] in 10.0; won by inches)

Inter-city relay race (440 x 220 x 220 x 880): 1st Glasgow (J. G. McColl, D. E. Duncan, C. H. Cowie, D. McPhee) (3:40.4); 2nd Edinburgh (C. B. Mein, A. M. Mackay, E. H. Liddell, C. S. Brown)

June 16:   Scottish Intervarsity Sports, Craiglockhart, Edinburgh
100yd: 1st (10.1) (record)
220yd: 1st (21.6) (record and Scottish native record)
440yd: 1st (50.2) (record)
One mile relay race (880 x 220 x 220 x 440): 1st EUAC (C. S. Brown, I. H. Osborne-Jones, E. H. Liddell, I. M. Robertson) (3:40.8) (record)

June 23:   SAAA Championships, Celtic Park, Glasgow
100yd: Heat 1: 1st (10.6)
100yd: Final: 1st (10.4)
220yd: Heat 1: 1st (walkover)
220yd: Final: 1st (22.4) (Championship best)
One mile relay race (880 x 220 x 220 x 440): 1st EUAC (C. S. Brown, E. H. Liddell, L. J. Dunn, I. M. Robertson) (3:43.6)

June 27:   Edinburgh Pharmacy A.C. Sports, Powderhall Grounds, Edinburgh
120yd (open) handicap: Heat 1: 1st (12.2) (off scratch)
120yd (open) handicap: Semi-final:1st (12.0) (off scratch)
120yd (open) handicap: Final: 1st (11.9) (off scratch)

June 30:   Heart of Midlothian F.C. Sports, Tynecastle Park, Edinburgh
100yd (open) handicap: Heat: 1st
100yd (open) handicap: Semi-final: unplaced (narrowly defeated)

July 6:   Amateur Athletic Association Championships, Stamford Bridge, London
220yd: Round 1: Heat 10: 1st (22.4)
220yd: Round 2: Heat 3: 1st (21.6)

July 7:   Amateur Athletic Association Championships, Stamford Bridge, London
100yd: Round 1: Heat 2: 1st (10.0)
100yd: Round 2: Heat 1: 1st (9.8) (equals Championship best and British record)
100yd: Final: 1st (9.7) (Championship best and British record)
220yd: Final: 1st (21.6)

July 14: Triangular International, Stoke-on-Trent
100yd: Heat 1: 2nd (Won by W. P. Nichol [E] in 10.8)
100yd: Final: 1st (10.4)
220yd: Heat 1: 1st (23.0)
220yd: Final: 1st (22.6)
440yd: 1st (51.2)

July 28: Greenock Glenpark Harriers Meeting, Cappielow Park, Greenock
100yd (open) handicap: Heat: 1st (10.6) (off scratch)
100yd (open) handicap: Semi-final: unplaced
100yd (invitation) handicap: unplaced (Won by D. E. Duncan [Maryhill H., 4yd] in 10.4)

August 4: Rangers Football Club Sports, Ibrox Park, Glasgow
120yd (open) handicap: Heat 3: 3rd (off scratch) (Won by J. McAlpine [Bellahouston H., 7½yd] in 12.2)
300yds (special) handicap: 4th (31.8) (off scratch) (Won by R. McLean [Glasgow H.S.F.P., 13yd] in 30.6; 2nd, L. S. Barden [W.S.H., 16yd]; 3rd, B. McGrath [Manchester A.C., 7yd]; Scottish record attempt)

August 6: British Games Meeting, Stamford Bridge, London
100yd (open): Round 1: 1st (10.2)
100yd (open): Round 2: Heat 1: 3rd (10.1) (fastest loser)(Won by W. P. Nichol [Highgate H.] in 10.0; 2nd, T. Matthewman [Huddersfield A.C.]; won by inches)
100yd (open): Final: 4th (1st, Matthewman, 10.2; 2nd, Nichol; 3rd, G. Varney [Poly. H.]; won by inches)
220yd (open): Liddell did not run owing to an injured leg

August 8: Hibernian Football Club Sports, Easter Road Park, Edinburgh
100yd (open) handicap: Heat 3: 1st (10.8) (off scratch)
100yd (open) handicap: Final: unplaced (Won by C. H. Cowie [Paisley Y.M.C.A., 4½yd] in 10.6)
100yd (invitation) handicap: unplaced (Won by C. H. Cowie [4½yd] in 10.8)

August 11: Celtic Football Club Sports, Celtic Park, Glasgow
100yd (invitation) handicap: 3rd (off scratch) (Won by J. Crawford [Queen's Park F.C., 3yd] in 10.4; 2nd, W. P. Nichol [Highgate H., scratch]; won by a yard, inches between 2nd and 3rd)

220yd (open) handicap: 3rd (off scratch) (Won by Nichol [2yd] in 22.6; 2nd, B. McGrath [Manchester A.C., 5yd]; won by a yard; inches between 2nd and 3rd)

1924

April 25-26: University of Pennsylvania Relays, Philadelphia, Pennsylvania
100yd (special event): 4th (Won by C. Bowman [Syracuse] in 10.0; 2nd, L. A. Clarke [Johns Hopkins College]; 3rd, W. Conway [Pennsylvania State]. About 30 inches covered the first four competitors)
220yd (special event): 2nd (Won by L. A. Clarke [Johns Hopkins College] in 21.6)

May 19:   Maryhill Harriers Meeting, Firhill Park, Glasgow
100yd (invitation) handicap: 2nd (off scratch) (Won by I. H. Osborne-Jones [E.U.A.C., 6½yd] in 10.2; won by half a yard)
Invitation relay race: 1st Maryhill Harriers, (J. C. Anderson, D. E. Duncan, A. H. Graham, C. H. Cowie) (2:08.8); 2nd EUAC (A. F. Clark, I. H. Osborne-Jones, A. L. Knipe, E. H. Liddell). Maryhill won by 7 yards. Liddell took over on the last leg 15 yards behind Cowie.

May 28:   Edinburgh University Athletic Club Sports, Craiglockhart, Edinburgh
100yd: 1st (10.2) (equals record)
220yd: 1st (23.0)
440yd: 1st (51.5) (record)

May 30-31: Scottish Intervarsity Sports, Hampden Park, Glasgow
100yd: 1st (10.2)
220yd: Heat 1: 1st (24.0)
220yd: Final: 1st (23.4)
440yd: 1st (51.2)
One mile relay race (880 x 220 x 220 x 440): 1st EUAC (M. H. Finkelstein, A. L. Knipe, A. F. Clark, E. H. Liddell) (3:52.8)

June 7:   Hawick Common Riding Amateur Sports, Volunteer Park, Hawick
100yd (open) handicap: Heat 4: 1st
100yd (open) handicap: Semi-final: 1st

100yd (open) handicap: Final: 2nd (Won by H. Innes [Teviotdale H., 10yd] in 10.2)

One mile relay race (440 x 220 x 220 x 880): 1st EUAC (E. H. Liddell, I. H. Osborne-Jones, A. L. Knipe, M. H. Finkelstein)

June 14:   SAAA Championships, Hampden Park, Glasgow
100yd: Heat 1: 1st (10.0) (equals Championship best and Scottish native record)
100yd: Final: 1st (10.0) (equals Championship best and Scottish native record)
220yd: Heat 2: 1st (23.2)
220yd: Final: 1st (22.6)
440yd: 1st (51.2)

June 20:   AAA Championships, Stamford Bridge, London
220yd: Round 1: Heat 1: 1st (22.3)
220yd: Round 2: Heat 1: 1st (21.8)
440yd: Round 1: Heat 3: 1st (51.0)
440yd: Round 2: Heat 1: 1st (49.6)

June 21:   AAA Championships, Stamford Bridge, London
220yd: Final: 2nd (22.0) (Won by H. P. Kinsman [South Africa] in 21.7; won by 2½yd)
440yd: Final: 1st (49.6).

June 25:   Edinburgh Pharmacy A.C. Sports, Powderhall Grounds, Edinburgh
150yd (open) handicap: Heat 3: 1st (15.4) (off scratch)
150yd (open) handicap: Final: 2nd (Won by I. H. Osborne-Jones [E.U.A.C., 8yd] in 15.6; won by a foot)

June 28:   Heart of Midlothian Football Club Sports Tynecastle Park, Edinburgh
300yd (invitation) handicap: 4th (off scratch) (Won by G. C. Fraser [E.N.H., 16yd] [33.0]; 2nd, A. M. Mackay [E.S.H., 14yd]; 3rd, R. S. Mein [E.H., 15yd])

OLYMPIC GAMES, Colombes Stadium, Paris

Tuesday, July 8:
200m: Round 1: Heat 3: 1st (22.2)
200m: Round 2: Heat 2: 2nd (Won by E. W. Carr [Australia] in 21.8)

Wednesday, July 9:

> 200m: Semi-final 2: 2nd (21.9) (Won by C. W. Paddock [USA] in 21.8, 1m)
>
> 200m: Final: 3rd (21.9) (1st, J. V. Scholz [USA] in 21.6; 2nd, Paddock, 21.7; won by 30 cm.; 1.5m between 2nd and 3rd)

Thursday, July 10:

> 400m: Round 1: Heat 14: 1st (50.2)
>
> 400m: Round 2: Heat 4: 2nd (49.3) (Won by A. Paulen [Netherlands] in 49.0)

Friday, July 11:

> 400m: Semi-final 2: 1st (48.2)
>
> 400m: Final: 1st (47.6) (World and Olympic record)

July 19:   British Empire versus United States of America (Relays), Stamford Bridge, London

One mile relay race (4 x 440 yards): 1st British Empire (E. J. Toms, R. N. Ripley, G. M. Butler, E. H. Liddell) (3:18.2); 2nd USA (E. C. Wilson, R. A. Robertson, W. E. Stevenson, H. M. Fitch). [*Liddell took over from Butler on the last leg 4 yards down on Fitch. He proceeded to overtake the American and won by 4 yards. His split time was taken at 47.6, his fastest over the imperial distance. The time recorded by the all-British (Empire) team was a mere two-tenths slower than the world record set in 1915. It was a UK best and remained such for ten years*].

One mile relay race (440 x 220 x 220 x 880): 1st USA (C. R. Brookins, G. L. Hill, J. V. Scholz, A. Helffrich); 2nd British Empire (E. H. Liddell, A. E. Porritt, G. M. Butler, D. G. A. Lowe). [*Liddell handed over to Porritt 2 yards behind Brookins*].

July 26:   Greenock Glenpark Harriers Meeting (incorporating a Scotland versus Canada international), Cappielow Park, Greenock

100yd: 3rd (Won by C. H. Coaffee [C] in 10.0; 2nd, J. Crawford [S]; won by a yard; inches separated 2nd and 3rd) [*Liddell's inches defeat by Crawford was only the second time he was defeated in a scratch race by a fellow-Scot, the other being by Stewart at the Edinburgh University Sports of 1921*].

440yd: 1st (51.2) (2nd, A. T. Christie (C); 3rd, H. Aylwin [C]; won by 10yd)

One mile relay race (880 x 220 x 220 x 440): 1st Scotland (D. Macrae, R. McLean, R. A. Robb, E. H. Liddell) (3:57.0); 2nd

Canada. [*Liddell ran the last leg, taking over 8 to 10 yards behind the Canadian, Christie. He speedily reduced the lead but was still 6 yards down with 150 yards to go. Eventually he came through to win by 5 yards*].

August 2: Rangers Football Club Sports, Ibrox Park, Glasgow
440yd (open) handicap: 1st (49.6) (off scratch); (2nd, C. W. Oldfield [South Africa, 5yd]; won by 1 foot)

August 5: West of Scotland Harriers Meeting, Ibrox Park, Glasgow
220yd (open) handicap: 3rd (off scratch) (Won by R. A. Robb [W.S.H., 11yd] in 22.6; 2nd, R. McLean [Glasgow H.S.F.P., 7yd]; inches covered all 3)
300yd (invitation) scratch: 1st (32.0); (2nd, W. P. Nichol [Highgate H.]; 3rd, C. W. Oldfield [South Africa]; won by 4 yards)

August 16: Gala Harriers Sports, Netherdale Park, Galashiels
100yd (open) handicap: Heat 5: 2nd (off scratch) (Won by R. Epton [E.N.H., 9yd]; won by 2 yards)
440yd invitation handicap: 1st (54.0) (off scratch) [*Run in a downpour of rain*]

1925

May 20: Edinburgh University Athletic Club Sports, Craiglockhart, Edinburgh
100yd: 1st (10.4)
220yd: 1st (23.0)
440yd: 1st (51.4) (record)

May 30: Scottish Intervarsity Sports, University Park, St Andrews
100yd: 1st (10.2)
220yd: 1st (22.0)
440yd: 1st (55.8)
[*In five years Eric Liddell had an unblemished record in these sports*]

June 6: Queen's Park Football Club Sports, Hampden Park, Glasgow
440yd (open) handicap: 3rd (50.2) (off scratch) (Won by R. A. Robb [G.U.A.C.,18yd] in 49.8; 2nd, J. D. Hope [W.S.H., 20yd]; won by ½ yard)
Inter-city relay race (880 x 220 x 220 x 440): 1st Edinburgh (C. B. Mein, F. B. Wardlaw, A. F. Clark, E. H. Liddell) (3:39.8) (Scottish best); 2nd Glasgow (R. B. McIntyre, R. McLean, R. A. Robb, D. Macrae)

June 13:   Corstorphine A.A.C. Sports, Union Park, Corstorphine, Edinburgh
440yd (East of Scotland Championship): 1st 53.5
600yd (open) handicap: 7th (off scratch) (Won by J. N. K. Clarkson [E.U.A.C., 45yd] in 1:16.8). Liddell was beaten by 8 yards. 34 starters!

June 20:   Edinburgh Southern Harriers Sports, Powderhall Grounds, Edinburgh
220yd (East of Scotland Championship): 1st (23.4)
220yd (open) handicap: Heat 3: 1st (22.8) (off scratch)
220yd (open) handicap: Final: 1st (22.25) (off scratch)
300yd (invitation) handicap: 1st (31.5) (off scratch)

June 24:   Edinburgh Pharmacy A.C. Sports, Powderhall Grounds, Edinburgh
120yd (open) handicap: Heat 5: 2nd (off scratch) (Won by A. Kennedy [K.O.S.B. & E.N.H., 8yd] in 12.0; won by 1 yard)
One mile invitation relay race (880 x 220 x 220 x 440): 1st EUAC (R. B. Hoole, R. D. Allison, I. H. Osborne-Jones, E. H. Liddell) (3:45.4) [*This marked Liddell's final appearance on an Edinburgh track before his departure for China*]

June 27:   SAAA Championships, Hampden Park, Glasgow
100yd: Heat 1: 1st (10.2)
100yd: Final: 1st (10.0) (equals Championship best and Scottish native record)
220yd: Heat 1: 1st (walkover)
220yd: Final: 1st (22.2) (Championship best)
440yd: 1st (49.2) (Championship best)
One mile relay race (880 x 220 x 220 x 440): 1st EUAC (R. B. Hoole, I. H. Osborne-Jones, A. F. Clark, E. H. Liddell) (3:40.2)
[*Between 1921 and 1925 Eric Liddell was undefeated in all his races at the Scottish Championships, including relays, 26 races and 16 titles in all!*]

CAREER HIGHLIGHTS: (2) RUGBY – REPRESENTATIVE MATCHES 1921-1923

SEASON 1921-22

1921

December 3: Inter-City match: Inverleith, Edinburgh
Edinburgh 3 Glasgow 8

December 10: International trial (1): Galashiels
'Scotland' 30 'North and South' 9 (EHL scored five tries for 'Scotland')

December 24: International trial (2): Inverleith, Edinburgh
'Scotland' 32 'The Rest' 6 (EHL scored five tries for 'Scotland')

1922

January 2: International: Colombes, Paris
Scotland 3 France 3

January 14: International trial (3): New Anniesland, Glasgow
'Scotland' 16 'The Rest' 8 (EHL scored one try for 'Scotland')

February 4: International: Inverleith, Edinburgh
Scotland 9 Wales 9

February 25: International: Inverleith, Edinburgh
Scotland 6 Ireland 3 (EHL scored one try)

March 18: International: Twickenham, London
Scotland 5 England 11 (EHL selected but withdrew through injury)

SEASON 1922–23

1922

December 2:   Inter-City match: New Anniesland, Glasgow
               Edinburgh 17 Glasgow 8 (EHL scored two tries for
               Edinburgh)

December 9:   International trial (1): Hawick
               'Scotland' 26 'The Rest' 6 (EHL scored one try for
               'Scotland')

December 23:   International Trial (2): Inverleith, Edinburgh
               'Scotland' 25 'The Rest' 14 (EHL scored three tries: two
               for 'Scotland' in the first half and one for 'The Rest' in the
               second half after the backs switched sides!)

1923

January 6:   International trial (3): New Anniesland, Glasgow
               'Scotland' 18 'The Rest' 3 (EHL scored one try for
               'Scotland')

January 20:   International: Inverleith, Edinburgh
               Scotland 16 France 3 (EHL scored one try)

February 3:   International: Cardiff
               Scotland 11 Wales 8 (EHL scored one try)

February 24:   International: Lansdowne Road, Dublin
               Scotland 13 Ireland 3 (EHL scored one try)

March 17:   International: Inverleith, Edinburgh
               Scotland 6 England 8

Note: *All the above matches were on Saturdays.*

END NOTES

Preface

1. Nigel Andrews, 'Running for Britain', *Financial Times*, Friday, 3 April 1981, p. 21.
2. E. H. Liddell, 'An "Eskimo" Runner', *All Sports Weekly*, July 3rd, 1926, p. 20.
3. The IAAF was founded as the 'International Amateur Athletics Federation' after the Stockholm Olympic Games of 1912. It became known as the 'International Association of Athletics Federations' after 2001, and is currently known as *World Athletics*, as from June 2019. It has been the guardian of track and field athletics globally in amateur days, and, since 2001, in the modern era of professionalism.

Chapter 1 – Encountering Eric Liddell

1. Catherine Marshall, *A Man Called Peter: The Story of Peter Marshall*, (London, 1964 [first published 1952]), p. 23. Peter Marshall was born in Scotland but became a Presbyterian minister in New York Avenue Presbyterian Church, Washington, D.C., and a chaplain to the US Senate. He died in 1949, aged forty-six.
2. See: www.bbc.co.uk/scotland/sportscotland/asportingnation/article/019.shtml (Accessed 10 November 2018).
3. The letter is dated 20 October 1973. Bruce was born and brought up in Elgin, Morayshire, in Scotland.
4. *Heart of an Athlete*. Daily Devotions for Peak Performance, Fellowship of Christian Athletes (Ventura, CA, 2005), pp. 113-14.
5. D. P. Thomson, *Scotland's Greatest Athlete. The Eric Liddell Story*, (Crieff, Perthshire: Research Unit, 1970, paperback); D. P. Thomson, *Eric H. Liddell. Athlete and Missionary* (Crieff, Perthshire: Research Unit, 1971, hardback). The latter, containing many illustrations, was a 'revised illustrated edition' of the earlier paperback, which had been brought out to coincide with the Commonwealth Games held in Edinburgh in 1970.
6. Kept at West Register House, Edinburgh, under *J. W. Keddie Papers (Athletics)*. The reference is GD 445.
7. The articles covered three issues: 15 January 1977, 22 January 1977 and 5 February 1977.
8. Lord Burghley did, however, win the 400 metres hurdles at the Games in Amsterdam four years later.

9. I competed for Edinburgh Southern Harriers between 1965 and 1970, and Mitcham Athletic Club between 1973 and 1975, when a serious accident curtailed all sporting participation. Among other things I won the Scottish junior triple jump in 1965, was placed fourth in the same event at the British Universities Championship in 1968 and ran in a silver-medal-winning 4 x 440 yards relay at the Scottish Championship of 1966. I also played senior rugby union for Boroughmuir School Former Pupils XV between 1966 and 1970.

10. The name originally mooted in the Treatment was the simple 'Runners'. That, however, eventually gave way to *Chariots of Fire*, doubtless suggested by a line in William Blake's enigmatic poem 'Jerusalem' (written in 1804) which itself would most likely have been prompted by the story of Elisha in 2 Kings 6.

11. The story of my involvement with Colin Welland is given in part by Sally Magnusson in *The Flying Scotsman* (London: Quartet Books, 1981), pp. 184-5.

12. The annual 'Triangular International' involved a contest between England (and Wales), Ireland and Scotland.

13. David M. Virkler, 'Chariots of Fire. Running the Race with Faith. The story of Eric Liddell's Olympic Victory and Chariots of Fire': http://www.wordandworld. homestead.com/Chariots.html. (Accessed 10 November 2018).

14. The numerous biographies of Liddell are listed in the bibliography.

15. I was responsible for the definitive history of the Scottish Amateur Athletic Association, 1883-1983, *Scottish Athletics*, which was published in 'coffee table' format in 1982 (Glasgow, 1982). This remains the only comprehensive study of the history of amateur athletics in Scotland. Besides some articles in *Athletics Weekly*, I have also from time to time contributed to *Track Stats*, the journal of the National Union of Track Statisticians.

Chapter 2 – 'It is surrender'

1. David Michell, *A Boy's War*, OMF, Singapore, 1988, pp. 1-2.
2. Thomson, *Eric H. Liddell: Athlete and Missionary*, pp. 186-7.
3. Reference may be made to Thomson, *Eric H. Liddell: Athlete and Missionary*, chapter 25.
4. As above, p. 197.
5. As above, p. 199.
6. As above, p. 230.

Chapter 3 – The shaping of a Christian sportsman

1. The Evangelical Union was an association of Congregational (independent) churches which had been formed in 1843, for the greater part from ministers and people formerly of a Scottish Presbyterian secession church. It was founded as a purely voluntary association of churches for 'mutual countenance, counsel and cooperation in supporting and spreading the glorious simple, soul-saving and heart-sanctifying gospel of the grace of God'. In general terms these churches had an evangelistic zeal, and were influential especially among working-class people. Their theology was akin to that of Charles G. Finney (1792-1875), the American revivalist preacher. The EU was notably committed to the temperance cause. No one involved in the liquor trade could be a member of their churches. There were ninety EU congregations at the time of its merger with the Congregational Union

on 1 January 1897. For further information on the Evangelical Union see the *Dictionary of Scottish Church History and Theology* (Edinburgh, 1993), pp. 305-6.

2. This became a United Free Church of Scotland in 1900 after a union of the United Presbyterian Church with the majority of the Free Church in Scotland.

3. Thomson, *Eric H. Liddell: Athlete and Missionary*, p. 6.

4. James named his third son, Ernest, after William Blair. Ernest Blair Liddell was born in Peking (Beijing) in 1912.

5. Thomson, *Eric H. Liddell. Athlete and Missionary*, p. 36.

6. Harlan P. Beach, *Princely Men in the Heavenly Kingdom* (New York, 1903), p. 105.

7. W. P. Nairne, *James Gilmour of the Mongols* (London, no date, but c1932), p. 109.

8. As above, p. 111.

9. From the entry on 'James Gilmour' in the website of Wholesome Words: https://www.wholesomewords.org/biography/biorpgilmour.html. (Accessed 10 November 2018).

10. Among accounts of experiences of Christian missionaries at that time in China, one of the most remarkable is that described by Archibald Glover, a China Inland Missionary at the time of the rebellion: A. E. Glover, *A Thousand Miles of Miracle*. This book, abridged by Leslie Lyall, was issued by the Overseas Missionary Fellowship in a 'centenary edition with new material', and published jointly with Christian Focus Publications in 2000.

11. This story is told by Margaret Aitchison in her biography of Tom Cochrane, *The Doctor & The Dragon. A Pioneer in Old Peking* (Pickering & Inglis, Basingstoke, 1983), p. 46ff.

12. Thomson, *Eric H. Liddell: Athlete and Missionary*, p. 16.

13. As above, p. 34.

14. As above, p. 36.

15. Eric Liddell, *The Disciplines of the Christian Life* (London, 1985), pp. 84-5 (the emphasis is in the original). This book was prepared by Eric in Tientsin in the fourteen months or so before he was finally sent to the Weihsien Internment Camp early in 1943.

16. As above, p. 109.

17. As above, p. 64ff.

18. Thomson, *Eric H. Liddell: Athlete and Missionary*, p. 37.

19. D. P. Thomson, *Personal Encounters* (Research Unit, Crieff, 1967), p. 79.

20. See Tony Ladd and James A. Mathisen, *Muscular Christianity. Evangelical Protestants and the Development of American Sport* (Grand Rapids, 1999). There are references to Eric Liddell on pages 147 and 214.

21. Obituary notice in the *Sunday Times*, 20 May 1945, quoted by D. P. Thomson, *Eric Liddell, The Making of an Athlete and the Training of a Missionary* (Glasgow: Eric Liddell Memorial Committee, 1945), p. 39.

22. Thomson, *Eric H. Liddell: Athlete and Missionary*, p. 39.

23. Sally Magnusson, *The Flying Scotsman* (London, 1981), p.100. The text referred to by Eric Liddell is Ecclesiastes 9:11.

24. Russell W. Ramsey, *God's Joyful Runner* (South Plainfield, NJ: Bridge Publishing, 1987), p. 55. The text referred to is 1 Corinthians 7:7.

25. Magnusson, *The Flying Scotsman*, p. 104.

26. Ray Palmer (1808-1887). There is a reference to this hymn in Eric Liddell's *The Disciplines of the Christian Life*, pp. 74-5.

Chapter 4 – An exciting prospect
1. Thomson, *Eric H. Liddell: Athlete and Missionary*, pp. 19-20. This account came from notes of a talk Eric later gave in Tientsin. None of the other biographers of Liddell gives this detail in full, yet it is an account full of colour, and it is in Eric's own words.
2. As above, p. 27.
3. Thomas Sword McKerchar was a native of Edinburgh. Born on 25 February 1877, Tom followed his father James into the printing trade. He became a 'paper ruler' (i.e. responsible for putting the lines on lined, or 'ruled', paper) in a printing business in the capital. He died on 13 August 1940 in his sixty-fourth year. Eric always said that he owed so much of his success on the track to the training and guidance of McKerchar.
4. Thomson, *Eric H. Liddell: Athlete and Missionary*, p. 26.
5. Any athlete could enter for an 'open' handicap event. In the case of 'invitation' events, the sports' organisers would issue invitations to selected athletes to take part in these events.
6. 'Men and Matters', under the heading of 'Field Sports', *Glasgow Herald*, Thursday, 11 August 1921. This was written two days before the final track meet of the season at Celtic Park, Glasgow.
7. Thomson, *Eric H. Liddell: Athlete and Missionary*, pp. 18-19.

Chapter 5 – Another string to his bow
1. *The Scotsman*, Thursday, 9 February 1922, p. 5. A 'try' is scored when a player touches the ball down over the opponents' line. A try is 'converted' by someone from the scoring team place-kicking the ball between the uprights and over the crossbar of the rugby posts. A try and a conversion constituted a 'goal'. In the 1920s, the drop goal (a drop kick from open play going between the posts) then carried rugby's highest points tariff of four points. A try was worth three, with two further points added for a conversion, and three for a penalty.
2. *The Scotsman*, Monday, 12 December 1921, p. 10.
3. *The Scotsman*, Tuesday, 27 December 1921, p. 8.
4. *The Scotsman*, Monday, 16 January 1922, p. 4. It was noted that A. L. Gracie had been unable to travel north for the trial.
5. It may be of passing interest that the author actually met three of the members of the Scotland team which played against Wales in 1922: J. M. Bannerman (1901-1969)(seated on the left); Jock Wemyss (1893-1974)(seated third from the left) and Col. Usher the captain that day. Jock Wemyss on one occasion reported on a Saturday rugby fixture in March 1969 in which the author played for Boroughmuir against Melrose. Among other things Wemyss reported that, 'Alan Irvine was in fine form at the heel of the 'Muir pack and he and John Keddie outshone the Melrose half-backs' (*Sunday Express*, 2 March 1969)! Boroughmuir won 16-11.
6. William Reid, 'A Tale of Two Cities', *The Scottish Field*, May 1937, p. 33.
7. E. H. Liddell, 'How I Won My Races', *All Sports Weekly*, May 29th, 1926, p. 9.

Chapter 6 – More brilliant running
1. *The Scotsman*, Monday, 10 July 1922, p. 10.
2. *The Scotsman*, Monday, 14 August 1922, p. 9.

Chapter 7 – Another rugby season
1. R. J. Phillips, *The Story of Scottish Rugby*, (Edinburgh & London, 1925), p. 223. Phillips is referring to W. A. Stewart, the Olympic sprinter who played for Scotland in four internationals in 1913-1914. His scoring rate must be unmatched in the annals of rugby union, for in the four internationals he scored no fewer than eight tries from the right-wing position!
2. As above, p. 213.
3. *The Scotsman*, Monday, 9 October 1922, p. 10. The match was at Jock's Lodge, home of the Royal High School F. P. team in Edinburgh.
4. A. A. Thomson, *Rugger My Pleasure* (London, 1955), p. 96.
5. *The Scotsman*, Monday, 8 January 1923, p. 8.
6. David Barnes and Peter Burns with John Griffiths, *Behind the Thistle. Playing Rugby for Scotland*, (Edinburgh, 2015), p. 46.
7. As above, p. 47.
8. *The Scotsman*, Monday, 23 February 1923, p. 10.
9. *The Scotsman*, Monday, 19 March 1923, p. 10.
10. *The Scotsman*, Monday, 28 January 1924, p. 4.
11. Thomson, *Rugger My Pleasure*, p. 96.
12. As above, pp. 95-6.
13. Barnes and Burns with John Griffiths, *Behind the Thistle. Playing Rugby for Scotland*, p. 47.

Chapter 8 – Beginning to fulfil the potential
1. Thomson, *Eric H. Liddell: Athlete and Missionary*, pp. 19-21. Thomson refers to this athlete as 'one of my correspondents', but does not identify him by name. In that 220 yards final there were in fact only two other athletes, William Nichol and Tom Matthewman, the other finalist, C. L. Steyn, having pulled out through injury. Also, Eric was in the second lane, and not the 'outside berth'. How fallible memories can be!
2. See chapter 8 of Mark Ryan's biography of Harold Abrahams, *Running with Fire* (London, 2011), 'Running Scared of Eric Liddell', pp. 74-88.
3. *The Scotsman*, Monday, 16 July 1923, p. 10.
4. 'Boring', in this context, means wrongfully knocking over or otherwise impeding another athlete in the course of a race. It may arise from carelessness, rather than intent, but would still lead to disqualification.
5. *The Scotsman*, Monday, 16 July 1923, p. 10.
6. R. L. Quercetani, *A World History of Track and Field Athletics, 1864-1964* (London, 1964), p. 53. This reference is omitted in his subsequent revised and updated *Athletics, A History of Modern Track and Field Athletics (1860–2000)* (Milan, 2000), pp. 79-80.
7. Thomson, *Eric H. Liddell: Athlete and Missionary*, pp. 44-5.
8. David McCasland, *Eric Liddell. Pure Gold* (Grand Rapids, MI: Discovery House Publications, 2001), p. 81.

9.   Magnusson, *The Flying Scotsman*, p. 45.

Chapter 9 – Reaching for the pinnacle

1.   *The Scotsman*, Wednesday, 13 February 1924, p. 12.
2.   E. H. Liddell, 'Record "Record Smashing"', *All Sports Weekly*, June 19th, 1926, p. 15.
3.   As above, p.15.
4.   E. H. Liddell, 'How I Won my Races. Eric Liddell's Own Story of his Greatest Feats', *All Sports Weekly*, May 29th, 1926, p. 9. The difference in the 400m in Paris was that he ran the whole of first 200m 'almost, if not quite, "all out"'!
5.   C. M. Usher (ed.), *The story of Edinburgh University Athletic Club* (Edinburgh, 1966), p. 66.
6.   Thomson, *Eric H. Liddell: Athlete and Missionary*, p. 46.
7.   Usher (ed.), *The story of Edinburgh University Athletic Club*, p. 61.
8.   Eric Liddell was also entered for the 100 yards, but so tight was the schedule that he wisely withdrew from the event. He had been due to run in heat 1 at 2.30 p.m. on the Saturday, but with a second round and the final to be run between then and 4 o'clock, this was rather too much, given that the final of the 220 yards was due to be held at 4.15, followed by the 440 yards a little later.
9.   Ryan, *Running with Fire*, pp. 113-14.

Chapter 10 – The man who was Friday

1.   Melvyn Watman, *History of British Athletics* (London, 1968), p. 45.
2.   *The Official Report of the Games of the 8th Olympiade*, Paris, 1924, p. 97.
3.   Mark Ryan, *Running with Fire*, p. 139.
4.   E. H. Liddell, 'Match Winning Athletes', *All Sports Weekly*, June 12th, 1926, p. 4.
5.   F. A. M. Webster, *Great Moments in Athletics* (London, 1947), p. 23.
6.   See John Kieran and Arthur Daley, *The Story of the Olympic Games, 776 B.C. to 1956 A.D.* (Philadelphia, 1957), pp. 157-8.
7.   E. H. Liddell, 'Record "Record Smashing"', *All Sports Weekly*, June 19th, 1926, p. 15.
8.   Webster, *Great Moments in Athletics*, p. 24.
9.   E. H. Liddell, 'Record "Record Smashing"', p. 15.
10. Thomson, *Eric H. Liddell: Athlete and Missionary*, pp. 55-6.
11. As reported in *The Scotsman*, Saturday, 19 July 1924, p. 11, under the headline, 'Athlete and Christian'.
12. *Athletics Weekly*, 17 April 1982, p. 26, reprinting an article by Harold Abrahams dating from October 1934.
13. E. H. Liddell, 'Record "Record Smashing"', p. 15.
14. Marshall Brant, *The Games: A Complete News History* (London, 1980), p. 56.
15. Liddell's time was accepted as a world record by the International Amateur Athletic Federation (IAAF) at its meetings in 1924, 1926 and 1928. Only later did the IAAF recognise officially that Ted Meredith's record of 47.4 seconds for the 440 yards, set in 1916 (round one bend but not on a stringed course) over a distance three yards longer than the metric equivalent, was intrinsically superior to the records of Imbach (48.0), Fitch (47.8) and Liddell (47.6). The IAAF became the International Association of Athletics Federations in 2001, since the sport was no longer exclusively 'amateur'. From 2019 it is known as World Athletics.

16. It may be noted that individual times in the semi-finals were not given officially, other than for the winners. Butler's time in the first semi-final, in which he finished second, has been variously estimated as 48.0 and 47.9, from press reports and a photograph of the finish. In this book we have taken a more conservative view, based on a national report (Finnish) in which all the times of the semi-finalists are recorded, including 48.2 for Guy Butler.
17. Horatio M. Fitch, 'I was there. The day we rode our Chariots of Fire', in *Modern Maturity*, April-May 1983, p. 32.
18. Roberto L. Quercetani, *A World History of the One-Lap Race, 1850-2004* (Milan, 2005), p. 12.
19. *Edinburgh Evening Dispatch*, Saturday, 12 July 1924.
20. E. H. Liddell, 'Record "Record Smashing"', p. 15.
21. Payton Jordan and Bud Spencer, *Champions in the Making* (London, 1969), p. 42.
22. E. H. Liddell, 'Record "Record Smashing"', p. 15.

Chapter 11 – Coming down from the mountaintop
1. *The Scotsman*, Friday, 18 July 1924, p. 10.
2. *The Scotsman*, Saturday, 19 July 1924, p. 11.
3. Sadly, this fine building was demolished in the early 1980s.

Chapter 12 – The final season
1. *Athletics Weekly*, 17 April 1982, p. 26.
2. Kieran and Daley, *The Story of the Olympic Game*s, p. 158.

Chapter 13 – Life is more than sport
1. Magnusson, *The Flying Scotsman*, p. 81. Elsa McKechnie later became Mrs Watson.
2. For some of the details of this work in Britain in 1924-25 see Thomson, *Eric H. Liddell: Athlete and Missionary* and McCasland, *Eric Liddell. Pure Gold*.
3. *The Scotsman*, Monday, 19 January 1925, p. 8.
4. Liddell, *The Disciplines of the Christian Life*, p. 47.
5. As above, p. 115.
6. *The Scotsman*, Thursday, 5 February 1925, p. 5.
7. *The Scotsman*, Tuesday, 19 May 1925, p. 8.
8. *The Scotsman*, Wednesday, 9 March 1932, p. 15.
9. In 1929 the majority of the United Free Church united with the Church of Scotland. After that date St George's became St George's West, Church of Scotland.
10. *The Scotsman*, Wednesday, 6 May 1925, p. 11.
11. Russell W. Ramsey, *God's Joyful Runner* (South Plainfield, NJ, 1987), p. 79. There is no indication where Ramsey gleaned this part of the address from. It is possibly from a newspaper report suitably put into the first and second person.
12. Thomson, *Eric H. Liddell: Athlete and Missionary*, p. 76.
13. As above, p. 77.
14. Quotations are from a typed letter which may be seen on the website of the Eric Liddell Centre: http://www.ericliddell.org/about-us/eric-liddell/personal-corre-spondence-of-eric-liddell/. (Accessed 10 November 2018).

Chapter 14 – Missionary life in China
1. After seven years of service the missionaries were given leave for a year, a 'sabbatical' year. Eric Liddell had such breaks in 1931-32 and 1939-40, returning to Scotland both times and also passing through Canada on his way back to China.
2. Magnusson, *The Flying Scotsman*, p. 102.
3. David Guest, 'Eric Liddell: A Chosen Vessel', Highbury College of Technology, Portsmouth, 1985, p. 1.
4. Thomson, *Eric H. Liddell: Athlete and Missionary*, p. 82.
5. Michell, *A Boy's War*, p. 110.
6. Thomson, *Eric H. Liddell: Athlete and Missionary*, pp. 107-8.
7. This is an undated circular letter, but was evidently written shortly after Eric began work at the Anglo-Chinese College in 1925. See: http://www.ericliddell.org/eric-liddell/eric-liddell-personal-correspondence.php.
8. This is an undated letter, but was evidently written some time in 1928: http://www.ericliddell.org/about-us/eric-liddell/personal-correspondence-of-eric-liddell/. (Accessed 10 November 2018).
9. Sun Hailin, *The Man who Brought the Olympics to China – The Story of Zhang Boling* (Beijing: New World Press, 2008), p. 20.
10. English translation by Joy Kuang of a passage from a Chinese book, *Chinese Olympic Pioneer – Zhang Boling*, pp.222-3. This volume is a fuller version of the abbreviated English translation, *The Man who Brought the Olympics to China*.
11. Thomson, *Eric H. Liddell: Athlete and Missionary*, p. 102.
12. Ross and Norris McWhirter, *Get to your Marks!* (London, 1951), p. 44.
13. Thomson, *Eric H. Liddell: Athlete and Missionary*, p.104. At the time Peltzer (1900-1970) was also the official world-record holder for 1,000 metres and 1,500 metres. Past his best in 1932, Peltzer finished ninth in the 800 metres at Los Angeles. He also ran in the German 4 x 400 metres relay team which finished fourth in the final of that event.
14. For details of these see the biographies by D. P. Thomson and David McCasland listed in the bibliography.
15. Letter dated 23 August 1930. http://www.ericliddell.org/about-us/eric-liddell/personal-correspondence-of-eric-liddell/ (Accessed 10 November 2018).
16. Thomson, *Eric H. Liddell: Athlete and Missionary*, p. 136.
17. As above, p. 140.
18. 'Missionary Adventure in China', in, *The Scotsman*, Wednesday, January 26, 1938, p. 11. This harrowing adventure is told with a fair bit of explicit detail in Duncan Hamilton's *For the Glory*, Transworld Publishers, 2016, pp. 182-188.
19. Eric Liddell, 'Back from the Dead' – The Peony Rose, Siaochang, February 13th, 1939. This was a story told by Eric Liddell and distributed in a duplicated form along with a lithograph of the flower picture mentioned in the story. The author received copies of these from D. P. Thomson in 1966.
20. Letter to his family back home from Siaochang dated December 1938. He introduces himself as Li-Mu-Shi (Pastor Liddell). See, http://www.ericliddell.org/about-us/eric-liddell/personal-correspondence-of-eric-liddell/ (Accessed 10 November 2018).
21. As above.
22. Thomson, *Eric H. Liddell: Athlete and Missionary*, p. 166.

23. As above, p. 176. The capital letters are in the original.

Chapter 15 – Internment
1. McCasland, *Eric Liddell. Pure Gold*, p. 258.
2. Ramsey, *God's Joyful Runner*, p. 154.
3. Thomson, *Eric H. Liddell: Athlete and Missionary*, p. 188.
4. Michell, *A Boy's War*, p. 117.
5. Thomson, *Eric H. Liddell: Athlete and Missionary*, p. 186.
6. As above, p. 199.
7. As above, pp. 201-2.
8. Michell, *A Boy's War*, p. 166.

Chapter 16 – A life well lived
1. Thomson, *Eric H. Liddell: Athlete and Missionary*, pp. 107-8.
2. As above, p. 209
3. McCasland, *Eric Liddell. Pure Gold*, pp. 289-90.
4. Thomson, *Eric H. Liddell: Athlete and Missionary*, p. 210 ff.
5. As above, pp. 211-12.
6. Thomson, *Personal Encounters*, p. 80.
7. Harold Abrahams, 'He ran like a man inspired', *World Sports*, June 1948, p. 13.
8. Usher (ed.), *The story of Edinburgh University Athletic Club*, p. 65.
9. Michell, *A Boy's War*, p. 156.
10. Graham Hutchings, 'Liddell honoured by skirl of pipes in a foreign field', *The Daily Telegraph*, Monday, 10 June 1991.
11. From Isaiah 40:31.
12. David Michell, 'Chefoo and Weihsien (Weifang) Revisited': www.weihsien-paintings.org/NormanCliff/Photos/1991/indexFrame1991.htm (Accessed 10 November 2018). The article is dated 28 June 1991. Sadly, David Michell died as a result of a car crash near his home in Toronto on 24 December 1997. He was sixty-four years old.
13. Ivo Tennant, 'College builds noble tradition', *The Times*, Monday, 1 July 1996. The title heading the article reads: 'Eltham invokes spirit of Liddell to encourage his heirs.'
14. Richard Spencer, 'Chariots of Fire hero is honoured by the Chinese', *The Daily Telegraph*, Thursday, 18 August 2005, p. 15.
15. Norman Cliff, 'Refining Gold'. This may be seen on the website of The Eric Liddell Centre: https://www.ericliddell.org/rev-dr-norman-cliff-a-transcript-of-a-talk-on-his-experiences-of-weihsien-camp-he-describes-eric-liddells-life-and-death-in-the-camp/. (Accessed 10 November 2018).
16. Thomson, *Eric H. Liddell: Athlete and Missionary*, p. 219-21.

Chapter 17 – 'More than an athlete'
1. *The Independent*, Monday, 24 March 2008, p. 40.
2. *The Daily Telegraph*, Monday, 21 July 2008, S18-S19.
3. Duncan Hamilton, *For the Glory* (London, 2016), pp. 171-2.
4. As above, p. 194. This incident is recorded in Thomson, *Eric H. Liddell: Athlete and Missionary*, p.136, from where Hamilton picked up the anecdote.
5. Liddell, *The Disciplines of Christian Life*, p. 66.

6. See Lian Xi's study of 'Liberalism in American Protestant Missions in China, 1907-1932': *Conversion of the Missionaries* (The Pennsylvania State University Press, 1997).

7. See, for example, David Aikman, *Jesus in Beijing* (Monarch Books, 2006) and Tony Lambert, *China's Christian Millions* (OMF, 2006). For a contemporary Reformed perspective see Bruce P. Baugus (Ed.), *China's Reforming Churches. Mission, Polity, and Ministry in the Next Christendom* (Grand Rapids, Michigan: Reformation Heritage Books, 2014). Aikman describes this book as 'the finest work on Christianity in China that I have seen in years.'

8. Eric Liddell, *The Disciplines of the Christian Life,* pp. 79-80.

BIOGRAPHICAL BIBLIOGRAPHY

BIOGRAPHIES (IN ORDER OF PUBLICATION)

Thomson, D. P. *Eric Liddell. The Making of an Athlete and the Training of a Missionary*, Eric Liddell Memorial Committee, Glasgow, 1945.

Thomson, D. P. *Scotland's Greatest Athlete. The Eric Liddell Story*, Research Unit, Crieff, 1970.

Thomson, D. P. *Eric H. Liddell. Athlete and Missionary*, Research Unit, Crieff, 1971.

Magnusson, Sally. *The Flying Scotsman*, Quartet Books, London, 1981.

Swift, Catherine. *Eric Liddell: God's Athlete*, Marshall, Morgan & Scott, Basingstoke, 1986.

Ramsey, Russell W. *God's Joyful Runner*, Bridge Publishing, South Plainfield, NJ, 1987.

Repp, Gloria. *His Best for God. The story of Eric Liddell*, Child Evangelism Fellowship, Warrenton, MO, 1989.

Williamson, Denise & Hsieh, Jim. *Chariots to China: A Story of Eric Liddell*, Wolgemuth & Hyatt, Publishers, Brentwood, TN, 1991.

Wilson, Julian. *Complete Surrender*, Monarch Publications, Crowborough, 1996.

Benge, Janet & Benge, Geoff. *Eric Liddell. Something Greater Than Gold*, YWAM Publishing, Seattle, WA, 1999.

Caughey, Ellen W. *Eric Liddell: Gold Medal Missionary*, Barbour Publishing, Uhrichsville, OH, 2000 (Reissued as *Run to Glory. The Story of Eric Liddell* in 2017).

Meloche, Renee Taft. *Eric Liddell: Running for a Higher Prize*, YWAM Publishing, Seattle, WA, 2001.

McCasland, David C. *Eric Liddell. Pure Gold*, Discovery House Publications, Grand Rapids, MI, 2001.

Keddie, John W. *Running the Race. Eric Liddell – Olympic Champion and Missionary*, Evangelical Press, Darlington, 2007.

Keddie, John W. *Finish the Race*, Christian Focus Publications, Fearn, Ross-shire, 2011 (*This has been produced as an unabridged audio book (2017) by Christian Audio. See www.christianaudio.com*).

Hamilton, Duncan. *For the Glory. The Life of Eric Liddell from Olympic Hero to Modern Martyr*, Transworld Publishers, London, 2016.

Eichinger, Eric T. with Eva Marie Everson. *The Final Race. The Incredible World War II Story of the Olympian Who Inspired* Chariots of Fire, Tyndale Momentum, Illinois, 2018.

FILMS / DVDS:

Chariots of Fire (20th Century Fox, 1981).

The Story of Eric Liddell (A Day of Discovery Television Production, 2004).

The Eric Liddell Story (The Torchlighters Heroes of the Faith, Christian History Institute, 2007).

On Wing of Eagles (Archstone Distribution, 2017).

ARCHIVE FOOTAGE

Unsurprisingly, actual archive footage of Eric in action is hard to find and is not exactly in high definition! However, there is some material out there to be viewed and readers may be interested in the following archive footage readily to be accessed on the internet:

Rugby:

Footage of filmed rugby events in the 1920s is understandably rare. There are, however, a couple of accessible clips involving Eric Liddell from 1920s internationals:

1. Scotland versus Wales, Inverleith, 1922: https://www.britishpathe. com/video/honours-even-8/query/Wales Apart from film of the teams (Eric is squatting on the right at the front in the Scotland team) there is a brief clip of Eric throwing in to a line-out 55 seconds in to the film.

2. Scotland versus Wales, Cardiff, 1923: https://www.britishpathe. com/video/thrilling-rugby-wales-v-scotland-aka-thrilling-r-2/query/ Wales In the film of the teams Eric is in the back row on the left.

Athletics:

There are clips/footage from the Paris Games of 1924 available on the International Olympic Committee web-site (www.olympic.org). The author has only succeeded in tracing one brief clip of the 200m final on the internet. It is on YouTube in the 7th programme of '*The Fastest Men on Earth*' series: https://www.youtube.com/watch?v= C5MaW97jIHQ&t=48s One can see the brief 200m clip between 7.36 and 7.49 into the programme.

The best clip available for the 400m is: https://www.olympic.org/ videos/paris-1924-liddell-eric This shows first of all the finish of the second semi-final of the 400m and then about half of the 400m final from the start. It shows how the race started straight into the back straight. This means that Eric's two fastest races have been caught and are available on film in reasonable quality, all things considered. The finish of the 400m semi-final shows how easy it was for Eric, bearing in mind that his time of 48.2 in that race was a whole second faster than his previous best! What is noticeable in this clip (semi-final and final) is the relatively poor attendance in the terraces, apart from the stand on the finishing straight. It also shows how soft the cinders were.

INDEX

TRUTHFORLIFE®

THE BIBLE-TEACHING MINISTRY OF **ALISTAIR BEGG**

The mission of Truth For Life is to teach the Bible with clarity and relevance so that unbelievers will be converted, believers will be established, and local churches will be strengthened.

Daily Program

Each day, Truth For Life distributes the Bible teaching of Alistair Begg across the U.S. and in several locations outside of the U.S. through 1,800 radio outlets. To find a radio station near you, visit **truthforlife.org/stationfinder**.

Free Teaching

The daily program, and Truth For Life's entire teaching archive of over 2,000 Bible-teaching messages, can be accessed for free online and through Truth For Life's full-feature mobile app. Download the free mobile app at **truthforlife.org/app** and listen free online at **truthforlife.org**.

At-Cost Resources

Books and full-length teaching from Alistair Begg on CD, DVD, and USB are available for purchase at cost, with no markup. Visit **truthforlife.org/store**.

Where to Begin?

If you're new to Truth For Life and would like to know where to begin listening and learning, find starting point suggestions at **truthforlife.org/firststep**. For a full list of ways to connect with Truth For Life, visit **truthforlife.org/subscribe**.

Contact Truth For Life

P.O. Box 398000 Cleveland, Ohio 44139
phone 1 (888) 588-7884 **email** letters@truthforlife.org
 /truthforlife @truthforlife truthforlife.org

Also by Christian Focus Publications...

olumba

The Faith of an Island Soldier

Bruce Ritchie

COLUMBA

THE FAITH OF AN ISLAND SOLDIER

BRUCE RITCHIE

Columba's name dominates the narrative of early Scottish Christianity. What was established on Iona through Columba's astonishing leadership, and through a succession of energetic and resourceful abbots, exerted a unique influence on the development of Christianity in Scotland and beyond. Bruce Ritchie's analytical biography is the key to understanding the real Columba, his theology, his spirituality, and the faith that drove him across the sea.

Bruce Ritchie has written a new, scholarly, ground–breaking biography of St Columba, weaving together historical narrative and theological exploration in a masterful way. We encounter the man, his times, his life, his teaching, and his legacy, set before us with depth, detail, and colour. This now surely has to be the starting point for all future studies of the Scottish saint. In my judgment, the book deserves the widest possible circulation among all serious students of Scottish church history.

Nick Needham
Lecturer in Church History, Highland Theological College, Dingwall, Scotland

978-1-5271-0387-0

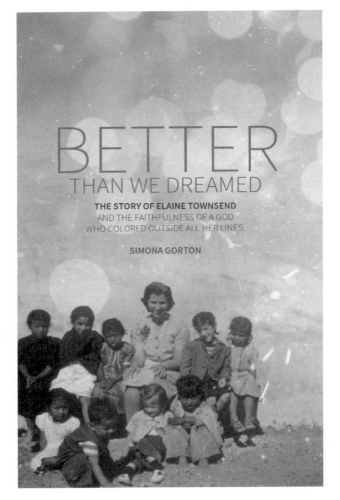

BETTER
THAN WE DREAMED

THE STORY OF ELAINE TOWNSEND
AND THE FAITHFULNESS OF A GOD
WHO COLORED OUTSIDE ALL HER LINES.

SIMONA GORTON

BETTER THAN WE DREAMED

THE STORY OF ELAINE TOWNSEND

SIMONA GORTON

Read the story of a life lived safely within the lines, that God turned upside down. From social star of 1930's Chicago to a Wycliffe missionary in South America and the USSR, Elaine Townsend's life was far from boring. Meet the woman who became Cameron Townsend's wife, and discover how a life can be filled with adventure, by simply saying 'yes' to God.

Through each stage of Elaine's life her trust and dependence on her Saviour shines as an example to believers everywhere, yet there are also weaknesses with which we can all identify. This account of her struggles and successes is filled with stories gathered from those who knew Elaine best, as well as insights into the mission work that renewed a generation's passion for Bible translation.

Both encouraging and challenging, this thorough biography leads the reader to rightly recognise Elaine Townsend as one of the great Christian women of the 20th century – a demonstration of what God can do with a willing heart.

This moving biography chronicles the life of one of the most impactful figures in modern missions and challenges readers to be like her: eager to see God's Word spread, faithful in pursuing the work, and humble before the sovereign God who accomplished it.

Bob Creson
President / CEO, Wycliffe Bible Translators USA

978-1-5271-0266-8

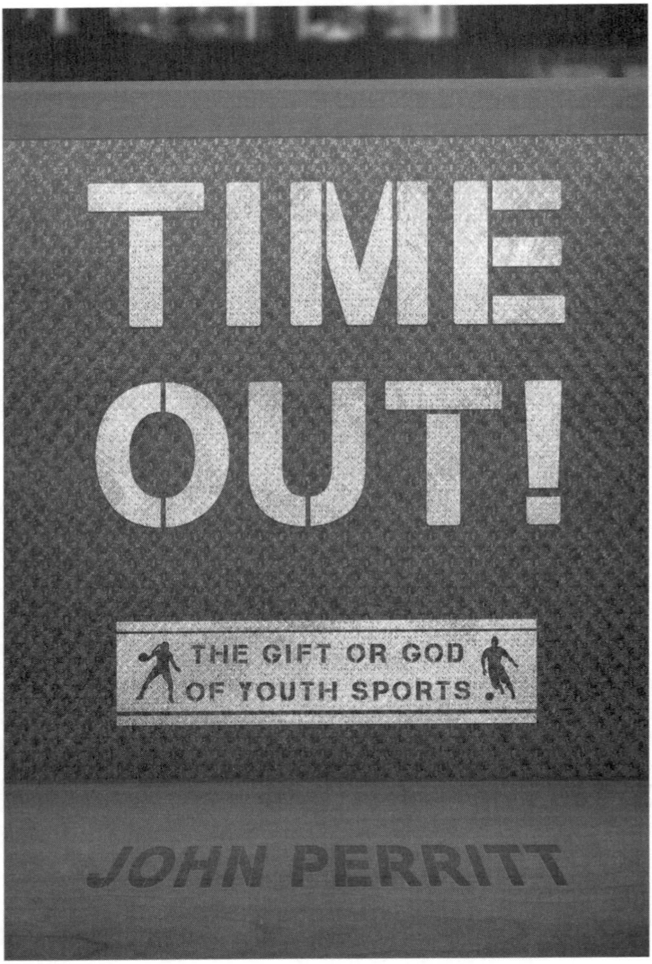
TIME OUT!
THE GIFT OR GOD
OF YOUTH SPORTS
JOHN PERRITT

TIME OUT!

THE GIFT OR GOD OF YOUTH SPORTS

JOHN PERRITT

Sport is one of the many evidences of a gracious God. It can unite people, sharing together in the enjoyment it brings. But it brings the challenge of proper stewardship under God, especially when working with young people. Are they being encouraged to use their gifts and time to God's glory? Are you ensuring that they are living by God's Word, rather than prioritising their sport? There is a lot to learn about how God wants us to live through sports – both on and off the field.

Perspective, we are often told, is everything. In this helpful book John Perritt helps Christians, and especially Christian parents, to put sports into perspective—a Christian perspective. This book is a very helpful contribution to a conversation Christians must eagerly engage with.

R. Albert Mohler
President, The Southern Baptist Theological Seminary, Louisville, Kentucky

978-1-5271-0177-7

Christian Focus Publications

Our mission statement –

STAYING FAITHFUL
In dependence upon God we seek to impact the world through literature faithful to His infallible Word, the Bible. Our aim is to ensure that the Lord Jesus Christ is presented as the only hope to obtain forgiveness of sin, live a useful life and look forward to heaven with Him.

Our Books are published in four imprints:

CHRISTIAN
FOCUS

popular works including biographies, commentaries, basic doctrine and Christian living.

CHRISTIAN
HERITAGE

books representing some of the best material from the rich heritage of the church.

MENTOR

books written at a level suitable for Bible College and seminary students, pastors, and other serious readers. The imprint includes commentaries, doctrinal studies, examination of current issues and church history.

CF4•K

children's books for quality Bible teaching and for all age groups: Sunday school curriculum, puzzle and activity books; personal and family devotional titles, biographies and inspirational stories – Because you are never too young to know Jesus!

Christian Focus Publications Ltd,
Geanies House, Fearn, Ross-shire,
IV20 1TW, Scotland, United Kingdom.
www.christianfocus.com